Palgrave Macmillan Studies in Banking and Financial Institutions

Series Editor: **Professor Philip Molyneux**

The Palgrave Macmillan Studies in Banking and Financial Institutions are international in orientation and include studies of banking within particular countries or regions, and studies of particular themes such as Corporate Banking, Risk Management, Mergers and Acquisitions, etc. The books' focus is on research and practice, and they include up-to-date and innovative studies on contemporary topics in banking that will have global impact and influence.

Titles include:

Yener Altunbaş, Alper Kara and Öslem Olgu
TURKISH BANKING
Banking under Political Instability and Chronic High Inflation

Paola Bongini, Stefano Chiarlone and Giovanni Ferri (*editors*)
EMERGING BANKING SYSTEMS

Vittorio Boscia, Alessandro Carretta and Paola Schwizer
COOPERATIVE BANKING: INNOVATIONS AND DEVELOPMENTS

Vittorio Boscia, Alessandro Carretta and Paola Schwizer
COOPERATIVE BANKING IN EUROPE: CASE STUDIES

Roberto Bottiglia, Elisabetta Gualandri and Gian Nereo Mazzocco (*editors*)
CONSOLIDATION IN THE EUROPEAN FINANCIAL INDUSTRY

Alessandro Carretta, Franco Fiordelisi and Gianluca Mattarocci (*editors*)
NEW DRIVERS OF PERFORMANCE IN A CHANGING FINANCIAL WORLD

Dimitris N. Chorafas
CAPITALISM WITHOUT CAPITAL

Dimitris N. Chorafas
FINANCIAL BOOM AND GLOOM
The Credit and Banking Crisis of 2007–2009 and Beyond

Vincenzo D'Apice and Giovanni Ferri
FINANCIAL INSTABILITY
Toolkit for Interpreting Boom and Bust Cycles

Peter Falush and Robert L. Carter OBE
THE BRITISH INSURANCE INDUSTRY SINCE 1900
The Era of Transformation

Franco Fiordelisi
MERGERS AND ACQUISITIONS IN EUROPEAN BANKING

Franco Fiordelisi, Philip Molyneux and Daniele Previati (*editors*)
NEW ISSUES IN FINANCIAL AND CREDIT MARKETS

Franco Fiordelisi, Philip Molyneux and Daniele Previati (*editors*)
NEW ISSUES IN FINANCIAL INSTITUTIONS MANAGEMENT

Hans Genberg and Cho-Hoi Hui
THE BANKING SECTOR IN HONG KONG
Competition, Efficiency, Performance and Risk

Carlo Gola and Alessandro Roselli
THE UK BANKING SYSTEM AND ITS REGULATORY AND SUPERVISORY FRAMEWORK

Elisabetta Gualandri and Valeria Venturelli (*editors*)
BRIDGING THE EQUITY GAP FOR INNOVATIVE SMEs

Kim Hawtrey
AFFORDABLE HOUSING FINANCE

Otto Hieronymi (*editor*)
GLOBALIZATION AND THE REFORM OF THE INTERNATIONAL BANKING AND MONETARY SYSTEM

Sven Janssen
BRITISH AND GERMAN BANKING STRATEGIES

Caterina Lucarelli and Gianni Brighetti (*editors*)
RISK TOLERANCE IN FINANCIAL DECISION MAKING

Anders Ögren (*editor*)
THE SWEDISH FINANCIAL REVOLUTION

Dominique Rambure and Alec Nacamuli
PAYMENT SYSTEMS
From the Salt Mines to the Board Room

Catherine Schenk (*editor*)
HONG KONG SAR's MONETARY AND EXCHANGE RATE CHALLENGES
Historical Perspectives

Noël K. Tshiani
BUILDING CREDIBLE CENTRAL BANKS
Policy Lessons for Emerging Economies

The full list of titles available is on the website:
www.palgrave.com/finance/sbfi.asp

Palgrave Macmillan Studies in Banking and Financial Institutions
Series Standing Order ISBN 978–1–4039–4872–4

You can receive future titles in this series as they are published by placing a standing order. Please contact your bookseller or, in case of difficulty, write to us at the address below with your name and address, the title of the series and the ISBN quoted above.

Customer Services Department, Macmillan Distribution Ltd, Houndmills, Basingstoke, Hampshire RG21 6XS, England

---

Risk Tolerance in Financial Decision Making

Edited by

Caterina Lucarelli
Associate Professor, Department of Economics, Polytechnic University of Marche, Italy

and

Gianni Brighetti
Associate Professor, Department of Psychology, University of Bologna, Italy

palgrave
macmillan

First published 2011 by
PALGRAVE MACMILLAN

Palgrave Macmillan in the UK is an imprint of Macmillan Publishers Limited, registered in England, company number 785998, of Houndmills, Basingstoke, Hampshire RG21 6XS.

Palgrave Macmillan in the US is a division of St Martin's Press LLC, 175 Fifth Avenue, New York, NY 10010.

Palgrave Macmillan is the global academic imprint of the above companies and has companies and representatives throughout the world.

Palgrave® and Macmillan® are registered trademarks in the United States, the United Kingdom, Europe and other countries.

ISBN 978–0–230–28113–4 hardback

This book is printed on paper suitable for recycling and made from fully managed and sustained forest sources. Logging, pulping and manufacturing processes are expected to conform to the environmental regulations of the country of origin.

A catalogue record for this book is available from the British Library.

A catalog record for this book is available from the Library of Congress.

10 9 8 7 6 5 4 3 2 1
20 19 18 17 16 15 14 13 12 11

Printed and bound in Great Britain by
CPI Antony Rowe, Chippenham and Eastbourne

Contents

Tables

Figures

Contributors

Luisa Anderloni is Full Professor of Corporate Finance at the Faculty of Political Sciences, University of Milan, Italy.

Gianni Brighetti is Associate Professor at the Department of Psychology, University of Bologna, Director of the post-graduate school in Health Psychology, University of Bologna. He is also Director of the BIOlab and the Center for Affective Neuroscience. He has published several contributions in national and international peer reviewed journals and books.

Rosita Borlimi is a psychotherapist at the Department of Psychology, University of Bologna, Italy.

Caterina Lucarelli is Associate Professor at the Department of Economics, Università Politecnica Marche, Ancona, Italy. She is the national coordinator of the research on 'Risk tolerance in investment and debt decision', supported by the Italian Ministry of University and Research. She has published several contributions in national and international peer reviewed journals and books.

Nicoletta Marinelli is Research Fellow in Economics of Financial Intermediaries at the Faculty of Economics, 'La Sapienza' University, Rome, Italy.

Camilla Mazzoli is Assistant Professor of Economics of Financial Intermediaries at the Faculty of Economics, Università Politecnica Marche, Ancona, Italy.

Valeria Nucifora is a psychotherapist at the Department of Psychology, University of Bologna, Italy.

Cristina Ottaviani is a PostDoc at the Department of Psychology, University of Bologna, Italy.

Giulio Palomba is Assistant Professor of Econometrics at the Faculty of Economics, Università Politecnica Marche, Ancona, Italy.

Daniela Vandone is Associate Professor of Economics of Financial Intermediaries at the Faculty of Political Sciences, Università degli Studi di Milano, Milan, Italy.

Introduction

Caterina Lucarelli

REFLECTIONS:
1st – that I was not for others what I had till then believed I was for myself;
2nd – that I could not see my self live;
3rd – that, being unable to see myself live, I remained an outsider to myself, namely one whom the others could see and know, each in his own way; and I couldn't;
...
CONCLUSIONS:
...
2nd – that I decided to discover who I was at least for those closest to me (...) and to amuse myself by dismantling spitefully the me that I was for them.[1]
from 'One, No one and One Hundred Thousand'
Luigi Pirandello, NOBEL Prize in Literature, 1934
(translated by W. Weaver, 1992)

This book sheds light on the emotional side of risk taking behaviour and is based on an innovative cross-disciplinary approach, mixing financial competences with others, related to psychology and affective neuroscience. A deep theoretical background on the issue of risk tolerance is provided, together with the singular results of an empirical research study which aims to investigate the emotional side of risk taking behaviour.

In the theoretical sections, traditional and behavioural approaches are employed to study both the investment and the debt decision process of individuals and households, respectively. The fallacy of traditional measures of responsible investing and borrowing suggests the choice of a novel approach and the introduction of a perspective emanating from psychology and affective neuroscience.

Mazzoli and Marinelli, in **Chapter 1**, illustrate the main theories with regard to financial risk in standard finance and they provide a description of the main critiques and solutions coming from the behavioural finance. In particular, Mazzoli depicts several dimensions which have been proposed to accurately define financial risk in the literature. She informs that the definition of risk itself is still a source of argument among academics: the main contrast arises when comparing the assumptions of standard finance with those of behavioural finance. In fact, with reference to the former, the traditional finance paradigm seeks to explain investors' risk exposure using models in which agents are rational. However, after years of effort, it has become clear that risk behaviour is strictly individual and that the traditional finance framework is not completely suitable for its understanding. In the following part of Chapter 1, Marinelli describes how behavioural finance has emerged to offer a response, at least in part, to the difficulties faced by the traditional paradigm when portraying financial markets. As the name suggests, behavioural finance aims to improve upon our understanding of financial markets and its participants by applying insights from behavioural sciences (for example psychology and sociology). In broad terms, it argues that some financial phenomena, such as the investment process and risk taking, can be better understood by using models in which some agents are not fully rational.

Vandone, in **Chapter 2**, offers a review of the traditional and behavioural literature on household indebtedness, and she aims to elucidate on the link between household risk tolerance and debt decisions. The theoretical economic framework for consumption, saving and indebtedness decisions is developed within the Life Cycle theory, proposed by Modigliani and Brumberg in 1954, and the Permanent Income Hypothesis, developed by Friedman in 1957. These inter temporal consumption choice models are founded on the idea that households make their consumption choices, and consequently those relating to saving and indebtedness, on the basis of their wealth, current disposable income and future income expectations so as to guarantee a uniform level of consumption over their lifetimes. Thus, the economic models are based on the economic rationality of individuals, who seek to increase living standards by smoothing consumption over different periods of their lives through appropriate saving and borrowing decisions. However, in recent years, a growing number of studies in the field of behavioural economics have emerged which focus on the psychological variables that may significantly influence individuals' decisions relating to spending, saving or indebtedness. The research models adopted within behavioural economics are based on empirical results and anomalies regarding consumer behaviour that conflict with traditional notions of economic rationality. Several studies have in fact shown how the behaviour of individuals deviates systematically from the 'rational choice' model of standard economic theories without implying that such behaviour is irrational. The effect of behavioural factors on household debt demand is likely to be different for secured and unsecured debt. The underlying idea is that the effects of secured debt decisions last for a long time and will follow the life cycle. Conversely, unsecured debt decisions are largely determined by short run benefits since debt is used for shopping and are thus more subject to variables like impulsivity, materialism, social comparison and satisfaction or self-esteem. In particular, there are concerns that some contract features in the consumer credit market may induce consumers to borrow too much and to make suboptimal contract and repayment choices. These concerns are effectively motivated in part by evidence which suggests that consumers first have a time inconsistent taste for immediate gratification, and secondly often naively underestimate the extent of this taste. In particular, with regard to unsecured debt, a specific concern relates to the rapid growth over recent years in the use of revolving credit cards on the back of strong growth in payment systems and card usage. The need to understand investors' attitudes towards risk has caused both academics and practitioners for many years to look for reliable tools which are able to reliably assess the risk tolerance of individuals. Marinelli and Mazzoli, in **Chapter 3**, construct a critical review of the traditional approaches which evaluate the risk tolerance in investment decisions. With specific reference to the European Union, the Markets in Financial Instruments Directive (MiFID) has formalised the need for financial firms to include their clients' risk tolerance in the information set required to determine whether an investment is 'suitable' for a particular client. Unfortunately, the Directive only dictates general rules as far as the content of client questionnaires are concerned; thus, each financial firm makes use of its own particular questionnaire that is likely to be different from its competitors'. In Chapter 3, after the analysis of the MiFID suitability questionnaires, Marinelli and Mazzoli develop an empirical analysis addressed to investigate how financial firms actually deal with their customer suitability obligations (and subsequently, with their client risk tolerance assessment). Their contribution is threefold. First, Marinelli conducts an analysis concerning the formalisation of the 'suitability' questionnaire among a sample of Italian financial firms. She analyses 14 'suitability' questionnaires provided by the first

14 Italian financial groups in terms of promoted assets in the area of portfolio management (90 per cent of the total market). Therefore she is able to compare the different approaches used to develop the questionnaires and to outline the main differences, specifically concerning the risk tolerance assessment. Then Mazzoli discusses the reliability of 'suitability' questionnaires among a sample of Italian financial intermediaries. She examines the consistency of the profiles that materialise from different questionnaires submitted to the same person. Finally, Chapter 3 concludes by opening up the analysis at the international level and deepening the post-MiFID Italian suitability assessment compared to the pre-MiFID and non-EU countries' practice.

In **Chapter 4** Anderloni and Vandone analyse the link between behaviour and over-indebtedness. Such behaviours often refer to social and psychological factors that act to reduce an individual's capacity to evaluate the consequences of his or her consumption and borrowing decisions. Additionally, these behaviours may not be considered to be completely rational from an economic point of view. In fact, individuals tend, on one hand, to overestimate their capacity to manage domestic financial resources and, on the other, to underestimate the possibility of being affected by negative events (such as illness or job loss). As a result, they systematically underestimate the risk of not being able to meet their financial commitments. Furthermore, they overestimate the immediate benefits and undervalue the future costs; such behaviour leads to the decision to purchase, using debt if necessary, regardless of the effect this choice may have on the sustainability of future debt levels. The empirical literature shows how individuals have little awareness of these psychological mechanisms. Indeed, individuals in financial difficulties tend to lay the blame on exogenous factors (for example, job difficulties) and rarely recognise their innate inability to manage money or to take appropriate financial decisions. Moreover, many studies show how irregular behavioural patterns persist even when individuals are aware of the risks they face. Individuals' incapacity to take corrective steps, even when they are aware of the over-indebtedness risks, should be taken into consideration when designing policies to prevent or manage situations of indebtedness which are, or are likely to become, detrimental.

The fallacies of traditional theoretical and operational approaches, which simplify the financial decision process of individuals by ignoring the mental processing of human beings, requires the essential contributions of psychology and neuroscience. Brighetti et al., in **Chapter 5**, analyse how risk perception is influenced by the characteristics of risk and the subjective/affective states of the perceiver. For example, in order to maintain their internal state, subjects in a positive mood become more risk seeking but only when the stakes are low. Thus, emotions do not necessarily damage thoughtful decision making. This concept seems intuitive, however it wasn't until the 1970s that evidence on the influence of emotions in decision making, in opposition to the normative economic rationalistic approach, began to materialise in international journals. Kahneman and Tversky were the first to demonstrate that decision making behaviour is linked with a non-linear probability weighting function. A more extreme and recent influential conceptualisation is Damasio's Somatic Marker Hypothesis. This specific hypothesis arose from the observation of patients with ventromedial prefrontal cortex lesions who where characterised by having both a generally flat affect and a repeated engagement in decisions that led to negative consequences, such as bankruptcy and indebtedness. This led Damasio to hypothesise that the primary dysfunction of these patients was an inability to use emotions to aid in decision making and to further postulate that somato-visceral signals from the body (affective reactions) ordinarily guide individuals' decisions making and risk engagement processes. More recent studies have demonstrated that there are specific circumstances under which individuals who have lost the capacity to process emotional information correctly might actually make better decisions than those individuals who retain this capacity. Moreover, it has been found that there is a group of healthy individuals who show the same performance as the patients at a decision making task (for example, risk seekers). Specifically, it seems that emotion is disruptive to decisions under risk, but not to decisions under ambiguity. This means that risk taking behaviour and impaired decision making are not synonymous. To clarify this apparent contradiction, Chapter 5 confronts the crucial issue of daydreaming that, given its pervasiveness, inevitably accompanies our usual daily experience and has the power to influence our behaviours. The concept of 'how people undo reality' becomes essential when the domain of analysis concerns economic choices. Many scholars have postulated a relationship between psychological processes, how investors buy and sell, and financial market price movements. Thus, economics, psychology and neuroscience have started to converge into a single field under the label of *neuroeconomics*, which aims to employ recent neuroscientific methods in order to analyse economically relevant brain processes. This innovative field has repeatedly revealed deviations from the classical theory of economists, highlighting that subjects show dysfunctional behaviors that are not explicable within the traditional paradigm.

The second part of the book describes our unique empirical research which involved more than 450 individuals: banks' customers, traders and asset managers. Lucarelli et al., in **Chapter 6**, describe how the empirical research was organised and the technical tools which were used to carry out the experiments: a psycho-physiological test, namely the Iowa Gambling Task (IGT), run together with a physiological test which measures the Skin's Conductance Response (SCR) while risky choices are made; a more traditional questionnaire, made up of a financial risk tolerance self-assessment test, an impulsivity test and finally a set of questions to understand both the socio economical features of the interviewed and his or her real life financial choices.

In **Chapter 7**, Lucarelli and Palomba propose traditional and innovative measures of risk tolerance. The most innovative is a measure of the 'unbiased risk tolerance' (UR) of individuals, which is fundamentally the attraction or aversion to risk shown during the controlled experiment (IGT) aimed at observing both the choices and the uncontrolled (somatic) responses to risky decisions. The research compares the unbiased risk tolerance with both a measure for the biased risk tolerance (BR), obtained by a financial risk tolerance self-evaluation test and a measure of the risk tolerance shown in real life investment/decision choices (RLR). Any difference between UR and BR shows whether individuals are able to properly self-evaluate their risk tolerance or not, and if they over/undervalue their personal capability to afford financial risk. The comparisons among UR, BR and RLR are essential to understand what drives real life risk taking behaviour: either who we are or who we suppose to be.

Results on the investment are provided in **Chapter 8**, where Lucarelli depicts the demographic, socio economic and cultural reasons which could explain incoherencies among UR, BR and RLR.

Vandone and Ottaviani, in **Chapter 9**, analyse the determinants of an individual's propensity to hold debt including the role of psychological factors, together with the explanatory variables commonly used in the applied economic literature. They also investigate whether the effect of such explanatory variables is different for secured debt (that is, mortgages) and unsecured debt (that is, consumer credit). The book concludes in **Chapter 10**, with comments on the main results as a whole, and with a discussion about the related implications of the research for market participants and regulators. These implications appear even more relevant if connected to the new regulation of financial markets, introduced by MiFID, in terms of transparency and communication between intermediaries and customers.

This research was supported by a grant from the Italian Ministry of University and Research as a 'Progetto di Ricerca di Interesse Nazionale' – PRIN 2007 (September 2008–September 2010). We are grateful to Banca Popolare di Ancona – UBI Group and to Twice SIM – Milan, for their cooperation in providing an assorted sample of individuals who participated in our test. In particular, we are grateful to Luciano Goffi, from Banca Popolare di Ancona – BPA, for sharing and supporting our research goals and for allowing several BPA-branches to take part in the experiments. The cooperation of Ivano Farotti, Alessandra Daniele and all the BPA staff, both in the headquarters and in the branches of the bank, was essential for our empirical results. We are also grateful to Enrico Petocchi and Annalisa Di Maggio, from Twice SIM, for promptly agreeing to cooperate with the research team, allowing us to run our experiments during the Trading Expo which was held in the Borsa Italiana – Milan in October 2008 and at the Italian Trading Forum which was held in Rimini in May 2009.

Great gratitude goes to the past President of Assogestioni, Prof. Marcello Messori, for his support and for giving us the chance to include in the analysis a relevant sample of asset managers. In particular, we are grateful to JPMorgan-ITALY, Pioneer, Eurizon Capital, Azimut, UbiPramerica, Arca and Prima sgr, their managing directors and their staff, for actively taking part in our research.

Moreover, we are grateful to all our research staff and specifically to Elisa Gabbi, Arianna Rizzoli and Sara Falcioni who have worked tirelessly for months on our long experiments (almost three-quarters of an hour each), for so many individuals, all over Italy. A special acknowledgement goes to Fergus McGuckian for his precious mother tongue revision.

Finally, a sincere 'Thank you!' goes to the 445 friends who actively gave us a considerable amount of their time, and who provided much enthusiasm for the tests we proposed, without fear of the possible outcomes or conclusions that would arise.

Note

1. *RIFLESSIONI:*
1ª - che io non ero per gli altri quel che finora avevo creduto di essere per me;
2ª - che non potevo vedermi vivere;
3ª - che non potendo vedermi vivere, restavo estraneo a me stesso,
cioè uno che gli altri potevano vedere e conoscere; ciascuno a modo suo; e io no;
...
CONCLUSIONI:
...
2°- che mi proposi di scoprire chi ero io almeno per quelli che mi stavano più vicini
(...)
e di spassarmi a scomporre dispettosamente quell'io che ero per loro.

1
The Role of Risk in the Investment Decision Process: Traditional vs Behavioural Finance

Camilla Mazzoli and Nicoletta Marinelli

1.1 Risk: the traditional finance perspective

1.1.1 Definition of financial risk

Risk and uncertainty exist whenever the future is unknown (Williams et al., 1997). Despite the intuitiveness of the concept, risk and its definition are still a debated issue in the literature. A first point to be discussed is the difference between risk and uncertainty. Knight (1921) maintains that *risk* refers to a situation for which the possible outcomes and their probabilities are known (measurable uncertainty); on the contrary, *uncertainty* exists when the probabilities associated to the outcomes are not known (unmeasurable uncertainty). In any case, not all academic authors agree on this distinction. Levy and Sarnat (1995) point out that, if one considers the existence of a subjective probability according to Savage (1954), the distinction between risk and uncertainty disappears. In fact, by assigning an individual subjective probability to decision problems, an uncertain situation can be transformed into a risky choice[1] and the distinction loses significance.

For years, economists, statisticians, engineers, physicists, and so on, have been defining risk and have measured it according to the specific features of their discipline; so far, there is a lack of a common definition and of a common measure of risk that is suitable for all the fields of study (Rohrmann and Renn, 2000; Vughan and Vaughan, 2000; Ricciardi, 2004).

In general, risk refers to a situation in which a decision is made and its consequences depend on the outcome of future events having known their probabilities (Lopes, 1987). Furthermore, the approach to risk changes to a substantial degree depending on the area of study. Technical disciplines usually concentrate on the quantification of risk and very often the definition of risk corresponds to its measure.[2] On the contrary, the social sciences are less concerned by the measurement of risk and focus more on its qualitative aspects.

From the traditional finance standpoint, financial risk is the variability of a financial outcome from its average value. Table 1.1 shows that financial risk can be classified depending on:

- the outcome of the financial event (pure and speculative risk)
- the events that are able to cause a variability of the outcome (market risk, credit risk, liquidity risk and operational risk)
- the possibility to reduce or not to reduce the risk (diversifiable or non-diversifiable risk)
- the moment when the risk is observed (*ex post*) or predicted (*ex ante*).

The distinction between pure and speculative risk has been formalised by Mowbray and Blanchard (1961). In both cases there is uncertainty as to the outcome of the event under consideration; nevertheless, in the case of *speculative risk* the uncertainty can lead to either a profit or a loss as far as the outcome is concerned while *pure risk* can only result in loss.[3] Thus far, pure risk typically applies to the insurance market while speculative risk is typical of securities and credit markets.

As far as the cause of variability of the outcome is concerned, the *market risk* (or price risk) deals with a change in the market value of a

Table 1.1 Financial risk classification

Possible outcome	**Cause of the variability**	**Possibility of reducing**	**Moment of observation**
Pure	Market	Diversifiable	Ex ante
Speculative	Credit	Non-diversifiable	Ex post
	Liquidity		
	Operational		

financial product due to unexpected changes in market conditions. As a general rule, five main market-risk categories can be identified:

- exchange rate risk
- interest rate risk
- equity risk
- commodity risk
- volatility risk.

Each of the five drivers reflects the risk of price variability of a financial product due to its sensitivity to the specific driver (Resti and Sironi, 2007).

Credit risk is the possibility that counterparties are unwilling or unable to fulfil their contractual obligations. Its effect is measured by the cost of replacing cash flows when the counterparty defaults. What is more, losses due to credit risk can occur even before the actual default. In general, a credit risk event occurs when there is a change in the counterparty's ability to perform its obligation.[4]

Liquidity risk takes two forms: 'asset liquidity risk' and 'funding liquidity risk'. The first one refers to the possibility that a transaction cannot be conducted at prevailing market prices due to its size. The second is the eventual inability to meet payment obligations which may force early liquidation, thus transforming paper losses into realised losses (Jorion, 2000). *Operational risk* ordinarily emanates from human and technological accidents or errors.[5] It includes fraud, inadequate procedures and controls, and management failure that can also produce market or credit risk. For example, an operational problem in a business transaction can cause an increase in the costs due to favourable market movements being missed.

The possibility of reducing risk sets apart diversifiable and non-diversifiable risk. A financial risk is *diversifiable* (firm specific) if it is possible to reduce it by holding a diversified portfolio of securities rather than individual securities. However, even in a well-diversified portfolio there is a risk that cannot be reduced through a further diversification (*non-diversifiable* or systematic risk) and it ordinarily depends on macroeconomic events.

Risk can also be observed (ex post) or predicted (ex ante). *Ex post* risk measures inform about the effective deviation of the historical series of outcomes from their average value; on the contrary, in the *ex ante* perspective, an estimation is given of the eventual future divergence of the outcomes from their expected value, given the possible scenarios one believes to happen.

Ricciardi (2004) maintains that risk, in the standard finance sense of the word, is:

- one-dimensional
- objective
- macro-perspective oriented.

It is *one-dimensional* as the only aspect that is taken into account to calculate the risk of a financial event is the series of its past occurrences. This information is then assembled and incorporated into quantitative models in order to estimate the risk of the event in the future. It is *objective* because the past occurrences of the event are observable in nature, they can be collected and statistical inference can be made in order to approximate the probability of the future event. Moreover, as investors are supposed to be perfectly rational, they make unbiased forecasts about the future that allow them to estimate the probability distributions of the outcomes (Barberis and Thaler, 1993). Finally, risk in the standard finance standpoint leads to a *macro-perspective* as it considers the behaviour of participants in the markets as a whole, based on the assumption that all individuals are rational decision makers; depending on their attitude towards risk, an individual can thus be classified as being risk averse, risk neutral or as a risk lover (Levy and Sarnat, 1995).

The description of financial risk that we provided up to now, applies to every possible financial event, both from the investment and the debt point of view. From now on, within this chapter, we will focus our attention only on the financial risk that deals with investment decisions[6] specifically. Moreover, we will observe the financial risk that is involved into investments from two different points of view: a traditional finance approach and a behavioural perspective.

1.1.2 Traditional financial risk measures

The securities industry has long been interested in measuring financial risk. The first measures that were proposed in the literature are generally termed *traditional risk measures*. They mainly relate to stock investments by measuring the variability of returns in terms of earning and dividends (Fuller and Farrel, 2003) and also in terms of price changes.[7] A key point in describing these measures is the ex ante or ex post perspective that one takes into account. In the *ex post* perspective, risk measures assess the risk that an investment has generated in terms of how much the outcome has diverged from its average value. This means that the computation is made starting from the historical series of returns that the investment has produced. The perspective completely changes when assessing the *ex ante* risk of an investment. In this case, as the return generated by the investment is uncertain, a crucial set of information is the investor's expectation in regards to the future return the asset may yield. Up to this point, *ex ante* financial risk measures have been strongly based on the probability distribution of returns (or the possible scenarios) that depend on the investor's projections about future stock dividend payments and future stock prices (Fuller and Farrel, 2003).

The financial risk measures that we will illustrate in this section are analysed in the *ex ante* perspective. Moreover some of these measures take into account the possible symmetric upside and downside diversions from the expected return and some others do not. The main reason for this second group of measures is that investors are usually much more interested in downside risk because every return above the expected one is desirable (Elton et al., 2007). Therefore, the traditional financial risk measures can be classified as:

- Symmetric risk measures: standard deviation (or variance[8]), tracking error variance
- Asymmetric risk measures: semi variances, lower partial moments, value at risk.

The *standard deviation* (SD) is a weighted average of the potential deviations of the conditional returns from their expected value; the weights are the probabilities of occurrence of the different scenarios, as follows:

$$\sigma = \sqrt{\sum_{i=1}^{n} \pi_i [r_i - E(r)]^2} \tag{1.1}$$

where:

$$E(r) = \sum_{i=1}^{n} r_i \pi_i \tag{1.2}$$

and:

π_i is the probability of the i scenario to occur (scenarios go from one to n);
r_i is the return associated to the probability of the i scenario.

This measure is commonly used as it is easy to compute but it also exhibits some limitations. One assumption is that investment returns must be symmetric (that is normally distributed).[9] Therefore, in the standard deviation upside risk matters just as much as downside risk. For this reason, it cannot be applied to securities or portfolio strategies that exhibit asymmetric (skewed) return distributions[10] (Warwick, 2003). For example, when trying to apply the SD to investments other than stocks some computational problems may arise as it cannot accommodate investment vehicles with asymmetric payoff profiles (such as derivatives and portfolio insurance).[11]

A modification of SD is the *tracking error variance* (TEV) relative to an underlying benchmark. The tracking error is defined as the difference between the expected return of the investment and the return of a specified benchmark or target position. Its variance is computed as follows:

$$TEV = \sum_{i=1}^{n} \pi_i [r_i - b_i]^2 \tag{1.3}$$

where:

π_i is the probability of the *i* scenario to occur (scenarios go from one to n);
r_i is the fund or portfolio return associated to the probability of the *i* scenario;
b_i is the benchmark return associated to the probability of the *i* scenario.

Still, TEV typically suffers from the same drawbacks that exist with normal variance. It treats deviations above the benchmark exactly like deviations below the benchmark return.

Alternative (asymmetric) measures of risk that are suitable for non-normally distributed results belong to the downside risk measures. The first measure dates back to 1952 when Roy proposed the *safety first technique*. The basic idea is that an investor does not prefer the portfolio with the higher return for a given level of risk but, on the contrary, he or she prefers the investment with the smallest probability of going below the target return. Some years later Markowitz (1959) recognised the importance of this idea and he agreed that investors are more concerned with downside risk rather than variance.[12] So, Markowitz himself proposed two measures of downside risk: a below target semi variance (BTSV) and a below mean semi variance (BMSV). The first one is computed by taking into account only the returns below the target and the second considers only the returns below the mean return. Since only a subset of return distributions is used, Markowitz calls them partial or semi variances.[13] The below mean semi variance is computed as:

$$BMSV = \sum_{i=1}^{n} \pi_i Max[0,(E(r) - r_i)]^2 \tag{1.4}$$

where:

$$E(r) = \sum_{i=1}^{n} r_i \pi_i \tag{1.5}$$

and:
π_i is the probability of the *i* scenario to occur (scenarios go from one to n);
r_i is the return associated to the probability of the *i* scenario.

The below target semi variance is:

$$BTSV = \sum_{i=1}^{n} \pi_i Max[0,(T - r_i)]^2 \tag{1.6}$$

where:
π_i is the probability of the *i* scenario to occur (scenarios go from one to n);
r_i is the return associated to the probability of the *i* scenario;
T is the target return.

Confirmations of the semi variance measures over the variance continued in the 1960s and 1970s (Quirk and Saposnik, 1962; Mao, 1970; Klemkosky, 1973). It is worth highlighting that all the variance and semi variance measures used in these years assume the strict hypothesis of investors' risk aversion.

A huge jump in the evolution of downside risk measures occurred with the development of the lower partial moments (LPM) introduced by Bawa (1975) and Fishburn (1977).[14] These measures reflect the popular negative meaning of risk since they only consider negative deviations of the return from a reference point (Unser, 2000). The general formula of the LPM is illustrated below:

$$LPM(a,t) = \sum_{i=1}^{n} \pi_i Max[0,(t - r_i)]^a \tag{1.7}$$

where:
LPM (a, t) is the lower partial moment associated to the target return *t* and to a degree *a*;
π_i is the probability of the *i* scenario occurrence (scenarios go from one to n);

ri is the return associated to the probability of the *i* scenario.
a is the degree of the LPM.

Despite semi variance measures having already highlighted this concept, what was new with the LPM was the possibility of considering not only risk averse investors because risk neutral and risk seekers can also be included. In fact, the value *a* is the critical element which sets apart the LPM from the semi variances. Deviations, instead of being squared as in the semi variance measures, can be raised to every possible value of *a*.[15] Fishburn (1977) identifies *a* with the single investor's risk preference. In particular, if an investor's main concern is the failure to meet the target without any particular regard to the amount, then a small value of *a* is appropriate (generally less than one); if small deviations below the target are relatively harmless when compared to large deviations, then a larger value of *a* is indicated (generally more than one) (Fishburn, 1977). In addition, *a* equal to one separates risk seeking from risk averse behaviour with regard to returns below the target. In this sense, the generalised *LPM(a,t)* represents an evolution of the semi variance as it includes the investors' preference. Still, it requires particular attention to how *a* is calculated. A first point that Fishburn (1977) underlines is that the risk propensity coefficient *a* is strictly dependent on the investor's total wealth; if the amount of wealth at risk is very small relative to a subject's total wealth, he or she will particularly be a risk seeker (*a* less than one) but, if the contrary happens, he or she will be more risk averse (*a* more than one). Therefore, the estimation of the coefficient *a* is dependent on the relationship between the value of the investment portfolio and the investor's total wealth.

Based on the findings of Fishburn (1977), Laughhunn et al. (1980) developed an interactive computer program to estimate each person's value of *a*. They studied a sample of corporate managers from the United States, Canada and Europe by giving them a number of small investment projects from which to choose both in the form of personal decisions and of corporate decisions.[16] By making use of the results of the computer experiment, managers were classified as risk seeker (*a* less than one) or as risk averse (*a* more than one). The results show that 71 per cent of the sample exhibit a risk seeking behaviour (except for the case of ruinous losses, where the percentage falls to 36 per cent) no matter the background of the managers, the magnitude of the loss and the context of the decision making process (personal or corporate). Furthermore, a regression analysis on the risk preferences shows that the country of origin of the manager and the organisational level are strongly associated with the risk preference. Nevertheless, the specific sample does not allow any generalisation of the results.

Some years later, downside risk measures started to appear in the practitioner literature (Sortino and Van Der Meer, 1991; Rom and Ferguson, 1993, 1997; Balzer, 1994; Merriken, 1994; Sortino and Price, 1994; Sortino and Forsey, 1996). Still, most of the authors mentioned above make us of the semi variance and they ignore the investor's risk propensity that is available to the user of LPM because of the lack of a reliable and universally valid method of assessing one's risk tolerance (Nawrocki, 1999).

Recently, Warwick (2003) and Bernstein and Damodaran (1998) propose a review of the alternative risk measures providing the following general formula for the LPM:

$$LPM_n = \begin{cases} E\,[(r-b)^n] \text{ over the range of probability } r<b \\ 0 \text{ over the range of probability } r \geq b \end{cases} \quad (1.8)$$

where:
r is the return of the investment based on the distribution of probabilities;
b is target return;
n represents the order of ranking of the relative LPM but no mention is made to its possible representation of one's risk tolerance, even if one can trace it from Fishburn (1977).

Depending on the value of n, different measures of downside risk can be derived. For example, the *shortfall probability* (Balzer, 1994) corresponds to the general case n equal to zero, as follows:

$$\text{shortfall probability} = \text{probability } (r<b) \quad (1.9)$$

Hence, the probability of shortfall is an incomplete measure of risk as it only informs about the probability of reaching a result that is below the target return but does not give any information about the distance between the target return and the lower one. This measure, according to Fishburn (1977), could describe the behaviour of a risk seeker investor who is only interested in the probability of loss but is not interested that much in the amount. On the contrary, the *expected shortfall* (ES) adds to the previous formula the capacity of estimating the magnitude of the potential shortfall if it occurs (Warwick, 2003).

It corresponds to the case *n* equal to one in the general formula of the LPM, as follows:

$$\textit{expected shortfall} = E[r-b] \textit{ over the range of probability } r-b<0 \qquad (1.10)$$

The ES could reflect a more risk averse behaviour of the investor as he or she is interested also in the magnitude of loss rather than only in its probability.

Around the end of the 1990s, another risk measure was added to the LPM. *Value at risk* (VaR) is closely related to the LPM in its attempt to concentrate on the downside risk. Still, the two groups of measures address two different questions; the LPM represents the probability of failing an *ex ante* target return while the VaR calculates the worst potential loss over a target horizon with a given level of confidence (Jorion, 2000).

Theoretical research on the Value at Risk was initiated by Jorion (1997), Dowd (1998) and Saunders (1999). VaR is the lowest quantile of the potential losses that can occur within a given portfolio during a specified time period. The time horizon can differ from a few hours for an active trading desk to a year for a pension fund. When the primary goal is to satisfy external regulatory requirements, such as bank capital requirements, the quantile is typically very small (for example, 1 per cent of the worst outcomes). However for an internal risk management model used by a company to control the risk exposure the typical number is around 5 per cent.[17] The formula is:

$$\textit{probability } [V_t \geq VaR] = 1-\alpha \qquad (1.11)$$

where V_t is the loss in t, t is the end of the period and α is the confidence level.

The two most important factors that have to be chosen when computing a VaR measure are the length of the horizon and the confidence level. In general VaR will increase with both the horizon and the confidence level. According to Jorion (2000) the choice of both the parameters depend on the use of the VaR number as:

- a benchmark measure
- a potential loss measure
- equity capital.

In the first case ('benchmark measure'), the VaR is used to compare risk in a cross-sectional or time difference context. For example an institution could need to know if a trading unit has a greater risk than another or if today's VaR is in line with a previous one. For this reason, the choice of the confidence level and the time horizon does not matter much. Another application of the VaR is to give an idea of the worst loss an institution can potentially incur ('potential loss measure'). In this case, the horizon depends upon the nature of the portfolio. It can be chosen by the liquidation period (the longest period that is necessary for an orderly portfolio liquidation) that is related to the liquidity of the securities or it can correspond to the period over which the portfolio remains relatively constant. Still, as VaR assumes that the portfolio is frozen over the horizon, this second choice loses significance as the horizon is extended. Finally, banks usually choose a daily VaR as it allows them to compare the VaR with their daily profit and loss measures. In the last case, VaR is used as a capital protection for the institution ('equity capital'). A loss exceeding the VaR would wipe out the equity capital possibly leading to bankruptcy. In this case the choice of the confidence level should reflect the degree of risk aversion of the company and the cost of exceeding VaR. Next to this, the choice of the horizon depends on the time that is required for corrective actions as losses start to develop; correcting actions can take the form both of reducing the risk profile or to raise new capital (Jorion, 2000).[18]

What has been described up to now might give an idea of the remarkable number of risk measures that have been proposed in the literature. In order to set apart more and less appropriate risk measures, Artzner et al. (1997) propose a series of axioms. Given X and Y as the future losses of two portfolios, a risk measure is consistent if:

1. risk is monotonic: if $X \leq Y$ then $\sigma(X) \leq \sigma(Y)$
2. risk is homogeneous: $\sigma(\lambda X) = \sigma \lambda(X)$ for $\lambda > 0$
3. riskless translation invariance exists: $\sigma(x + X) = \sigma(X) + x$, where x is a riskless bond
4. risk is subadditive: $\sigma(X+Y) \leq \sigma(X) + \sigma(Y)$.

The first point represents the *monotonicity axiom* and it imposes that risk and return are connected. The *homogeneity axiom* ensures that one cannot increase or decrease risk by investing differing amounts in the same stock; in other words the risk arises from the stock itself and is not a function of the quantity that is purchased. The *translation invariance axiom* can be explained by the fact that the investment in a riskless bond bears no loss. The *subadditivity* is the most important axiom because it ensures that a coherent risk measure takes into account portfolio diversification.

Risk measures that do not comply with the axioms can be modified in order to become coherent. For example, if we apply the four axioms to the VaR we find that it cannot be considered a coherent risk measure because it does not respect the subadditivity axiom (Mitra, 2009). The problem can be solved by taking into account the diversification effect when calculating the VaR of portfolios (Allen et al., 2004).[19]

The subadditivity axiom also demonstrates the importance of capturing dependencies between securities when measuring the risk of a portfolio; this evidence has given rise to the field of studies referred to the 'copulas' (Nelsen, 2006). These functions allow the mapping of a set of marginal distributions into a multivariate distribution and vice versa. In fact, a copula is used to separate the pure randomness of one variable (for example, a financial asset) from the interdependencies between it and the other variables. By doing so, one can model each variable separately and, in addition, have a measure of the relations between those variables. Technically, this means that the univariate probability distribution, that informs about the probabilities of outcomes of one variable, can be modelled by a distribution type, while another variable can be described by another type of probability distribution. By doing so, one can choose for each asset the most appropriate type of distribution, not influencing the interdependencies between those assets that are represented by a multivariate probability distribution function. A variety of copulas already exists at the moment; examples include the Gaussian copula (Frey et al., 2001) and Clayton copula (Cuvelier and Noirhomme-Fraiture, 2005). Others will probably be proposed in the future as it continues to be an area of active research (Mitra, 2009).

1.1.3 The risk return trade off

With the seminal article about portfolio selection, Markowitz (1952b) introduces the Modern Portfolio Theory (MPT), whose main contribution deals with:

- the mean–variance relationship
- the portfolio diversification.

Both these concepts were already known even before 1952. In particular, diversification of investments was a well-established practice long before Markowitz published his paper (Rubinstein, 2002). Daniel Bernoulli in his 1738 article argues by example that risk averse investors will want to diversify: '... *it is advisable to divide goods which are exposed to some small danger into several portions rather than to risk them all together*'.[20]

What was lacking before Markowitz (1952b) was an adequate and formalised theory of investments that covered the effects of diversification and analysed risk–return trade-offs on the portfolio as a whole (Markowitz, 1999) rather than concentrating on single securities. Markowitz's work shows that it is not a security's own risk that is important to an investor, but rather the contribution the security makes to the variance of his or her entire portfolio.

There are three main hypotheses under the Modern Portfolio Theory (MPT):

- Investors select their portfolios based on the expected return and expected risk (that is measured by the standard deviation[21])
- Investors are risk averse (risk is considered a negative variable) and try to maximise their expected utility (they are rational)
- The investors' investment horizon is one and unique.

The first and second hypotheses represent the foundation of the mean–variance relationship; between two investment strategies (or portfolios) the one showing the highest return and the lowest risk is preferred by all investors. In brief, investors try to maximise the investment return by bearing the lowest risk that is possible. Starting from these assumptions, Markowitz proposes the way to calculate a portfolio expected return and risk and, by doing this, he introduces the second main contribution of his theory: diversification. The expected return of a portfolio is the weighted average of the expected returns of individual securities based on the single weights (1.12); the variance of the portfolio is a weighted average of the single securities risk sided by the covariance of the single securities as in (1.13) (that is the degree to which the single securities move together or not, measured by the correlation coefficient $\rho_{i,j}$). The weight represents the quantity of each asset that is included in the portfolio.

$$E(r_p) = \sum_{i=1}^{n} E(r_i) * w_i \tag{1.12}$$

where:
r_p is the return of the portfolio p;
r_i is the return of the security i with i=1 ... ... n;
w_i is the weight of the security i in the portfolio p.

$$\sigma_p = \sqrt{\sum_{i=1}^{n}(w_i\sigma_i)^2 + \sum_{i=1}^{n}\sum_{j=1}^{n} w_i w_j \sigma_i \sigma_j \rho_{i,j}} \tag{1.13}$$

where:
σ_p is the standard deviation of the portfolio *p;*
w_i is the weight of the security *i* in the portfolio *p*;
$\rho_{i,j}$ is the correlation coefficient between securities *i* and *j* with *i* and *j*=1 ...... n.

If we manage a portfolio of perfectly correlated securities (having a correlation coefficient ρ equal to one) the different portfolios we can obtain by changing the single securities weights are the AB line shown in Figure 1.1 (A is the lowest risk–return portfolio and B is the higest risk–return portfolio):

This means that, if the securities are perfectly correlated, by increasing the return of the portfolio the investor is accepting a proportional increase in the risk he or she is bearing. Moreover, all the porfolios are equally desirable because portfolios with higher risk are also featured by higher return and investors will choose their preferred based on their personal degree of risk aversion.[22]

By adding another series of portfolios with securities that are not perfectly correlated we can obtain more efficient results; in fact, while the return remains the same (because the correlation coefficient is not included in (1.12)), the risk lowers due to the diversification effect, as shown by the solid line in Figure 1.2. As they are not perfectly correlated, some securities compensate their risk determining a decrease in the total risk of the portfolio and allowing the AB line to curve to the left (thus becoming ADB),[23] as Figure 1.2 shows.

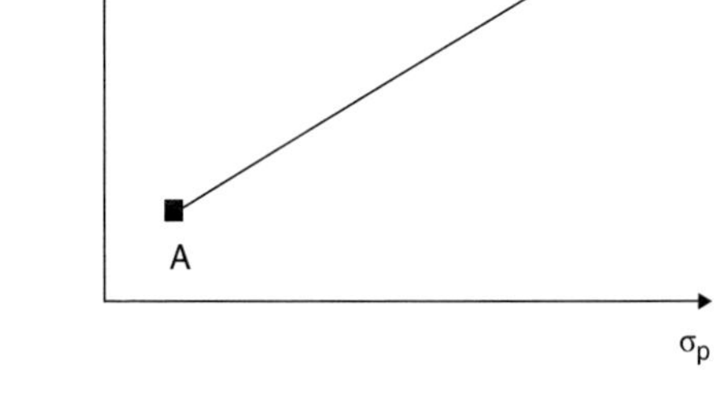

Figure 1.1 Portfolios of perfectly correlated securities

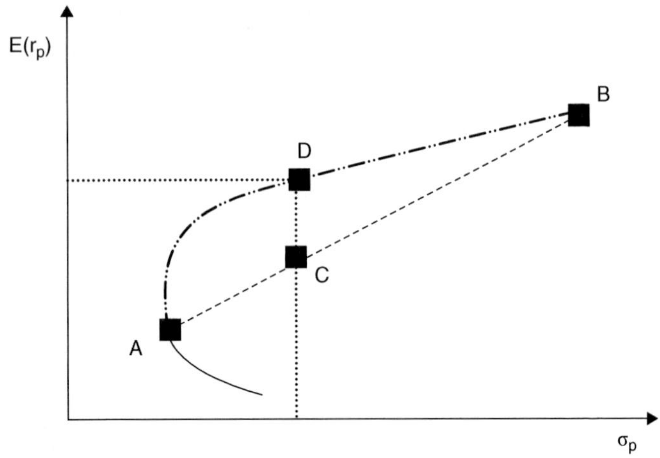

Figure 1.2 Frontier of efficient portfolios

This way, some portfolios (C and D in Figure 1.2) show the same level of risk but different levels of return. The best portfolios are those that maximise the return for a given level of risk or minimise risk for a given level of return (solid line curve). Markowitz (1952b) calls these portfolios *efficient* as they provide the most efficient mean–variance combinations for a risk averse investor.[24] The portofolios lying on the efficient frontier are all desirable to investors as they represent optimal combinations of risk and return. At this point, the choice of every single investor will depend upon the personal degree of risk aversion. The economic theory of choices states that an investor chooses among the different opportunities by specifying a series of curves (called utility functions or indifference curves).[25] So, given an opportunity set (the different options an investor can choose among), the preferences the investors exhibit for the alternatives allow to build their set of indifference curves informing about their degree of risk aversion (Elton and Gruber, 1995).

In general, there are three basic configurations of the curve of indifference, as shown in Figure 1.3. All three charts show that the utility of a subject increases with the expected return of the investment, according to the assumptions of Markowitz (1952b); nevertheless, if we compare the mean and variance in Figure 1.4, in order to bear a given level of risk σ_x, the risk averse subjects (top three curves) require a higher expected return compared to the risk seeker subjects (lower three curves).

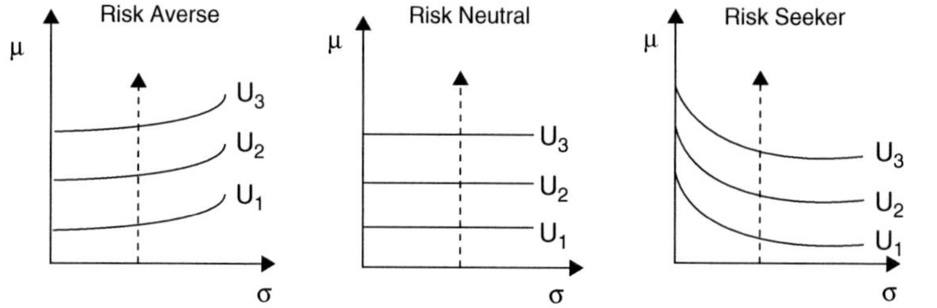

Figure 1.3 Indifference curves for a risk seeker, risk neutral and risk averse subject

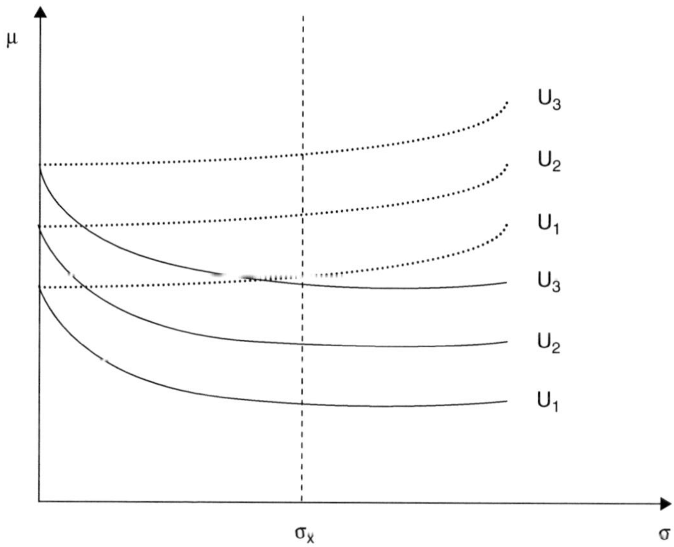

Figure 1.4 Comparison of risk averse and risk seeker subjects

The mean–variance relationship introduces for the first time a subjective element into finance theory. In fact, there are cases where the choice among different alternatives cannot be predicted a priori but need to consider one's level of risk aversion thus implying a subjective choice instead of an objective one. The indifference curves that are involved in the MPT are based on a quadratic utility function (1.14) whose slope is determined by the coefficient of absolute risk aversion (A) that is positive by definition[26] (Pilbeam, 1998). The utility function that is used in

Markowitz (1952b) is based on the Von Neumann–Morgensten (1944) utility function that assigns a value of utility to each payoff (Bernstein and Damodaran, 1998).

$$U = E(r) - \frac{1}{2}A\sigma^2 \qquad (1.14)$$

where:
U is the utility deriving from the investment;
E(r) is the expected return of the investment;
A is the level of risk aversion for the investor we are considering;
σ^2 is the risk fo the investment.

This function reflects two important points:

(a) Investors's utility is based on the risk and return of the investment (according to the first hypothesis of the MPT).
(b) Risk is something that investors dislike, as shown by the negative relationship between utility and risk (according to the second hypothesis of the MPT)

The tangent point between the curve of indifference and the efficient frontier represents the most efficient portfolio for the investors we are considering (subjective dimension of choice), as shown in Figure 1.5.

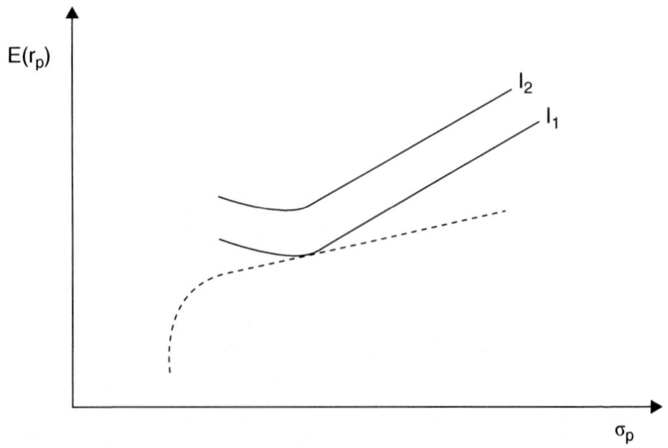

Figure 1.5 Efficient frontier and curves of indifference

In spite of this, a major problem with the MPT is the huge amount of covariances that have to be calculated when assessing the risk of a portfolio. In the case where we have two securities in the portfolio there is only one covariance but when the portfolio is made by n securities the covariances that need to be calculated are much more.[27] As a consequence, the amount of calculation required for the Markowitz method was one of the factors stimulating other approaches to investment management (Pilbeam, 1998).

The first attempt to simplify the MPT was proposed by Sharpe (1963).[28] Based on the concept of correlation between securities formalised by Markowitz, he introduced the idea that shares are not only correlated between themselves but also with the market. So, the return of a security is linked to the return of the market by a coefficient (beta) that informs about the degree of correlation with the market, as in (1.15):

$$E(r_i) = \alpha_i + \beta_i E(r_m) + e_i \tag{1.15}$$

So, if the share has a beta equal to one it will move similarly to the market but if the beta is more or less than one it will be more or less volatile that the market as a whole. Equation (1.15) is usually termed the *characteristic line* and clearly highlights the two components of risk: the systematic risk[29] and the specific risk.[30] As the specific risk of a security can be reduced to zero by an appropriate diversification, the return of a security (that is the compensation for the risk the investors is bearing) is mainly due to the market risk that cannot be diversified. Nonetheless, even if the market model dramatically reduces the number of variables required to evaluate a portfolio, it lacks a clear theoretical base and it does have a few limitations, especially with reference to the definition of market return (Pilbeam, 1998). Some of these problems are fixed by the Capital Asset Pricing Model (CAPM).

The CAPM is based on the work of Sharpe (1964), Lintner (1965) and Mossin (1966). It attempts to explain how securities should be priced, based on their relative riskiness in combination with the return on risk free assets. The hypotheses that are under the model partially reflect those already formulated by Markowitz (1952b) but an additional few are added. All investors are assumed to have homogeneous expectations, and as being economic agents who maximise the expected utility of their end of period wealth. Thus all investors have identical opportunity sets. They further assume the presence of risk free assets and investors may borrow or lend unlimited amounts of this asset at a constant rate: the risk free rate and assets' returns are normally distributed.[31]

The first point to be considered is how the risk and return of a portfolio change if we introduce a risk free asset. Under the hypothesis of homogeneous expectations, all investors hold the same risky portfolio that in equilibrium[32] includes all the securities that are in the market in proportion to their market value (for this reason it is called market portfolio). By adding a risk free asset to the market portfolio *m*, equation (1.12) becomes:

$$E(r_p) = [w_f(r_f)] + [(1 - w_f)E(r_{mp})] \tag{1.16}$$

and equation (1.13) becomes:

$$\sigma_p = \sqrt{(w_f \sigma_f)^2 + [(1 - .w_f)\sigma_{mp}]^2 + w_f(1 - w_f)\sigma_{mp}\sigma_f \rho_{mp,f}} \tag{1.17}$$

That is reduced to (1.18) because of σ_f being zero.

$$\sigma_p = [(1 - w_f)\sigma_{mp}] \tag{1.18}$$

In this case, the variance of the portfolio entirely depends on the proportion that is invested into the market portolfio. If we substitute in (1.18) $w_f = 1 - \frac{\sigma_p}{\sigma_{mp}}$

we obtain:

$$E(r_p) = r_f + \left(\frac{E(r_{mp}) - r_f}{\sigma_{mp}}\right)\sigma_p \tag{1.19}$$

In this case, the return of the portfolio is made up of the return of the risk free asset and the risk premium obtained by investing into the market portfolio.[33] Equation (1.19) represents the *capital market line* (CML) whose intercept is the return of the risk free asset (*R*f) and its slope is the risk premium. The market portfolio (*mp*) is the tangent point between the CML and the efficient frontier. Each point in the CML between *r*f and *mp* represents a different combination (in terms of percentages) of risk free asset and market portfolio.

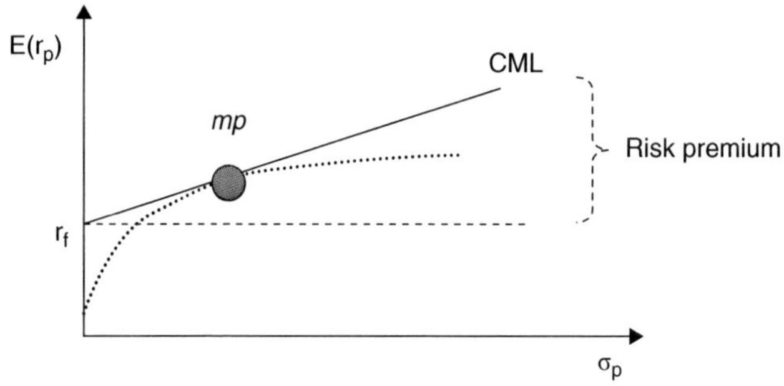

Figure 1.6 Capital market line

This way, the optimal risky portfolio (*mp*) is the same for all the investors given their homogeneous expectations. Differences in individual tastes emerge when determining the proportion of risk free asset[34] to be included in the porfolio. So, the indifference curves enter the analysis when the proportion of the market portfolio and risk free asset are established. The indifference curve in its tangent point with the CML will suggest the mix of *mp* and risk free assets that is suitable to that particular investor (Levy and Sarnat, 1995).

In this case, the only risk we are considering depends on the systematic risk, because the specific risk is eliminated through the diversification (as the market portfolio contains all the risky assets in the market).

Problems may arise when considering portfolios that are not efficient (poorly diversified or made up of only a few securities) and whose risk is due to both the market and specific components. In this case, the formula of the return has to consider explicitely the correlation coefficient linking a single security (or poorly diversified portfolio) with the market. This equation is expressed as:

$$E(r_p) = r_f + \left\{ [E(r_m) - r_f]^* \rho_{p,m} \frac{\sigma_p}{\sigma_m} \right\} \tag{1.20}$$

Where $\rho_{p,m} \frac{\sigma_p}{\sigma_m}$ is termed beta and represents the systematic risk of the portfolio depending on its correlation with the market. Equation (1.20) indicates the *security market line* (SML), which differs from the CML in that it can have a possibile application to every portfolio (and not only to efficient ones). Equation (1.20) is also called *market model* (MM) and provides a way to correctly price a financial asset; its return is a function of the risk free asset return and of the degree to which the asset (or portfolio) is linked to the market return (systematic risk). The specific component of risk is not priced by the market as it can be totally eliminated through an appropriate diversification (under the hypothesis of no transaction costs).[35]

Perhaps the most important difference between the CAPM and the MM is the 'market return'. The market model refers to market return as a stock index return thus confining its possible application to the stock market; on the contrary, the CAPM refers to a generic market portfolio that can include every risky financial asset.[36] In theory, the CAPM has infinite possibile applications because it can be used for every financial activity. Nevertheless, in practice, the beta that is proposed in the MM is very often used as a proxy of the CAPM beta due to the difficulty of defining a porfolio that includes all the possibile risky assets that one can find in the market or to the subjectivity apparent in selecting only some of them. As a consequence, a stock market index that is compatible for geographic area, sector, and so on, with the portfolio or security is often used as a proxy. This last point represents one of the major limits of the CAPM that the following Arbitrage Pricing Theory (APT) of Ross (1976) tries to overcome. As far as the limits of the CAPM are concerned, altough the assumptions of the CAPM are sometimes too tight to hold in the real word, criticisms of the CAPM cannot be attributed solely to its assumptions; in fact, some studies (Black et al., 1972; Fama, 1970) have concluded that the CAPM might hold even if some assumptions are relaxed (Mirza, 2005). The major critique comes from the weakness of the empirical tests that have been conducted on the model over the years. These tests have revealed a series of problems that can be grouped as follows:

(a) Returns are not statistically positively related to beta
(b) The CAPM is rejected when the porfolio that is used as a market proxy is inefficient
(c) Since the market portfolio is not measurable, the CAPM can never be empirically proven or disproven

As far as the first point is concerned, the problem arises from the practice of estimating future betas based on their historical values. Although the model postulates a positive linear relationship between beta and returns, researchers are concerned about the stability of this link over time. If beta is found to be not stable its estimation reliability is questioned. Blume (1971), Baesel (1974) and Roenfeldt (1978) used different datasets over various time periods and observed that beta is not totally stable over time. Futhermore, in the 1990s, Fama and French (1992, 1996), Jegadeesh (1992) and Faff and Brooks (1998) came to the same results and concluded with a doubt about the attitude of the beta to be an appropriate measure of risk.

With reference to the second point, many authors (Roll, 1977; Ross, 1976; Fama and Macbeth, 1973; Black, 1993, Roll and Ross, 1994) find out that the use of an inefficient proxy for the market portfolio deeply changes the relationship that is postulated for the CAPM. For example, Roll and Ross (1994) and Kandel and Stambaugh (1996) demonstrate that even small deviations from efficiency can produce an insignificant relationship between risk and expected returns.

The third critique refers to the impossibility of testing the real CAPM. In fact, as already mentioned above, in order to maximise its diversification, the efficient market portfolio should be made of all the possible assets that are negotiated in the market (such as securities, fine arts, real estate, jewels, and so on). Nevertheless, as the real market portfolio is not observable in nature, a proxy of it is usually used in the application of the model. As a consequence, what has been tested in the literature is a 'synthetic CAPM' instead of the real one (Roll and Ross, 1980).

Some solutions have been proposed over the years to overcome the limits mentioned above; these can be grouped as follows:

- multifactor CAPM
- CAPM with higher co-movements
- conditional CAPM.

A first group of studies (*multifactor CAPM*) show that the cross-sectional variation in average security returns cannot be explained by the market beta alone. The first and most important multifactor model that has been proposed in the literature is the Arbitrage Pricing Theory (APT) of Ross (1976). The basic idea under the APT is that market risk itself is made of a number of systematic factors and the beta alone is not able to incorporate all the market risk. He comments that asset pricing should not be attributed to a single factor (beta), but rather it is a function of various economic factors. Thus, the expected return of a financial asset can be a linear function of various factors, where sensitivity to changes in each factor is represented by a specific beta coefficient. This leads to an important advantage that is introduced by the APT; in fact, this last model does not require the identification of an efficient market portfolio thus avoiding one of the most criticised points of the CAPM. The model derived rate of return is then used to price the asset correctly. At this point, if the price diverges from its correct value, arbitrage should bring it back into line. The APT also differs from the CAPM in that it is less restrictive in its assumptions. It assumes that each investor will hold a unique portfolio with its own particular array of betas, as opposed to the identical 'market portfolio'.

Nevertheless, the model by Ross does not give any indication about the number or typology of factors that should explain the return of an asset (Pilbeam, 1998). The following studies sought to identify the factors that could be involved in the explanation of an asset's return. Roll and Ross (1980) suggest that possible relevant factors can be the unanticipated changes in the industrial production, unanticipated changes in interest rates, the slope of the yield curve, the unanticipated inflation and the unanticipated changes in the spread between high and low grade bonds. Other authors propose some further variables such as the firm size (Banz, 1981), the book-to-market ratio (Chan et al., 1991) and the price to earning ratio (Basu, 1983). Fama and French (1995) in their three factor model demonstrate that SMB (the difference between the return of a portolfio of small stocks and the return of a portfolio of large stocks) and HML (the difference between the return of a portolfio of high book-to-market stocks and a portfolio of low book-to-market stocks) are useful factors when explaining a cross-section of equity returns.

A second group of studies (*CAPM with higher order co-movements*) pay attention to the non-normality of the return distribution and to the unsuitability of the mean–variance to characterise the return distribution. Kraus and Litzenberg (1976), Friend and Westerfield (1981), Sears and Wei (1985) and Harvey and Siddique (2000) test the CAPM with third moment (skewness) and fourth moment (kurtosis) and show that systematic variance, skewness and kurtosis contribute to the risk premium of an asset, even when factors based on size, book-to-market ratio, ans so on, are considered.

Moreover, following the suggestion made by Levy (1974) to compute separate betas for bull and bear markets, Fabozzi and Francis (1977) formally estimate and test the stability of betas over the bull and bear markets (*conditional asset pricing models*). They find no evidence supporting beta instability. However, in an empirical analysis of the cross-sectional relationship between the expected returns and beta, Fabozzi and Francis (1978) conclude that investors appreciate a positive premium for accepting downside risk, while a negative premium was associated with the up market beta; this suggests that downside risk (as measured by the beta corresponding to the bear market) may be a more appropriate measure of portfolio risk than the conventional single beta. After Fabozzi and Francis (1978), other authors continue to conduct tests in the same vein (Kim and Zumwalt, 1979; Chen, 1982) and they reach similar conclusions. Bhardwaj and Brooks (1993) observe that the systematic risks in bull and bear time periods are statistically different. Furthermore, following the introduction of ARCH and GARCH processes by Engle (1982), some authors have tested a GARCH based CAPM and they provide stronger evidence of the risk–return relationship than the unconditional models. For example, Fraser et al. (2004) compared the cross-sectional risk–return relationship obtained with an unconditional specification of the asset's betas with betas obtained through Quantitative Threshold ARCH (QTARCH8) and GARCH-M9 models. In all specifications, they consider the possibility of negative return–risk relationships when excess return on the market is negative. They observe that CAPM holds better in downward moving markets than in upward markets; this evidence suggests that beta as a risk measure is more appropriate in the bear markets. Further critics to the traditional CAPM come from the behavioural standpoint and will be discussed in section 1.2.4.

1.2 Risk: the behavioural finance viewpoint

1.2.1 Definition of risk

Before the rise of modern finance, some reputable economists, such as Adam Smith, Irving Fisher, John Maynard Keynes and Harry Markowitz, thought that the psychology of individuals affects the market. Some years before publishing *The Wealth of Nations*, Smith proposed a theory of human behaviour (*The Theory of Moral Sentiments, 1759*), where he argued that behaviour was determined by the struggle between the myopic 'passions' (such as emotions, motivational feelings, the 'overweening conceit' of mankind) and the 'impartial spectator' (a sort of farsighted planner and judge that scrutinises each move). Fisher wrote a book on 'money illusion' (*The Money Illusion, 1928*) where he argued that nominal interest rates systematically fail to adjust sufficiently for inflation, and explained savings behaviour in relation to some personal factors, such as self-control, foresight and habits (*The Theory of Interest, 1930*). Keynes (*The General Theory of Employment, Interest and Money, 1936*) famously commented on animal spirits in stock markets. Markowitz (1952a) proposed that people focus on gains and losses relative to a reference point, and that this in turn helps to explain the pricing of insurance and lotteries.

The creators of modern financial theory seem to have lost this train of thought. The traditional finance paradigm seeks to understand financial markets and to explain risk exposure using models in which agents are 'rational'. Rationality means primarily four things. First, when they receive new information, agents update their beliefs correctly, in the manner described by Bayes' law (*unbiased expectations*). Secondly, given their beliefs, agents make choices that are normatively acceptable, in the sense that they are consistent with Von Neumann and Morgenstern's expected utility theory (EU, henceforth), if the objective probabilities are known, and with Savage's notion of subjective expected utility (SEU, henceforth), if true probabilities are unknown but are estimated subjectively (*rational decision*). Thirdly, agents only value money or consumption and additionally, the value they attach to monetary outcomes or consumption is not influenced by aspects like mood, experience with a specific scenario, sudden increase in fear and regret or the feeling of others (*financial objectives*). Finally, agents work as optimisers, in the sense that they always optimise their own interests over all possible alternatives (*optimal outcome*).

This traditional framework is appealingly simple, and it would be very satisfying if its predictions were confirmed in the data. Unfortunately, after years of effort and countless studies, it has become clear that basic facts about the aggregate stock market, the cross-section of average returns and the risk behaviour of individuals are not easily understood in this framework.

Behavioural finance is a new approach to financial markets that has emerged, at least in part, in response to the difficulties faced by the traditional paradigm. As the name suggests, behavioural finance aims to improve our understanding of financial markets and its participants by applying insights from behavioural sciences (for example, psychology and sociology). In broad terms, it argues that some financial phenomena, such as the investment process and risk taking, can be better understood using models in which some agents are *not* fully rational. More specifically, behavioural finance analyses what happens when we relax one, or more, of the four assumptions underlying the theory of rational choice (Table 1.2). In some behavioural finance models, agents fail to update their beliefs correctly (*limited knowledge of possible outcomes and biased expectations*); alternatively, they apply Bayes' law properly but make choices that are normatively questionable, in that they are incompatible with SEU. Underlyingly, there is a rationality that

Table 1.2 Fundamentals of the fully rational approach and parallel fundamentals of the behavioural approach

Fundamentals of the fully rational approach	Fundamentals of the behavioural approach
Unbiased expectations	Limited knowledge of possible outcomes and biased expectations
Rational decisions	Bounded rationality
Financial objectives	Emotional profile
Optimal outcome	Satisfactory outcome

Table 1.3 The new concept of risk in the behavioural perspective

Traditional finance	Behavioural finance
Objective	Subjective
One-dimensional	Multidimensional
Macro-perspective oriented	Micro-perspective oriented

is not full, but limited by the information people have, the cognitive limitations of their minds, and the finite amount of time they have to make decisions (*bounded rationality*). Furthermore, some studies propose a financial decision maker that is influenced by personal factors (such as emotions) during the decision process (*emotional profile*) or one who merely addresses a satisfactory final outcome, rather than an optimal one (*satisfactory outcome*).[37]

Within this framework, the concept of risk also turns out to be different. Behavioural finance looks at risk in greater depth and finds that attitudes towards risk are not always logical: real individuals usually have to address risk in situations that they have never encountered before, for which statistical techniques are largely irrelevant. As a consequence, there is evidently much more to risk than traditional finance has considered and a significant proportion of this involves how people form images of the events that they are expected to assess the risk of. If the risk in the traditional financial perspective may be defined as objective, one-dimensional and macro-perspective oriented, the opposite stands for the behavioural viewpoint (Table 1.3).

First, behavioural finance assumes that a vital aspect of investment decision making is the *subjective* nature of perceived risk by the investors rather than exclusively the objective risk emphasised by standard finance theorists. In the traditional financial paradigm, risk exists 'out there', independent of our minds and cultures, waiting to be measured. In contrast, the behavioural perspective broadens the concept of risk and improves the overall area of risk judgement, by recognising the subjective nature of an individual's own perception of risk as a supplement to the traditional measures of objective risk.

Secondly, the concept of risk in the behavioural perspective is *multidimensional,* as it includes not only past occurrences of an event and its statistical measures, but also the misvaluation deriving from limitations of both knowledge and cognitive capacity.

Finally, the concept of risk is depicted from a *microeconomic perspective,* as behavioural risk research concentrates on the individual decision maker (for example, an expert professional or an individual investor) in order to gain better understanding into the valuation process. In this perspective, a substantial part of the behavioural finance literature is based upon laboratory experiments and mailed surveys that document the wide range of behavioural indicators that influence an individual's perception of risk.

1.2.2 Investment decision making biases

To make sharp predictions, behavioural models need to specify how agents deviate from the prescriptions of fully rational models. For guidance on this, behavioural economists typically turn to the extensive experimental evidence compiled by cognitive psychologists on the biases that arise when people form beliefs or on how they make decisions, given their beliefs. We review the psychological findings most relevant to the investment decision process in the current section, calling them investment decision making 'biases', as opposed to the objective 'risk measures' used by a fully rational agent in the investment decision process and outlined in section 1.1.2. These biases may be grouped into two main building blocks, as outlined in Figure 1.7.

The first building block (*mental processes*) addresses all cognitive limitations that set restrictions on the capacity to manage complex information and on the ability to make optimal decisions, which consequently

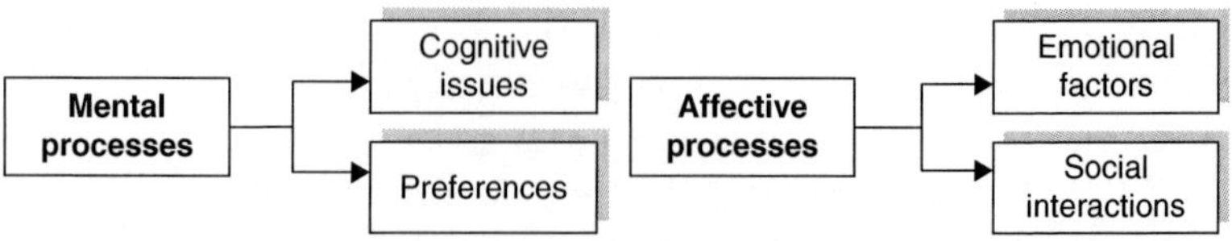

Figure 1.7 Investment decision making biases: the main building blocks

can lead to frequent judgement errors (Ricciardi, 2008). Traditional financial theory is based on the premise that individuals employ the use of financial analysis in a rational and systematic manner; on the contrary, behavioural finance shows that investors do not always process this information logically, efficiently and neatly, as people possess a limited working memory and limited computational capabilities (Simon, 1955; Arthur, 1994; Conlisk, 1996).

The second building block (*affective processes*) includes some factors, external to mental processes, which may influence the final decision as well. Behavioural finance focuses on the issues of emotional factors and social interactions that affect the risk judgement and the decision making process of investors (Ricciardi, 2008); both affective processes may lead to sub-optimal choices and results.

A summary of the fundamental decision making biases that may be of particular interest to the investment decision making process is reported in Table 1.4.

[A] Cognitive issues

A crucial component of any model of investment decisions is a specification of how agents process information and evaluate alternative choices. We now summarise what psychologists have learnt about how people appear to form beliefs in practice.

Heuristics A heuristic can be defined as a simple and general rule people employ to solve a specific category of problems; they are especially relevant when it comes to situations that involve a high degree of risk taking or uncertainty. Following the definition proposed by Ricciardi and Simon (2001), heuristics are 'mental shortcuts or strategies derived from our past experience that get us where we need to go quickly, but at the cost of sending us in the wrong direction'. Since time and cognitive resources are limited, we cannot analyse the data which the environment provides us with optimality. Instead, natural selection has developed our minds to implement rules of thumbs, or heuristics in the formal sense, that are very common in all types of problems. In many situations these heuristics yield optimal behaviour, but in some situations they do not, consequently resulting in systematic errors (called 'biases' or 'cognitive illusions'). The significance of heuristics in judgements under risk taking or uncertainty has been a major source of research in the area of decision making over the past four decades in works by Tversky and Kahneman (1973), Kahneman et al. (1982) and Gilovich et al. (2002).

Table 1.4 Investment decision making biases

Investment decision making biases	Event type	Biased effects
[A] Cognitive issues	Heuristics: - Availability heuristic - Representativeness	*Ease of recall bias* *Base rate neglect* *Sample size neglect* *Gambler's fallacy effect* *Trend chasing* *Halo effect*
	Framing	*Soothing effect* *Narrow framing* *Money illusion* *Preference reversals* *Context effects*
	Anchoring	*Conservatism*
	Overconfidence	*Miscalibration* *Self-attribution bias* *Hindsight bias* *Cognitive dissonance* *Rationalisation* *Confirmation bias*
	Ambiguity aversion	*Familiarity bias*
	Perceived control	*Locus of control* *Illusion of control*
	Mental accounting	*Sequential choices*
[B] Preferences	Prospect theory	*Utility over gains/losses* *Risk aversion/seeking over gains/losses* *Loss aversion* *Small probabilities overweighting* *Certainty effect*
[C] Emotional factors	Current feelings and mood Anticipation of future feelings	*Misattribution bias* *Risk/loss aversion* *House money effect* *Break-even effect* *Omission bias* *Endowment effect* *Status quo bias*
[D] Social interactions	Person to person contagion Media contagion	*Herding* *Rigid thinking* *Fundamental attribution error* *False consensus effect*

Two types of heuristics that have an effect on a person's perception of risk are the *availability heuristic* and *representativeness.* The *availability heuristic* was initially proposed in the work of Tversky and Kahneman (1973) and it is utilised in order to judge the likelihood or frequency of an event. Individuals who employ the *availability heuristic* judge the degree of risk of an event as highly probable, or indeed frequent, if examples of it are easy to remember or to visualise. In other words, items that are easier to recall are judged to be more common. While this is a perfectly sensible procedure, it can produce biased estimates because not all memories are equally retrievable or 'available', in the language of Tversky and Kahneman (1973); more recent events and more salient events will weigh more heavily and distort the estimate (*ease of recall bias*).[38]

On the other hand, *representativeness* is a cognitive bias that causes people to form an opinion regarding events in terms of how much they resemble other events with which they are familiar; the human brain has an automatic inclination to make judgements based on the similarity of items, assuming that similar situations are de facto identical, even though substantial differences may be present. Much of the time, *representativeness* is a helpful heuristic, but sometimes it can generate some severe biases. The first is the *base rate neglect*, which occurs when people assess the conditional probability of a hypothesis given some evidence without taking sufficient account of the 'base rate' or 'prior probability' of such evidence.[39] *Representativeness* also leads to another bias, the *sample size neglect.* When judging the likelihood that a dataset was generated by a particular model, people often fail to take the size of the sample into account: they think that, after all, a small sample can be just as representative as a large one. *Sample size neglect* means that in cases where people do not initially know the data generating process, they will tend to infer and make conclusions from it too quickly on the basis of too few data points. This belief that even a small sample will reflect the properties of the parent population is sometimes known as the 'law of small numbers' (Rabin, 2002). In situations where people do know the data generating process in advance, the law of small numbers generates a *gambler's fallacy effect* (Barberis and Thaler, 2002). This is the belief that, in an independent sample, the recent occurrence of one outcome increases the odds that the next outcome will differ; in fact, people avoid betting on a lottery number that was also a winner sometime over the preceding few days (Clotfelter and Cook, 1993). Use of *representativeness* can further lead to *trend chasing,* because people are too ready to believe that trends have systematic causes. Statisticians refer to the 'clustering illusion', wherein people perceive random clusters as reflecting a causal pattern; for instance, people mistakenly believe in 'hot hands' among sport players (meaning that a player is more likely to make his or her next point given that he or she has been recently successful) even when actual performance is very close to serially independent (Gilovich et al. 1985) or try to spot trends in random processes (for example, stock prices), expecting past price change to continue (called the *extrapolation bias*, as in DeBondt, 1998).[40] A final bias eventually connected with the use of *representativeness* is the *halo effect*, which causes someone who likes one outstanding characteristic of an individual to extend this favourable evaluation to the individual's other characteristics (Nisbett and Wilson, 1977).

Framing Another factor that may influence a person's decision making process and perception of risk is the format in which a situation or choice is presented, known as *framing*. Kahneman and Tvesrky (1979) depict framing effects from two perspectives: on the one hand, authors underline the environment or context where the decision has to be assumed; on the other hand, they consider the format in which the question is framed or worded. In this second perspective, for example, a chance of succeeding with a 50 per cent of probability sounds different from a chance of failing with a 50 per cent of probability: the success frame of the former option makes it seem more appealing than the failure frame of the latter, although the probability of success versus failure is the same for both. It follows that sometimes people choose the selection that is more psychologically soothing and pleasing rather than it being the best option (a sort of *soothing effect*). A second effect relates to the evidence that people tend to analyse problems in a manner which is too isolated, taking decisions one at a time without considering the big picture (the so-called *narrow bracketing* or *narrow framing*). As a consequence, if choices come one at a time, people bracket them narrowly, and if choices come many at a time, people bracket them more broadly (Redelmeier and Tversky, 1992; Read et al., 1999; Kahneman, 2003); for example, when choosing among several items, people tend to choose more variety when their decision is presented simultaneously than when choosing them sequentially.

Related to the concept of *framing*, there are other consequential effects that may affect the decision making process and risk perception also. *Money illusion* is another documented example of sensitivity to irrelevant description features and refers to the tendency to think in terms of nominal rather than real monetary values (Shafir et al., 1997).

By using different presentation, experimenters can also elicit *preference reversals*: faced with a choice between a binary lottery, with a high probability buy relatively low maximum payoff, versus another with lower probability and higher maximum payoff, subjects often tend to prefer the high probability lottery, yet place a higher valuation on the high maximum payoff lottery. Finally, there are some *context effects* in which the presence of a non-selected choice alternative affects which alternative is selected (Hirshleifer, 2001).

A critical implication of *framing* is that the presentation of information can be utilised to modify an individual's perception of risk; as outlined by Slovich et al. (1982), 'subtle differences in how risks are presented can have marked effects on how they are perceived'. Among relevant studies, the work of Sitkin and Weingart (1995) specifically investigates the association between the framing problem, risk perception and risk taking behaviour.[41] More recently, Bischof and Ebert (2009) investigate whether the label under which a financial instrument is presented affects the risk perception of investors.[42]

Anchoring Kahneman and Tversky (1974) argue that when forming estimates, people often start with some initial, possibly arbitrary belief, and then with an upcoming decision they adjust away from it; experimental evidence shows that the adjustment is often insufficient and people tend to 'anchor' too much on their initial belief. One of the most frequent anchors is a series of past events; for example, when projecting sales of a product for the coming year, a marketer often begins by looking at sales volume for past years, resulting in putting too much weight on past history and giving insufficient weight to other factors. Hammond et al. (1998) illustrate an additional example of anchoring; in their experiment, subjects are asked whether the population of Turkey is greater than 35 million and then to provide a precise estimate of Turkey's population. Their subsequent precise estimates are significantly affected by the initial random number of 35 million included in the first question, as in 50 per cent of the experiments the 35 million figure is utilised, revealing that when people make judgements their minds give inappropriate significance or overweight the importance of the initial information it obtains.

Conservatism is the manifestation of *anchoring* upon an initial probability estimate. It implies that individuals do not change their beliefs as much as a rational Bayesian would in the face of new evidence. One explanation for *conservatism* is that processing new information and updating beliefs is costly; as a consequence, *conservatism* is particularly evident when new information is presented in a cognitively costly form.

Overconfidence As the name suggests, *overconfidence* can be described as the belief in oneself and one's abilities with extreme and excessive conviction (Ricciardi, 2008). According to Daniel and Titman (1999), within the behavioural finance literature *overconfidence* is one of the most documented biases. This appears in two guises of *miscalibration*. First, the confidence intervals people assign to their estimates of quantities are far too narrow: their 98 per cent confidence intervals, for example, include the true quantity only about 60 per cent of the time (Alpert and Raiffa, 1982). Secondly, people are poorly calibrated when estimating probabilities: events that they think are certain to occur actually occur only around 80 per cent of the time, and events they deem impossible occur approximately 20 per cent of the time (Fischhoff et al., 1977). Experts can be more prone to *overconfidence* than non-experts when predictability is low and evidence ambiguous. Moreover, men tend to be more overconfident than women; though the size of the difference depends on whether the task is perceived to be masculine or feminine (Griffin and Tversky, 1992).

Overconfidence is often strengthened by the tendency of people: (1) to ascribe success to their own skills while blaming failure on bad luck (called the *self-attribution bias*); (2) to believe they predicted an event beforehand, but after it actually happened, following a retrospective picture of events (called the *hindsight bias*); (3) to develop twisted reasoning or to adjust attitudes to match past actions in order to be persuaded that they are a skilful decision maker (known as *cognitive dissonance*); (4) to construct a plausible *ex post* rationale for past choices to help them feel better about their decision competence (called *rationalisation*); (5) to interpret ambiguous evidence in a fashion consistent with their own prior beliefs (referred to as the *confirmation bias*).

Ambiguity aversion As reported in Barberis and Thaler (2002), people do not like situations where they are uncertain about the probability distribution of a gamble. Such situations are known as situations of ambiguity and are generally disliked. A possible explanation for *ambiguity aversion* is that the obvious absence of an identifiable parameter of the decision problem may often be associated with higher risk and the possibility of hostile manipulation. Heath and Tversky (1991) argue that, in the real world, *ambiguity aversion* has much to do with how competent individuals feel they are at assessing the relevant distribution; in this sense, *ambiguity aversion* in relation to a bet can be strengthened by highlighting subjects' feeling of incompetence, either showing them other bets in which they have more expertise, or by mentioning other people who are more qualified to evaluate the bet (Fox and Tversky, 1995).

Further evidence that supports the competence hypothesis is that in situations where people feel especially competent in evaluating a gamble, the opposite of *ambiguity aversion*, namely a *familiarity bias*, has been observed. The notion of *familiarity bias* has been a prevailing area of investigation in academic studies on risk perception. Individuals are more risk tolerant when they are personally familiar with a specific activity or circumstances, as risks that are familiar are feared less than those that are unfamiliar.

Perceived control The issue of *perceived control* incorporates two main forms of control which are: first, external versus internal control (that is *locus of control*), which explains the degree to which people perceive that they exert control over their own behaviour and personal outcomes of a specific situation compared with chance or outside factors (Rotter, 1971); second, perceived control (that is *illusion of control*), that induces a person to perceive that one has control over the outcome of a situation, even if the events are uncontrollable or random (Baker and Nofsinger, 2002). Within the literature on finance and investment decision making, the notion of how control influences an investor's perception of risk has become well noted and an established area of examination since the early 1980s. The relationship between locus of control and risk taking behaviour is analysed in works by McInish (1982), Maital et al. (1986), Grable and Joo (2000). The attempt to provide proxies for the illusion of control is the focus of other works, such as Forlani (2002) and Weber et al. (2002).

Mental accounting *Mental accounting* (Thaler, 1985) is a kind of cognitive issue that involves keeping track of gains and losses related to decisions in separate mental accounts, and to re-examine each account only intermittently when an action becomes relevant. For instance, people tend to divide monetary resources into different classes depending on their source or their destination; there are essentially three typical categories of mental accounts people refer to: consumption accounts, addressed to general expenses; income account, related to revenues; wealth account, including different sources of wealth. Each category may undergo some misvaluation effects when it is considered separately from another. Specifically, in the case of consumption accounts a frequent judgement mistake is related to the overvaluation of repeated or hedonic consumption (this is the so-called *hedonic framing*). Income is generally split according to the source: the propensity to use income to buy an item seems to be stronger when that income has been obtained occasionally (for example, by a lottery win rather than by a salary increase). Also wealth tends to be divided into mental accounts, being relevant to the kind of wealth involved: liquidity tends to be spent more easily, while consumption is less likely to be financed by disinvesting a real property or borrowing and dipping into one's future wealth.

These considerations seem to be absolutely coherent with the way people manage their resources in everyday life; vice versa, they conflict with the basic assumption of traditional economic theory under which money is perfectly fungible, apart from its provenance or destination. As a consequence, *mental accounting* may lead to sub-optimal outcomes, as it involves a sequential decision process that neglects the interactions between accounts and the relative effects upon choices (Linciano, 2010).

[B] Preferences

Traditional models assume that investors evaluate risky gambles according to EU, if the objective probabilities are known. Unfortunately, experimental work in the decades after the development of EU has shown that people systematically violate EU theory when choosing among risky gambles. In response to this, there has been an explosion of works on so-called non-EU theories, all of them trying to do a better job of matching the experimental evidence. Some of the better-known models include weighted utility theory (Chew and MacCrimmon, 1979; Chew, 1983), implicit EU (Dekel, 1986; Chew, 1989), disappointment aversion (Gul, 1991), regret theory (Bell, 1982; Loomes and Sugden, 1982), rank dependent utility theory (Quiggin, 1982; Yaari, 1987; Segal, 1989), case based decision theory (Gilboa and Schmeidler, 1995) and prospect theory (Kahneman and Tversky, 1979; Tversky and Kahneman, 1992). Of all of the non-EU theories, prospect theory may be the most promising for financial applications and we will discuss it in detail. The reason we focus on this theory is, quite simply, that it is the most successful at capturing the experimental results. In a way, this is not surprising. Most of the other non-EU models are what might be called 'quasi-normative', in that they try to capture some of the anomalous experimental evidence by slightly weakening the EU axioms. The difficulty with such models is that in trying to achieve two goals, that is to be normative and descriptive simultaneously, they end up doing an unsatisfactory job at both. In contrast, prospect theory has no aspiration as a normative theory: it simply tries to capture people's attitude to risky gambles.[43]

Prospect theory builds on Markowitz (1952a), which in turn builds on Friedman and Savage (1948). Friedman and Savage (1948) describe the shape of a utility function consistent with buying both lottery tickets and insurance; the utility function has both concave (insurance policies) and convex (lottery tickets) regions, with an inflection point that is invariant to wealth. Subsequently, Markowitz (1952a) modifies the Friedman–Savage function by locating one of the inflection points at 'customary wealth' which usually coincides with current wealth.[44] Figure 1.8 depicts the shapes of the associated utility functions.

Kahneman and Tversky (1979) follow the intuitions under an S-shaped utility function and lay out the original version of prospect theory, designed for gambles with at most two non-zero outcomes. They propose that when offered a gamble like:

$$(x, p; y, q), \tag{1.21}$$

to be read as 'get outcome x with probability p, outcome y with probability q', where $x \leq 0 \leq y$ or $y \leq 0 \leq x$, people assign it a value of:

$$\pi(p)v(x) + \pi(q)v(y) \tag{1.22}$$

where v and π are the value function and the probability weighting function respectively, as shown in Figure 1.9.

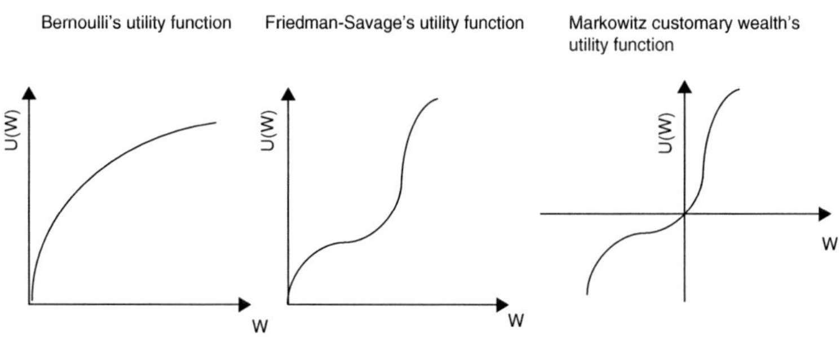

Figure 1.8 Examples of utility function with different shapes

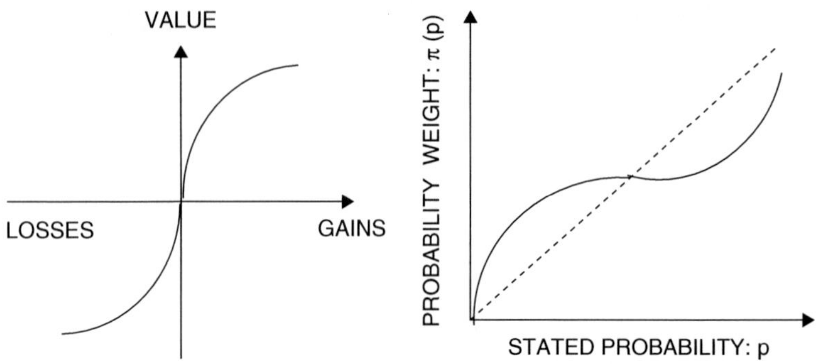

Figure 1.9 Kahneman and Tversky's (1979) proposed value function v and probability weighting function π

This formulation has a number of important features from a risk taking perspective. The main implications can be summarised as follows:

1. Utility is defined over gains and losses in reference to a starting point rather than over a final wealth position, an idea first proposed by Markowitz (1952a). This fits naturally with the way gambles are often presented and discussed in everyday life.
2. The second important feature is the shape of the value function v, namely its concavity in the domain of gains and convexity in the domain of losses. This means that people are risk averse over gains, and risk seeking over losses.
3. Another characteristic of the value function v is that it has a kink at the origin (*reference point*), indicating a greater sensitivity to losses than to gains, a phenomenon known as *loss aversion. Loss aversion* implies that people tend to assign more significance to avoiding loss than to achieving gain.
4. The final aspect of prospect theory is the non-linear probability transformation that is summarised in π. Small probabilities are overweighted. Moreover, people are more sensitive to differences in probabilities at higher probability levels; in particular, people place much more weight on outcomes that are certain relative to outcomes that are merely probable, a feature sometimes knows as the 'certainty effect'. Combining considerations about both functions, v and π, preferences for insurance and for buying lottery tickets are also simultaneously explained. Although the concavity of v in the region of gains generally produces risk aversion, for lotteries which offer a

small chance of a large gain, the overweighting of small probabilities in Figure 1.9 dominates, leading to a risk seeking behaviour. Along the same line, while convexity of *v* in the region of losses typically leads to risk seeking, the same overweighting of small probabilities introduces risk aversion over gambles which have a small chance of a large loss, explaining the propensity towards insurance.

In subsequent years, prospect theory is later built upon and develops into a cumulative prospect theory (Tversky and Kahneman, 1992). The main innovation is in regard to the probability weighting function, which takes cumulative probabilities into account and shows different patterns between gains and losses. This allows the model to formally depict a greater variety of attitudes towards risk.[45]

[C] Emotional factors

Brehmer (1987) is critical that many of the academic endeavours on perceived risk mostly concentrate on *cognitive issues* and disregard the *emotional factors* of investment decisions and risk perception. However, in the past decade, this trend has reversed itself by academics following the concept of 'risk as feeling', pointed out by works of Loewenstein et al. (2001) and of Slovic et al.(2004), among others. Thus, within the behavioural finance literature a growing area of investigation is the influence of emotions into the field of investment decision making and risk perception, as in a sample of works by MacGregor et al. (2000), Olsen (2000), and Dowling and Lucey (2004).

The influence of *emotional factors* upon the decision making process is twofold. First, mood and emotions felt today affect people's perceptions of and choices with respect to investment decisions and risk. For example, sales of state of Ohio lottery tickets are found to increase in the days following a football victory by Ohio State University (Arkes et al., 1988). More generally, people who are in good moods are more optimistic in their choices and judgements than those in bad moods (see, among others, Lerner et al. 2003), as bad moods are associated with more critical strategies of evaluating information; this may lead to incorrect judgements or *misattribution biases* (Ross, 1977), as pre-existing affective states may induce people to attribute their optimism about a choice to the wrong source. Moreover, mood states tend to affect relatively abstract judgements more than specific ones for which people have concrete information; this is indeed the case regarding financial investment decisions. Edmans et al. (2008) find that bad moods, caused by international soccer losses in important games, predict poor returns in the losing country the next day, especially among small stocks. In the study by Lo et al. (2005), automatic emotional negative responses among traders, such as fear and greed, 'short-circuit' more rational decision making faculties, resulting in a poorer trading performance.

Secondly, the anticipation of possible negative feelings associated with an outcome may also exert an influence upon the final decision, a phenomenon generally called *regret aversion*. In this perspective, *risk aversion* and *loss aversion* may be seen as the consequence of avoiding unpleasant future feelings. Related arguments can also explain the *house money effect* (Thaler and Johnson, 1990), which is a greater willingness to gamble with money that was recently won: the unpleasantness of a loss of recently won money may be diluted by aggregating it with the earlier gain. The same holds for situations in which people have experienced a loss and have a chance to make up this loss, even if it implies a greater assumption of risk (called the *break-even* effect). Regret is stronger for decisions that involve action rather than passivity; this effect is sometimes called the *omission bias* (Ritov and Baron, 1990). Regret aversion can also explain the *endowment effect*, a preference for people to hold on to what they have rather than exchange for a better alternative, as with the refusal of individuals to swap a lottery ticket for an equivalent one plus cash.[46] In a similar perspective, the *status quo bias* (Samuelson and Zeckhauser, 1988) involves preferring the choice designated as the default or status quo among a list of alternatives, in order to avoid the chance of being responsible for a worse outcome which would have materialised from choosing one of the other available options.

[D] Social interactions

Person to person and media contagion of ideas and behaviour seems to be important for the decision making process and, more specifically, for investment decisions. In a survey of individual investors, Shiller and Pound (1989) found that almost all of the investors who recently purchased a stock had their attention drawn to it through direct interpersonal communication; similarly, examples of large price movements triggered by Internet chat comes to mind. There are rational informational reasons to learn by observing the actions of others; nevertheless, sometimes people tend to pay too much attention to ideas or facts that are reinforced by conversation, ritual and symbols. This may lead to some biases that, having a social basis, can be self-reinforcing. For example, environmental pressure can cause group members to experience a sort of *herding* or even of *rigid thinking* that is an adherence to habitual behaviours (see Argote et al., 1988). Social interactions may also induce a *fundamental attribution error* (Ross, 1977), that is the tendency for individuals to underestimate the importance of external circumstances and overestimate the importance of disposition in determining the behaviour of others. Finally, Ross et al. (1977) outline the possibility of a *false consensus effect*, occurring when people mistakenly believe that others share their beliefs more than they really do; *overconfidence* may encourage this by making the individual reluctant to consider the possibility that he or she is making a mistake.

As a side note to this overview of all the possible investment decision making biases, an argument often heard within the traditional finance paradigm is that the psychological findings described above will be eliminated by learning and experience. However, psychological work shows otherwise that many biases are not easily eliminated by learning, repetition or bigger incentives, and they even exist among experts with substantial experience (Tversky and Kahneman, 1974; Rabin, 1998; Barberis and Thaler, 2002).

1.2.3 The risk–return trade-off anomalies

The investment decision making biases commented on in the previous section are useful tools to interpret some challenging patterns that contradict the basic assumptions of traditional finance. The emphasis here is on the interplay between the theory outlined in Section 1.1.3 and empirical works, with a specific focus on the trade-off between risk and return. Traditional financial theorists develop models with testable predictions; empirical researchers document 'puzzles', that is stylised facts that fail to fit established theories, and this stimulates the development of new theories and interpretations. In this section, we compare what we know about what investors actually do (*positive investment decision process*) with the body of knowledge about what investors should do (*normative investment decision process*). A distinction is made between micro-perspective puzzles (that is anomalies related to the investment decisions of a single individual) and macro-perspective puzzles (that is anomalies regarding the market as a whole).

[A] Evidence of risk and investment decisions: micro-perspective puzzles

As far as investment decisions are concerned, empirical works have reported anomalies in asset allocation and trading behaviour of individuals that is not explained by normative models of portfolio choice. We now summarise some evidence on the actions of investors that conflict with traditional theories and the behavioural ideas that have been used to explain them (Table 1.5). Our discussion of each finding is necessarily brief. For a deeper understanding of the phenomena we touch on, we refer the reader to the single references.

Table 1.5 Micro-perspective puzzles

Micro-perspective puzzles	Behavioural explanation
Under-diversification: the propensity to invest heavily in only a few assets (Benartzi, 2001; Benartzi and Thaler, 2002; Polkovnichenko, 2005)	• *Familiarity*: investors tend to put too much faith in familiar stocks, believing that they are less risky than other companies or even safer than a diversified portfolio (Baker and Nofsinger, 2002). • *Overconfidence*: overconfident investors would intentionally choose to hold focused and under-diversified portfolios, because they might mistakenly believe that they will earn superior performance by active trading and underweight evidence suggesting that stock is actually a bad investment (Goetzmann and Kumar, 2008).[47] • *Trend chasing*: investors with a greater sensitivity to past price trends seem to hold less diversified portfolios (Goetzmann and Kumar, 2008). • *Status quo bias*: in many retirement programmes, participants tend to maintain their previous asset allocations, despite large variations in returns and hence in their portfolio's risk–return characteristics (Samuelson and Zeckhauser, 1988). • *Narrow framing*: investors tend to take care about fluctuations in the individual stocks they hold instead of fluctuations in their total portfolios, sometimes yielding sub-optimal and under-diversified portfolios. Moreover, stocks selected are not only few, but also remarkably similar in their volatilities (the *preferred risk habitat hypothesis*; see Dorn and Huberman, 2009). • *Herding*: certain groups of investors change their behaviours in parallel (*herding*), without accurately weighing the effects of these parallel behaviours upon the overall portfolio (see Grinblatt et al., 1995; Nofsinger and Sias, 1999; Grinblatt and Keloharju, 2000).
Naive diversification: a tendency to diversify in a naive and simplified fashion, without following the normative rule of the mean–variance approach	• *1/n diversification heuristic:* in their study about the asset allocation of US 401 (k) plans, Benartzi and Thaler (2001) find that people tend to equally divide their resources among the investment lines offered by the plan.

Continued

Table 1.5 Continued

Micro-perspective puzzles	Behavioural explanation
Excessive trading: trading more than can be justified on rational grounds (Barber and Odean, 2000)	• *Overconfidence*: people believe that they have information strong enough to justify a trade, whereas in fact the information is too weak to warrant any action (Odean, 1999; Barber and Odean, 2000). • *Trend chasing*: investors tend to extrapolate long-term trends from short-term evidences, resulting in a high portfolio turnover following the market, in the illusion of anticipating future trends.
The selling decision: holding on to stocks that have fallen in value too long and selling stocks that have risen in value too soon (the *disposition effect*; see, for example, Shefrin and Statman, 1985, and for the house market, Geneseve and Mayer, 2001)	• *Prospect theory:* Barberis and Xiong (2009) find that this behaviour can be explained by people disliking incurring losses much more than they enjoy making gains, in combination with people's willingness to gamble in the domain of losses and to avoid risks in the domain of gains. • *Regret aversion:* postponing the sale of a losing investment may even be a way to postpone the sense of regret.
The buying decision: the propensity of individuals to buy a stock that has caught their attention ('attention getting strategy') without taking the main prescriptions of the mean–variance optimal strategy (mean, variance, correlations) into account (Odean, 1999; Barber and Odean, 2000).	• *Availability:* investors are more likely to buy high attention stocks as their memories are more 'available'.

Some works try to integrate the behavioural interpretations of puzzles within a theoretical model. For instance, in a recent paper, Boyle et al. (2009) try to formalise the link between investors' 'familiarity' towards assets and the different degrees of portfolio diversification. In their model, when investors are equally ambiguous about all assets, then the optimal portfolio corresponds to Markowitz's fully diversified portfolio. In contrast, when investors exhibit a different degree of familiarity across assets, the optimal portfolio is no more fully diversified. The greater the standard volatility of the expected returns and the difference between the ambiguity levels of the familiar and unfamiliar assets increase, the more the optimal choice shifts towards a portfolio concentrated in a few

Table 1.6 Macro-perspective puzzles

Macro-perspective puzzles	Description
Size effect	Stocks with a small market capitalisation appear to earn higher (risk adjusted) returns than bigger stocks.
Value effect	Stocks with a higher measure of fundamental value relative to market value earn higher returns than stocks with a low measure.
Momentum effect	Stocks that have performed well over the past year earn higher returns than stocks that have performed poorly.
Volatility effect	Stocks with low historical volatility exhibit superior risk adjusted returns.
Long-term reversal effect	Stocks that have performed badly during the past three to five years outperform stocks that performed well.
Post-earning announcement effect	Stocks with surprisingly good earnings outperform stocks with surprisingly bad earnings during the next 60 days.
Equity puzzle effect	Stocks outperform bonds over long horizons by a difference that is too large to be explained by any rational asset pricing theory.

familiar assets (*flight to familiarity*), until the extreme case in which the ambiguity about all assets and the standard deviation of the estimated mean are so high that no risky asset is held (*non-participation*).

[B] Evidence of risk and mispricing effect: macro-perspective puzzles

Cumulative evidence shows that the most important traditional asset pricing theory, the CAPM, is inconsistent with many empirical regularities found in cross-sectional asset pricing data, showing that one group of stocks systematically earn higher (risk adjusted) returns than another. We classify the evidence bearing on asset pricing puzzles into seven categories (Table 1.6). Our emphasis here is on findings that have received confirmation, over time becoming more widely accepted, and that are related to the theoretical framework outlined in Section 1.1.3.

The puzzles described above all share the same evidence of a return difference that is not explained by a rational change in equilibrium risk premium. For some of them, behavioural proponents suggest a specific explanation based on the typical investment decision biases. For example, Barberis et al. (2001) and Benartzi and Thaler (2002) show how a disproportionately large *aversion to losses*, in combination with an annual investment horizon (myopia), can explain the puzzling high returns of equities over bonds: in their view, the higher risk premium is the reward an investor asks to compensate for possible short run losses deriving from a stock investment. The same form of *narrow framing* described for the insufficient diversification helps also to explain the historically high returns on stocks with favourable multiples of fundamentals over market value, as shown by Barberis and Huang (2001). Barberis et al. (1998) find an important consequence of *representativeness* in some of the puzzles cited above; more precisely, they show that the *representativeness* bias can create the higher (lower) returns on stocks after they displayed good (bad) earnings announcement, the higher (lower) returns for recent winners (losers) and the reversal of these recent winner (loser) returns over longer horizons.

However, in a specific investment setting, it can be hard to judge which documented psychological bias is relevant. As a consequence, most of the puzzles summarised here are better explained within a general theoretical framework that is wide enough to explain a range of empirical patterns. Showing the progressive steps in the behavioural finance literature towards this ambitious purpose is the aim of the next section.

1.2.4 Behavioural financial theories on the risk–return trade-off

We now describe the behavioural counterparts of the traditional financial models used to theoretically found the risk–return trade-off, declining it in the form of optimal portfolio composition and asset pricing.

[A] Behavioural Portfolio Theory

Shefrin and Statman (2000) develop a positive Behavioural Portfolio Theory (BPT, henceforth), as an alternative to Modern Portfolio Theory (MPT, henceforth). They present BPT in two versions: a single mental account BPT version (BPT-SA), still comparable with MPT and built on Lopes's (1987) two-factors theory of risky choice (SP/A theory[48]), and a multiple mental account BPT version (BPT-MA), where they conclusively depart from traditional portfolio models and combine Lopes's (1987) model with Kahneman and Tversky's (1979) prospect theory.

In the BPT-SA version, investors consider the portfolio as a single mental account, specifically as a whole; this means that they take covariances into consideration, as Markowitz (1952b) prescribes. Portfolio selection in a BPT-SA framework is similar to portfolio selection in a mean–variance framework in regard to the optimisation process; however it differs in terms of the variables used as inputs of the optimisation, which are derived from Lopes's (1987) SP/A theory. In this theory, people are driven by three forces: *security*, that is, a general concern about avoiding low levels of wealth; *potential*, that is, a general desire to reach high levels of wealth; and *aspiration*, related to the goal of achieving a specific target level. Lopes's choice model focuses on an expected utility wealth function (E(W)), where two emotions tend to operate: on the one hand, fear (that is, concern for security), that leads individuals to overweight the probabilities attached to the worst outcomes (h_sD); on the other hand, hope (that is, concern for potential), that induces higher weighting of higher outcomes (h_pD). Lopes argues that each emotion serves to modify the decumulative weighting function (D), so that the final shape of the decumulative transformation function is:

$$h(D)=\delta h_s(D)+(1-\delta)h_p(D) \tag{1.23}$$

In SP/A theory, investors substitute E(W) with $E_h(W)$; that is, the expected value of W under the transformed decumulative function h(d). Lopes postulates that risky outcomes are evaluated not only in terms of $E_h(W)$, but also considering the probability that the payoff will be higher than a certain level of aspiration, A.[49] Shefrin and Statman (2000) translate these concepts into the traditional mean–variance framework where inputs for optimisation are expected returns (μ) and standard deviation (σ); the counterpart in BPT-SA to μ is $E_h(W)$, while σ is substituted by the probability that wealth might fall below the aspiration level (Prob (W≤A)). Hence, if the mean–variance frontier is obtained by maximising μ for fixed σ, the BPT-SA frontier is obtained by maximising $E_h(W)$ for fixed (Prob (W≤A)). Typically, a BPT-SA efficient portfolio is not mean–variance efficient, as analytically discussed by Shefrin and Staman (2000).

While the single account version of behavioural portfolio theory is useful for comparisons with mean–variance portfolio theory, Shefrin and Statman (2000) observe that investors in practice think of their portfolio not as single account but as a pyramid of many accounts or many layers. This leads to the second version of their BPT (namely, BPT-MA), where investors segregate their portfolios into distinct mental accounts, that is they act as if they overlook covariances.[50]

In the simple version of BPT-MA, investors divide their money into two layers, a 'downside protection' layer, designed to protect them from poverty, and an 'upside potential' layer, designed to have a chance at being rich. Each layer has specific goals and levels of aspiration. Shefrin and Statman (2000) express analytically this concept assuming that an investor is moved by three entities: a 'planner' and two 'doers'. Each doer is associated with one mental account, whereby the first has a low aspiration level and the second doer has a high aspiration level; the planner balances the two doers to maximise overall utility, dividing current wealth between the two accounts.

The utility of doers follows a Cobb–Douglas function representation:

$$U_s = P_s^{1-\gamma} E_h (W_s^{\gamma}) \quad \text{(for the low aspiration level)} \tag{1.24}$$

$$U_r = P_r^{1-\beta} E_h (W_r^{\beta}) \quad \text{(for the high aspiration level)} \tag{1.25}$$

where P_s and P_r are respectively the probability of falling short of the low aspiration level (A_s) and of the high aspiration level (A_p), W_s and W_r are the terminal wealth for the low and for the high aspiration doers, γ and β are two non negative weighting parameters.

The utility function of the planner combines the utilities of the two doers, where the weight attached to the high aspiration doer is much higher than the weight attached to the low aspiration doer. Hence, the planner's utility function takes the form:

$$U = \left[1 + K_{dr} \left(P_r^{1-\beta} E_h (W_r^{\beta})\right)\right] K_{ds} \left[P_s^{1-\gamma} E_h (W_s^{\gamma})\right] \tag{1.26}$$

The planner divides initial wealth W_0 into two portions, $W_{s,0}$ and $W_{r,0}$, respectively, one for the low aspiration account and the other for the high aspiration account.[51] Since the two mental accounts are not integrated, the final portfolio allocation may be far different from the one derived from a mean–variance optimisation.

A comparison between MPT, BPT-SA and BPT-MA is drawn in Table 1.7.

Table 1.7 MPT versus BPT-SA/BPT-MA: analogies and differences

MPT	BPT-SA	BPT-MA
• Optimisation inputs: μ and σ • Mean–variance efficient frontier • Uni-dimensional risk • Consistent attitude toward risk	• Optimisation inputs: $E_h(W)$ and Prob $(W \leq A)$ • Behavioural efficient frontier • Multidimensional risk • Consistent attitude toward risk	• No optimisation process • No efficient frontier • Multidimensional risk • Inconsistent attitude toward risk • Multiple mental accounts (layered pyramid)
Both models use a single mental account, meaning that investors consider their portfolio as a whole and take covariances into consideration. Moreover, both models implement the same optimisation process, built on the mathematical tools proposed by MPT to maximise utility for a fixed level of risk.		

The main difference between MPT and BPT-SA is the measurement of risk. In a traditional mean–variance framework, investors' attitude towards risk is measured by a single parameter, so that investors' preferences are expressed by equation (1.14) of Section 1.1.3 and the risk results in a uni-dimensional concept (A). In contrast, in BPT-SA the concept of risk is multidimensional, in line with the basic assumption of behavioural finance. The portfolio risk is the result of more parameters, influencing each other: the strength of fear (need for security), the strength for hope (need for potential), the strength of fear relative to hope, the aspiration level and the strength of the desire to reach the aspiration level relative to fear and hope.

BPT-MA has nothing in common with the traditional portfolio model. First of all, MPT is a prescriptive theory, involving an optimisation process, while BPT-MA takes a mere descriptive approach, never suggesting optimal solutions; as a consequence, contrary to MPT and to BMP-SA, BPT-MA does not derive an efficient frontier where optimal portfolios are located, however it simply describes the way people divide their wealth. Secondly, MPT and BPT-SA investors evaluate portfolios as a whole and consider covariances between assets as they construct their portfolios. On the contrary, BPT-MA investors build portfolios as pyramids of assets, layer by layer, where layers are associated with particular goals; it follows that covariances among securities are often overlooked. Moreover, MPT investors have a consistent attitude toward risk, in the sense that they are always averse to risk; conversely, a BPT-MA investor has a range of attitudes toward risk, which vary across the layers of the portfolio. As a consequence, while MPT banishes risk seeking and gambling from theory, risk seeking may be optimal for BPT investors. So, for example, BPT-MA investors may choose a riskless bond in the low aspiration layer of their portfolios and a risky asset that resembles a lottery ticket in the high aspiration layer. The shift of risk attitude from a consistent attitude to an inconsistent one brings a further implication: mean–variance portfolio theory posits that security returns follow a normal distribution, nevertheless BPT-MA investors seem to prefer securities with non-normal, asymmetric distributions that combine downside protection, in the form of a floor, with upside potential (Statman, 2003).

The main drawback of BPT-MA is that, even if it describes better the way people make portfolio choices, it is not able to derive optimal solutions; as we said before, BPT-MA is solely a descriptive theory without any prescriptive indication. As a result, it cannot be used to infer asset allocation in practice. On the contrary, MPT attracts investors and practitioners by its logic and practical application; the drawback in this case is that the measure of the single parameter for risk aversion (A) is not trivial.

Recently, Das et al. (2010) tried to overcome this contrast between MPT and BPT-MA, proposing a model where they integrate appealing features of MPT and BPT-MA into a new framework that they call mental accounting (MA). Features of BPT-MA include a mental accounting structure portfolio, a definition of risk as the probability of failing to reach the threshold level, and attitudes towards risk that vary by account. Features of MPT include the mathematical tools for portfolio optimisation over two moment distributions, which allows us to derive optimal portfolios. The starting point of their approach is that it is easy to chart the mean–variance frontier and this justifies its practical usage. Nevertheless, investors find it difficult to derive their optimal aggregate portfolio, mainly because the way in which they have to express their risk attitude in the MPT framework is not familiar to them. First, investors have more than one level of risk aversion; for example, the level of risk aversion associated with money dedicated to retirement is high but the risk aversion with money dedicated to inheritance is much lower. Moreover, investors find it difficult to specify their level of risk aversion even in the mental account sub-portfolios when they are asked to specify their level of risk aversion in units of variance or more generically in terms of a single numeric parameter; leading to misspecifications of their risk attitude and consequently of their optimal aggregate portfolios.[52]

The strength of the MA framework is that it is able to capture the investor's degree of risk in a more familiar way as implied by BPT-MA theory, but at the same time the language used is converted into a mathematical one that can be inserted as an input into the MPT optimisation process. In other terms, Das et al.(2010) show that solving the MA problem is analogous to solving a standard MPT problem with a specific 'implied' risk aversion coefficient: once the investor specifies his or her sub-portfolio threshold levels and probabilities, the problem may be translated into a standard mean–variance problem with an 'implied' risk aversion coefficient that is derived exactly through the parameter pair (threshold and probabilities). Aggregate portfolios composed of mean–variance efficient sub-portfolios are also mean–variance efficient; that is, mental accounting does not introduce inefficiency, but they may be different from those derived from a traditional MPT.[53]

Both BPT-MA and MA models work in a static framework; an attempt to develop a behavioural portfolio theory in a dynamic setting has recently been carried out by De Giorgi (2009). Besides the fact that he proposes a continuous time model where investment goals at different time horizons are considered, his framework departs from the ones above cited because it utilises cumulative prospect theory rather than the SP/A theory of Lopes (1987). Moreover, his model hypothesises a satisficing behaviour among investors and an endogenous allocation of wealth among investment goals. Nevertheless, the mental accounting approach is saved, suggesting a growing consensus among researchers about the fact that mental accounting should be addressed when structuring the asset allocation problem.

[B] Behavioural Asset Pricing Theory

Behavioural finance and neoclassical finance also have very different implications in relation to asset pricing in general and indeed the relationship between risk and return in particular. As there is a broad literature on behavioural asset pricing, this section will focus on a few models which, on the one hand, give an historical evolution of the main streams of thought in the field and, on the other hand, represent the current status of research.

Some pioneering analytic models capture the imperfect rationality in asset pricing by relaxing some of the hypotheses underlying the classical approach. Merton (1987) provides us with a static asset pricing model with incomplete information. The key behavioural assumption of his model is that an investor only uses a certain security. If all investors' information sets were complete, then the model would reduce to the standard CAPM. The non-participation can be viewed as reflecting limited attention or preference for the familiar. However, in the long run the efficient market equilibrium should be reached again. It seems clear from the structure of the model, and from its emphasis on the information assumption, that Merton is defending the traditional view by means of the behaviouralists' arguments, that is to say he tries to improve the CAPM by including incomplete information.

Odean (1998) studies the static effect of overconfidence when there is a single risky security. To explore how market prices are affected by overconfidence, he analyses market models in which investors are rational in all respects except the manner in which they value information. When price taking investors think the signal is more accurate than it really is, the market price overreacts to the signal. Eventually, when the true state of the world resolves, the price corrects. This mechanism causes excess price volatility and negative long-term return autocorrelation. The problem this model has to solve is that overconfidence is assumed exogenously which means that the different processes which are initiated by the different sources of overconfidence are not covered.

Instead of a general tendency to overestimate signal precision, in Daniel et al. (1998), overconfidence is limited to private information signals. This means that if investors overestimate their ability to generate information, or to identify the significance of existing data that others neglect, they will underestimate public signals and consequently their forecast errors. Overconfidence upon private signals causes the stock price to overreact on private information. Nevertheless, returns on private information arrival dates tend to reverse: when public information in opposition to overconfidence mispricing arrives, the inefficient deviation of the price from its fundamental value is partially corrected on average. Their central finding, the overreaction–correction pattern explained above, is consistent with short run momentum and long-term reversal in stock returns. The main shortcoming concerns empirical testability, as the group of overconfident investors is not identifiable.

Contrary to previous works, Shefrin and Statman (1994) try to provide a behavioural asset pricing framework which is truly that: behavioural. They analyse the general effect of mistaken beliefs on equilibrium prices in securities markets. Mistaken beliefs result from the existence of noise traders, who interact with information traders in the market. The central theme of their article is to provide a structural asset pricing model. Their main proposition is the notion of a behavioural beta. Their result is that when prices are inefficient, mispricing is related to a 'beta correction'. Therefore, the benchmark portfolio of the traditional CAPM needs to change so that it tilts in the direction of underpriced securities and away from overpriced securities. Again the argument concerning empirical testification takes place.

Additionally Daniel et al. (2001) provide an analogue to the CAPM, but for the case in which investors are deemed to be overconfident. Their model integrates risk aversion, multiple risky securities, and the effects of arbitrageurs. The central overconfidence assumption implies that an overconfident individual always thinks that the security is less risky than it really is. Hence, the greater the fraction of overconfident individuals in the population, and the greater their overconfidence, the lower the risk premium will be. This leads to the following conclusions: a security's expected return is linearly increasing in the security's beta with the market, and the security's current mispricing. Variables containing market price are proxies for the security's misvaluation. An extreme case would be very strong overconfidence and perfect proxy for the unconditional expected value resulting in the vanishing ability of beta to predict future returns. In theory, the model looks acceptable; however, it faces the major difficulty in the provision of appropriate proxies to measure the vague term 'mispricing' and therefore most of the implications remain to be tested.

The stream of studies cited above is at first a tempting way to illustrate some crucial insights about pricing. However, in full generality, the modelling approach is very elastic: several models have been proposed because there has been no generally accepted behavioural asset pricing theory and psychological assumptions vary considerably from model to model. Moreover, this modelling approach lacks the power of analytical techniques and a unified, coherent framework, compared with the approach followed by traditional finance proponents. In the hope of being less fragmented and more accurately predictive, some successive research has explicitly tried to bring together the psychological assumptions from behavioural finance, and the rigorous integrated methodology from neoclassical finance. The framework used is the kernel-based asset pricing described in Cochrane (2005). At the heart of the framework is the concept of a stochastic discount factor (SDF, henceforth) which is used to price any asset.

The basic SDF-based asset pricing equation is the following:

$$p = E\,(mx) \tag{1.27}$$

Equation (1.27) states that the price p of an asset with payoff x is the expected value of its discounted payoff, where m is the discount factor used to capture the effects of both time value of money and risk (Shefrin, 2008).

What makes an SDF-based asset pricing theory behavioural is that the SDF reflects not only fundamentals but also market sentiment. As outlined in Shefrin (2008), sentiment pertains to erroneous beliefs. In this sense, the sentiment of an individual investor can be described as the difference between two probability density functions: the objective probability density function (Π), which is correct, and the individual investors' subjective probability density function, that may be correct or incorrect. If it is correct, the beliefs of those investors are said to feature zero sentiment, otherwise they feature non-zero sentiment. The same notion of sentiment that applies to individual investors also applies to the market as a whole and it may be thought of as an aggregated market error: it is this market probability density function (PM) that underlies equation (1.27). Shefrin (2005) demonstrates that the equilibrium PM is a generalised weighted Hölder average of the individual investors' probability density function, with the weights reflecting relative wealth or consumption, and the exponents being coefficients of relative risk aversion.

One way to formally define a sentiment function Λ is through the function ln (PM/ Π), the log of the ratio of the two probability density function values at each point in the domain. In general terms, ln (PM/ Π) measures the percentage by which, in equilibrium, the market probability density function exceeds the objective probability density function, and is a log change of measure.

This notion of sentiment is applied by Shefrin (2005) to the calculation of SDF. Shefrin (2005) established that when all investors have power utility,[54] the log SDF can be expressed as the sum of a term reflecting market fundamentals and sentiment Λ. The fundamental variables entering the SDF are aggregate consumption growth (g), the market coefficient of relative risk aversion (γ_m) and the market time discount factor (δ_m). Formally, the equation relating the log SDF and sentiment has the construction:

$$\text{In}(m) = \text{In}(\delta_M) - \gamma_M \text{In}(g) + \Lambda \tag{1.28}$$

It implies that the neoclassical SDF only reflects the fundamental component of risk and is linear, whereas the behavioural SDF reflects both the fundamentals and the sentiment component, exhibiting a non-linear pattern (Shefrin, 2008).

A central issue for the robustness of this approach is how to measure empirical sentiment. Baker and Wurgler (2007) provide a discussion of different proxies for sentiment and the construction of what they call a 'top down' measure. Other studies offer an indirect empirical confirmation and evaluation of sentiment: Aït-Sahalia and Lo (2000) and Rosenberg and Engle (2002) estimate the empirical SDF, or more precisely its projection in respect to returns on the S&P500. Both papers find that the empirical SDF has the non-linear behavioural shape implied by equation (1.28). Moreover, Rosenberg and Engle (2002) estimate the SDF both in the neoclassical restricted and in the free form: the difference between the two estimated SDFs may be interpreted as an indirect estimate of the sentiment function Λ.[55]

If market prices reflect both fundamentals and sentiment, as theoretically and empirically discussed above, sentiment also has an influence upon asset return and, as a consequence, upon the nature of risk premiums across securities. To make this prediction clear, Shefrin (2008) uses the SDF to generate the return distribution for a mean–variance portfolio.[56] As the return to a mean–variance portfolio is a linear function of the SDF, with a negative coefficient, the shapes of the mean–variance return patterns are inverted images of their respective SDF function.

This approach has two main points worthy of note. First, the behavioural return pattern is more volatile than its traditional counterpart: in the middle, the return pattern is quite similar between the two portfolios, but at the extremes the behavioural mean–variance portfolio differs and shows much more volatility than the traditional one. Secondly, the behavioural return pattern is negatively skewed relative to the market portfolio: returns are not only extremely low in low growth states, but fall off quickly as the consumption growth declines (Shefrin, 2008). It is mostly this second implication that gives rise to the most innovative aspect compared to the traditional risk–return trade-off. Indeed, skewness pertains to the third moment and traditional mean–variance preferences are neutral in respect to all moments higher than the second; this traditional assumption generally holds for certain distributions, such as the normal distribution. But, if the distribution of returns to a portfolio is not normal but asymmetric, as implied in the behavioural approach, then the third moment and the sign of its coefficient must be considered.

In terms of the risk–return trade-off, the assumption of an asymmetric return distribution implies that if asset returns have systematic skewness, expected returns should include rewards for accepting this risk. In other words, the potential for large losses (negative skew) represents an unattractive feature for investors; to induce investors to invest in assets with negative skew, a large positive risk premium must be expected. Therefore, the risk premium for a stock will be determined not only by how much market risk the stock adds to a well diversified portfolio, but also by how much skewness the stock adds to a properly diversified portfolio. The measure of how much market risk a stock adds is beta; the measure of how much skewness a stock adds is the co-skewness. The co-skewness of a stock measures the impact its return distribution has on the already negative skewness of a behavioural mean–variance portfolio. Co-skewness has a beta-like formula that involves the squared market return instead of the market return (Harvey and Siddique, 2000): with this definition, co-skewness measures the extent to which a security's return covaries with the squared market return.

Barberis and Huang (2008) show that probability weighting leads investors to prefer positive skewness in individual securities. This results in the empirically observed relatively low returns on positively skewed securities; relevant studies, among others, have investigated this in relation to IPOs (Ritter, 1991), distressed stocks (Campbell et al., 2008) and private equity holdings (Moskowitz and Vissing Jorgensen, 2002). The momentum effect also has an explanation in terms of co-skewness: recent winners feature lower co-skewness than recent losers. In essence, the market and co-skewness are both fundamental factors that capture some aspects of systematic risk, but not all, as the evidence reported by Barone-Adesi et al. (2004) suggests.

The inclusion of co-skewness in the asset portfolio theory may be defined as a 'backward looking innovation': it is an 'innovation', because traditional mean–variance preferences are neutral in respect to all moments higher than the second; but it is also 'backward looking' because the same idea was originally proposed by a pioneering handful of studies formally developed in the 1980s out of behavioural finance and this idea has only more recently been rediscovered. Kraus and Litzenberger (1976), Scott and Horvath (1980), Kraus and Litzenberger (1983) and Barone-Adesi (1985) originally hypothesised and empirically tested the negative relationship between systematic skewness and asset returns. As a consequence, one may wonder if the concept of co-skewness is neoclassical or behavioural in nature. Probably this is a further example of convergence between the two views, and it further indicates that the two points of view are becoming more complementary rather than opposite.

Notes

Mazzoli is the author of Section 1.1 and Marinelli is the author of Section 1.2.

1. That is a choice whose probabilities are known.
2. For example, Markowitz (1952b) identifies financial risk with the variance measure and proposes the rule: *'the investor does (or should) consider expected return as a desirable thing and variance of return an undesirable thing'.* Additionally: *'The concept of risk appears frequently in financial writing; if the term risk was replaced by variance little change of apparent meaning would result'.*
3. In other words, a *pure risk* exists when there is a chance of loss and no chance of gain, while speculative risk exists when there is a chance of gain and also a chance of loss (Williams et al., 1997).
4. Resti and Sironi (2007) define credit risk as the possibility that an unexpected change in the counterparty's creditworthiness may generate a corresponding unexpected change in the market value associated with credit exposure. In addition, they draw attention to two prominent concepts that feature credit risk:
   - default risk or migration risk: credit risk is not only limited to the possibility of counterparty's default but it is even a mere deterioration of credit worthiness
   - risk as an unexpected event: in order to be considered as a risk the variation of the counterparty's credit worthiness must be unexpected.

5. It is the *'risk of loss resulting from inadequate or failed internal processes, people and systems or from external events'* (Basel Committee, September 2001).
6. The financial risk in the debt decision process will be illustrated in Chapter 2.
7. For this reason other important risk measures that are not informative about the dispersion (such as the duration of bond securities) are not considered in this analysis. Moreover, in order to properly measure the return generated by an investment one must account for both the price change and the cash flow derived from the asset during the period it was held.
8. Variance is obtained by squaring the standard deviation.
9. In this case, the chances of a positive outcome being a certain distance away from the centre of the distribution are as great as the chances of a negative outcome of an equal distance in the opposite direction.
10. The skewness measures the asymmetry of the probability distribution of a random variable.
11. This problem can be partially solved by a mathematical transformation from return to log-return as most of the securities returns are log-normally distributed. Still, not all the investments are normally or log-normally distributed.
12. Markowitz's theory will be deeply illustrated in Section 1.1.3.
13. Despite the fact that Markowitz proposes the semi variance measures and recognises their importance, he continues to use the variance as a risk measure because it is computationally simpler. With the lack of cost-effective computer power and the fact that the variance was already mathematically very complex, this was a significant consideration until the 1980s with the advent of microcomputers (Nawrocki, 1999).
14. The term partial is used here to reflect that the measures relate to only one side of the return distribution relative to a given target level; lower indicates that the side of the interest is the downside.
15. Of course, the case *a* equal to two gives the traditional semi variance.
16. In particular, the estimation procedure involves a computer program designed to present to the individual decision maker a series of pairs of alternatives to choose from. Each pair of alternatives consists of a sure option and an uncertain option.
17. For example, a one-day 5 per cent VaR of 1 million euros means that there is a 5 per cent probability that the portfolio will fall in value by more than 1 million euros over a one-day period.
18. Recognition of such models by the financial and regulatory communities is evidence of their growing use. Since 1997 the Securities and Exchange Commission has required different financial structures, including banks and other large capitalisation registrants, to quantify and report their market-risk exposure with VaR disclosure being one measure in order to comply. Therefore regulators also view VaR as a useful summary measure. Risk monitoring realised by the use of VaR is encouraged by regulators as well. In a risk-based capital proposal (1996), the Basel Committee on Banking Supervision endorsed the use of VaR models, contingent on important qualitative and quantitative standards.

    In addition, the Bank for International Settlements assisted in promoting the use of the VaR method publicly through financial intermediaries. This allows large banks the option to use a VaR measure to set the capital reserves necessary to cover their market-risk exposure. Regulators expect social benefits assuming that VaR (based risk management will reduce the likelihood of large-scale financial failures).

19. Nevertheless, the axioms proposed by Artzner et al. rise to new risk coherent measures that are not subadditive but capture the advantages of VaR at the same time. In particular, a variety of VaR related risk measures are suggested. Examples include TVaR (tail value at risk), WCE (worst conditional expectation) and CVaR (conditional value at risk).
20. As Markowitz (1999) points out, Bernoulli is not the first to appreciate the benefits of diversification. In *The Merchant of Venice*, Act I, Scene I, William Shakespeare as Antonio says:

    '... I thank my fortune for it,
    My ventures are not in one bottom trusted,
    Nor to one place; nor is my whole estate
    Upon the fortune of my present year...'
21. Markowitz himself is not persuaded that standard deviation is totally appropriate but he recognises that it is easy to compute.
22. How to measure one's risk aversion is illustrated below.
23. Markowitz maintains that the case of ρ equal to minus one is not observable in nature because it is equivalent to a zero risk portfolio. That is why this case is not considered at all.
24. The curve was later termed *efficient frontier.*
25. In other words, it is necessary to draw the indifference curve for each investor (the different combinations of risk and return an investor is indifferent to).
26. This is due to the fact that most investors are risk averse.
27. $(n^2\text{-}n)/2$ (that is 4,950 covariances for 100 securities).
28. It was Treynor (1961 and 1962) who proposed the method first; unfortunately these papers remained unpublished.
29. That is the link with the market return (r_m).
30. That is due to the specific company one is considering, which can be reduced by an appropriate diversification and is catched by the error term (e_i).
31. More importantly they assume that all assets are perfectly divisible and priced in a perfectly competitive market. Another implicit assumption of the CAPM is that there are no imperfections in the market such as taxes, regulations or short selling restrictions and the markets are deemed frictionless with costless information available, simultaneously to all investors (Mirza, 2005).
32. In a perfect market, the risky portfolio of all the investors will include the same securities independent on their tastes. In fact, if a security is not included in any of the investors' portfolios, its price will drop down because of the low demand. Therefore, its return will increase as long as it becomes sufficiently attractive to be included in the portfolio M. It follows that in equilibrium, all the securities that are available in the market will be included into the M portfolio.
33. Risk premium is the difference between the return of the market portfolio and the return of the risk free asset.

34. Or money to be borrowed if we consider the line beyond point *mp*.
35. When it comes to inefficient portfolios or single securities, total risk is no longer an appropriate measure for calculating the required rate of return; this is because an inefficient portfolio is not well diversified and so contains both specific and market risk. Since the specific risk could be easily diversified away, then only the systematic component of total risk, as reflected in the beta of the security of portfolio, will be priced by the market. All inefficient portfolios contain both specific and market risk but no one will pay for the component of risk that can be easily diversified at a low cost and the market will pay only for the systematic risk (Pilbeam, 1998).
36. Including real estate, fine arts, jewels, and so on.
37. Sortino (2001) wrote: 'Recent research in the behavioural finance area claims that investors do not seek the highest return for a given level of risk, as portfolio theory assumes... Rather than maximise the expected return, they want to maximise a "satisfying" strategy.'
38. A financial example of this bias is related to derivative usage: the general association of derivatives with higher probability of loss is said to be due to the cognitive availability of substantial losses in derivative transactions supported by broad and negative media coverage, especially during the recent financial crisis when loss announcements by banks engaged in credit derivatives were extensively covered in the news (Bischof and Ebert, 2009).
39. To illustrate the base rate neglect Kahneman and Tversky (1974) present this description of a person named Linda: 'Linda is 31 years old, single, outspoken, and very bright. She majored in philosophy. As a student, she was deeply concerned with issues of discrimination and social justice, and also participated in anti-nuclear demonstrations'. When asked which of 'Linda is a bank teller' (statement A) and 'Linda is a bank teller and is an active in the feminist movement' (statement B) is more likely, subjects typically assign greater probability to B. This is, of course, impossible and incoherent with Bayes law, under which the probability of joint events is always lower than the probability of single events (statement B is a 'subcase' of statement A); representativeness may give an explanation: the description of Linda sounds like the description of a feminist (it is representative of a feminist) and induce people to put too little weight on the base rate (probability of the single event, statement A). See also Barberis and Thaler (2002).
40. In an experimental market, consistent with *gambler's fallacy*, Andreassen and Kraus (1990) find that when exogenous prices fluctuate modestly, subjects buy on dips and sell on rises. However, when a trend appears, subjects do less of this tracking and possibly switch to chasing trends. There is further evidence from experiments and from surveys that real estate investors also extrapolate trends in forecasting price movements; see Case and Shiller (1990).
41. The subjects of their study are 63 college students who are provided with a car racing scenario in which the continued sponsorship of the venture is dependent on the success of winning. The findings reveal that situations that are framed positively are perceived as concerning higher risks than circumstances that are framed negatively; moreover, the degree to which subjects make risky decisions is negatively related with their level of perceived risk.

42. They use an experimental methodology to test if actual European reporting practices affect the risk perception of individuals and find that investors infer a different level of risk from financial reports of economically identical investments according to the application and presentation of different measurement categories.
43. In this sense, Tversky and Kahneman (1986) argue that normative approaches are doomed to failure, because people routinely make choices that are simply impossible to justify on normative grounds.
44. Markowitz's name is so closely associated with mean–variance theory that it is easy to overlook the fact that Markowitz (1952a) not only recognises that investors display both risk averse and risk seeking behaviour, but also makes an important contribution on the road that evolved from Friedman and Savage to prospect theory.
45. For a deeper understanding of the cumulative prospect theory, we refer the reader to the recent survey of Linciano (2010).
46. See Kahneman et al. (1991) and Bar-Hillel and Neter (1996).
47. In contrast, Goetzmann and Kumar (2008) find that traditional factors advocated by classical portfolio theory to justify under-diversification, such as small portfolio size and high transaction costs, are not strongly correlated with investors' diversification choices.
48. In SP/A theory, the S stands for *security*, P for *potential* and A for *aspiration*.
49. Note that the formalisations underlying the SP/A theory are virtually analogous of some other optimisation models, proposed almost in the same time period as an alternative to the mean–variance approach. We refer to the *safety first* portfolio theory, originally proposed by Roy (1952) and then developed by Telser (1955) and Arzac and Bawa (1977). For a deeper discussion of the *safety first* models, see Shefrin and Statman (2000).
50. For empirical evidence about individual investors who overlook covariances, see Kroll et al. (1988). An analogous finding for the case of institutional investors and pension plans is also reported in Jorion (1994) and Shefrin and Statman (2000).
51. Note that the BPT-MA model contemplates a safety first component anyway: for construction, the utility of the planner is zero when the utility of the low aspiration level is zero, but is not necessarily zero when the utility of the high aspiration level is zero. In other words, achieving safety comes first.
52. It is worth mentioning a promising field of financial risk studies that approaches the problem of deriving new risk measures which are able to fit better with the investor's attitude towards risk. We refer to the so-called 'spectral risk measures', recently proposed by Acerbi (2002, 2004) to replace the use of variance; the spectral risk measure is a weighted average of the quantiles of a loss distribution, the weights of which depend on the user's risk aversion. Spectral risk measures therefore are able to link the mathematical risk measure to the user's attitude towards risk. For a discussion, see, among others, Cotter and Dowd (2007) and Dowd et al. (2008).
53. When constraints are placed on short selling, aggregates of sub-portfolios are inefficient in comparison to a single optimal portfolio. Nevertheless, Das et al. (2010) find that portfolio inefficiency arising from investors' inability to specify accurately their risk attitude in the aggregate portfolio level, as potentially implied in the traditional approach, could be much higher.

54. The power utility function is also known as the constant relative risk aversion (CRRA) function.
55. Rosenberg and Engle (2002) find that the value for the SDF corresponding to a market return of –9.8 per cent is 2.5 for the neoclassical restricted SDF estimate but 5.0 for the free form SDF estimate featuring the behavioural shape. The log-difference between the two values is 80 per cent (= log (5.0/2.5)= 1.61–0.81). So, the market overestimates the probability density associated with a return of -9.8 per cent by 80 per cent.
56. The SDF can be used to price all assets, including portfolios.

2
Household Behaviour and Debt Demand

Daniela Vandone

2.1 Traditional economic models: behind the determinants of household debt demand

The theoretical economic framework for consumption, saving and indebtedness decisions is developed within the Life Cycle theory, proposed by Modigliani and Brumberg in 1954, and the Permanent Income Hypothesis, developed by Friedman in 1957.

These inter-temporal consumption choice models are based on the idea that households make their consumption choices, and consequently those relating to saving and indebtedness, on the basis of their wealth, current disposable income and future income expectations so as to guarantee a uniform level of consumption over their lifetimes.

The underlying assumption of these models is that income is generally low in an individual's early working life and tends to rise towards retirement. Individuals at the start of their working life, expecting higher future income receipts, finance the purchase of assets in order to raise consumption over the level offered by current income. Nearing the end of their working lives, inversely, individuals raise savings levels in preparation for retirement when spending will be greater than earnings. Within this framework, saving and indebtedness guarantee heightened economic welfare by smoothing out consumption over time. In particular, they may decide in a certain year to spend more than available income by running down all or part of their assets and/or by borrowing, provided that such a solution is temporary and that they die solvent (see Bagliano and Bertola, 2004).

Thus, the economic models referred to are based on the economic rationality of individuals, who seek to increase living standards by smoothing consumption over different periods of their lives through saving and borrowing.

According to these economic models, the applied literature highlights that household debt demand and supply is determined by household characteristics, household preferences and institutional factors.

2.1.1 Household characteristics

Household characteristics are individual variables related to the characteristics of a household. They are typically classified in:

- socio demographic variables
- economic variables.

As for the former, variables normally used in empirical analysis in order to find the drivers of household debt demand are: age, level of education, size of family and geographical area.

The age of the household is generally included in the analysis to take account of the life cycle model of consumption. The theoretical model predicts that demand for debt should be higher for young households expecting their income to grow, with demand dropping over time both because income becomes sufficient to cover expenditures and because households adopt a more conservative attitude as regards borrowing. In fact, empirical analysis shows that young people are more likely to borrow than members of older age groups (Crook, 2006; Fabbri and Padula, 2004), with the percentage of individuals with unsecured debt peaking for individuals aged between 30 and 40 years of age (Del Rio and Young, 2006; Magri, 2007). As for cross-country evidence, Crook (2006) points out that, although the probability of having debt in all countries is greater for young people, the maximum percentage is reached in the United Kingdom and Germany (those aged 30 to 40) and later (those aged 40 to 50) in the United States, Japan and the Netherlands.

As regards education, higher education reflects a quicker increase in future income, greater employment stability, and reduced entry costs in the market due to a better ability to understand financial information. Grant (2003) and Del Rio and Young (2006), however, suggest that this relationship exists for secured debt and is less significant for unsecured debt, that is consumer credit. Levels of education in general can reasonably be seen to have a positive impact on individuals' financial knowledge: the higher this level of knowledge is, the easier it is to access and evaluate financial products and services. This aspect should logically play an important role where complex products or large loan amounts, such as mortgages, are concerned. In fact, educational qualifications appear to be a less important factor for simple, easy to understand small loan packages, which are distributed not only by lenders over the counter, but also directly by retail stores.

With regard to household size, indebtedness is higher or the capacity to save is lower also in the case of large families with children at pre-school or school age when in this life cycle phase spending is typically high; Fabbri and Padula (2004) find that there is a positive relation between levels of indebtedness and the number of household members. This being said, however, the presence of children may also be an incentive for greater saving in order to satisfy intergenerational asset transfer.

The geographical area influences demand of debt since it affects the propensity to borrow, the availability of credit and market entry costs. Cavalletti et al. (2008) analyse the Italian household credit market and find that the probability of borrowing increases moving from the north to the centre and to the south of the country. Moreover, Fabbri and Padula (2004) analyse the effect of town and city size on indebtedness and find that residents in smaller towns have a lower probability of having debt.

As for the second group of determinants, the economic variables usually included in the analysis of the determinants of household debt demand are net wealth, income, work status and the number of income earners.

Net wealth generally has an ambiguous effect on the demand for debt. One would expect an increase in wealth to be accompanied by a reduction in households' debt demand due to their improved ability to finance consumption. However, empirical evidence and theoretical reasons suggest a possible opposite relationship: as wealth increases, the demand for debt increases as well, in particular for medium-low levels of wealth where the marginal utility of consumption is higher than that of wealth. Magri (2002) shows that rises in wealth are tracked by falls in the demand for debt as spending can be financed autonomously. However, households with intermediate wealth levels are more likely to participate in the consumer credit market due to increased spending patterns that characterise improvements in life style. Del Rio and Young (2006) focus their analysis on households with a portfolio of financial assets and find that households that do not own such a portfolio have a greater probability of having unsecured debt than those who do.

Current income is expected to have a negative effect on household debt demand: if the current income increases, demand for debt drops because, as for wealth, individuals are able to meet their needs with greater autonomy. However, empirical findings show that the sign can be ambiguous. With regard to low income as a factor for indebtedness, Del Rio and Young (2006) show that there is less probability of the poorer paid having debt due to the fact that low earnings are typically associated with highly unstable employment conditions that tend to reduce both the demand for and the supply of credit. Cox and Jappelli (1993), on the other hand, find a negative relationship between low income and probability of having debt as individuals currently at the bottom of the salary scale have expectations of increased earnings in the future and consequently borrow to smooth consumption over their lifetimes.

For medium-low income levels the sign can be ambiguous too. On the one hand, a positive sign can be expected, that is an increase in borrowing with an increase in income, due to the effect of the marginal utility which could boost consumption rather than saving; on the other, however, low incomes are usually also volatile and this tends to reduce demand for loans. Fabbri and Padula (2004), consistent with many studies carried out in the United States, reveal a positive relation between levels of debt and current income. Del Rio and Young (2006) and Magri (2007) show that for middle range levels of income, the marginal utility of consumption is high and income rises can generate higher spending and subsequent increased demand for credit. Crook (2006) also shows that high income individuals have a greater probability of having debt also due to the probability of facing fewer supply side constraints. The effect of the income variable, however, becomes less marked for middle to high earners, who, as their incomes rise, are able to satisfy spending needs from income.

For the variable work status, participation in the consumer credit market is higher for employees compared to the self-employed, whose income is subject to greater variability (Crook, 2006; Del Rio and Young, 2006). With reference to labour market status and the amount borrowed, Magri (2007) finds that the amount of consumer credit is higher for the self-employed and suggests this is because individuals in this category use unsecured debt also as a means of funding their work activities. With reference to cross-country differences, though the retired have a generally low probability of having debt, the share of those with debt is higher in the United Kingdom and Germany. There is less probability of the self-employed having debt in Italy and the Netherlands, whereas the unemployed have greater problems in accessing credit in Spain and the United States (Crook and Hochguertel, 2007).

2.1.2 Household preferences

Household debt demand also depends on household preferences, which explain cross-sectional differences in borrowing patterns across individuals. In particular, within the life cycle hypothesis household preferences depend, among other things, on the rate of time preference and on the household's rate of risk aversion.

As regards time preferences, according to the expected utility model, individuals have time consistent preferences and the utility of the different alternatives in time, assessed at the moment the decision is made, is simply the weighted sum of the values of the utility of each time period, discounted on the basis of the time when the utility arises. On the basis of this model, an individual's behaviour is dynamically rational when his or her investment or indebtedness plan is consistent with the current situation ('preference rationality'). In choosing how much to spend today and how much to save, every individual takes into account his or her own personal discount rate. This rate indicates the quantity of money an individual is prepared to give up tomorrow for an additional unit of money today. The more impatient the individual is, the greater he or she will discount the future over the present, and the higher his or her subjective discount rate for future utility will be.

As regards risk aversion, on a theoretical level, the link between risk preference and debt accumulation is clear, given that uncertainty surrounds the decision to acquire debt.

Households typically acquire debt to increase current consumption with repayment being made in the future. Given that debt repayments are generally financed from household income, it is apparent that if income in the future is subject to risk (that is, unemployment, death, disease ...), then the risk preference of individuals should play a key role in the decision to acquire debt. Intuitively, one might expect that the more risk averse a household is, the lower the debt an individual will incur if there is a non-zero probability that the individual cannot repay debt in the future. In sum, in the presence of uncertain future income streams, the nature of an individual's risk preferences arguably plays an important role in the decision to use debt to finance current consumption.

Taking into account risk preferences helps to explain why, all things being equal, there are some individuals who borrow more than others and those that borrow less. This link is, however, empirically difficult to study[1] and in fact the literature in this area is extremely limited. To our knowledge there are two recent papers that measure risk aversion.

Brown et al. (2008) find that risk preference is an important determinant of the level of debt, specifically unsecured debt, acquired at the household level and is negatively correlated: the higher the level of risk aversion, the lower the level of debt accumulation by households.

Donkers and Van Soest (1999) also analyse the relationship between risk taking and debt decisions. The authors use information on risk aversion and time preference in order to measure household preferences and to investigate whether these variables are helpful to explain households' financial decisions. They find that household characteristics (family composition, income, labour market status) are given, household preferences (time preference, risk aversion) may vary with these characteristics, and household financial decisions (both investment and debt decisions) are driven by family characteristics and household preferences.

2.1.3 Institutional factors

Household debt demand finally depends on institutional factors, which influence the demand for credit by creating the conditions for the market to sanction opportunistic behaviour. In fact, a household may decide to take out a loan not as a way of anticipating spending based on expectations of increased future income receipts, but because the household knows that the loan will not be repaid; a phenomenon aptly termed as 'strategic insolvency' (Gropp et al., 1997). An evaluation of the costs and benefits of insolvency will influence an individual's decision on whether to respect the contractual terms of the loan or whether to default and, in this perspective, whether to demand for debt. Such a decision is influenced by the credit market's capacity to sanction effectively opportunistic behaviour.

Among institutional factors, the literature usually focuses on two main factors: the justice system and the quality of information sharing mechanisms amongst financial institutions. In particular, empirical studies show that the probability of default is negatively correlated with the level of efficiency of the justice system and the existence of effective information sharing mechanisms.

With regard to the efficiency of the justice system, the probability of late payments or insolvency increases when credit recovery procedures are costly and lengthy. Specifically with regard to the efficiency of the justice system, Duygan and Grant (2008) show that the probability of late payment or insolvency increases as legal costs and repossession or foreclosure times rise; both facts act as incentives for opportunistic behaviour on the part of borrowers. The authors also find that a sudden fall in income, due to, for instance, job loss, will more probably lead to default in legal systems where creditor protection is weak. Grant and Padula (2006), however, underline that the effect of this institutional factor is limited to mortgages and has little impact on unsecured debt forms, such as consumer credit. Gropp et al. (1997) and Fay et al. (2002) refer specifically to 'strategic default' and, with regard to the United States, find that the probability of insolvency is higher when disciplinary mechanisms are ineffective, such as bankruptcy laws which favour the insolvent individual by fixing relatively high levels of income and wealth outside the threshold fixed in bankruptcy proceedings, and when the individual's social context is marked by high levels of insolvency and therefore where there is less stigma relating to the phenomenon.

Information sharing mechanisms among lenders reduces a household's incentive to over-borrow by demanding credit from more than one institution at the same time as each lender will be in a position to know the applicant's total system-wide exposure. Jappelli and Pagano (2006) show how the existence of information sharing mechanisms reduces an individual's incentive to over-borrow by applying for credit at more than one institution at the same time as each lender is in a position to know the individual's total debt exposure to the system. Duygan and Grant (2008) also show that the likelihood of insolvency is less when the financial system is equipped to know about previous episodes of insolvency and whether such events are due to adverse events, such as job loss.

2.2 Do individuals behave rationally? Some behavioural economics findings

As we have pointed out in the previous sections, traditional economic models posit that individuals behave rationally and choose their level of consumption, and thus of saving and debt, in order to maximise their expected utility, based on time consistent preferences. Within this framework, individual risk aversion reduces debt demand.

In recent years, there has been a growing number of studies in the field of behavioural economics which focuses on variables, other than those outlined by traditional economic models, that may significantly influence individuals' decisions relating to spending, saving or indebtedness.

These research models are based on empirical results that evidence anomalies regarding individuals' behaviour that conflict with traditional notions of economic rationality. Several studies have in fact shown how the behaviour of individuals deviates systematically from the 'rational choice' model of standard economic theories: although this does not imply that such behaviour is irrational,[2] the result is that individuals do not maximise their expected utility (Kahneman and Tversky, 1974, 1979; Kahneman et al., 1990; Barberis and Thaler, 2003; Etzioni, 2010; Franken et al., 2008; Rohde, 2009).

The anomalies regarding behaviour can be classified in:

(a) cognitive bias
(b) preference bias.

As regards cognitive bias, the rationality hypothesis typical of traditional economic models appears in contradiction with the tendency individuals have of acquiring and elaborating information by using only a limited number of intuitive rules (that is heuristics).

As numerous experiments have shown, information collection is often carried out on the basis of the availability heuristic, while the same information is elaborated on the basis of the representativeness heuristic.

Both heuristics, being the result of approximations, reduce the complexity of the problem but at the same time may generate significant, systematic errors which lead to forecasting distortions regarding the probability of an event and, therefore, its consequences.

The availability heuristic means that individuals tend to estimate the probability of an event on the basis of the availability of the experience, that is the ease or difficulty with which they remember an event, rather than on the basis of the real likelihood of the event's taking place (Meier and Sprenger, 2007, Kilborn, 2005). The 'availability' of the recollection is influenced by the frequency and significance of negative events as well as how recently they occurred. The more frequently and recently the event occurred, the more likely it is that individuals will overestimate the probability of a similar event happening again; vice versa, the less frequent and more remote in time the event took place, the more likely it is that individuals will underestimate the probability of a similar event's reoccurring. Consequently, if experiences of certain adverse events, such as liquidity crises, financial difficulties or over-indebtedness, are not available, individuals will tend to underestimate the chances of being affected by such events.

What is more, even if the same individuals were regularly exposed to statistics illustrating insolvency rates amongst other people, the impersonal nature of such information may mean it is not effective. Taking into account both excess optimism and the availability heuristic, it is clear that the probability of individuals' underestimating their exposure to insolvency risk is high.

The representativeness heuristic describes individuals' aptitude to judge probability on the basis of stereotypes and family situations. In other words, assessing the probability of an event depends on the extent such an event is similar to a certain class of events rather than their objective recurrence and the robustness of the sample. Individuals tend therefore to draw possible conclusions on the basis of an on–off event or a limited set of experiences. One of the several errors that this heuristic generates is excessive optimism.

As regards debt, individuals tend to be overoptimistic about their own exposure to risk and believe that they are capable of managing their level of indebtedness. As a result, they systematically underestimate the probability of being hit by adverse events (illness, job loss, and so on) that can lead to financial fragility and over-indebtedness and overestimate their capacities in managing household resources.

As for the second group of anomalies (that is preference bias), several studies in the field of experimental economics, inspired above all by the work carried out by Kahneman and Tversky (1974 and 1979), have identified different classes of choice related problems where preferences systematically contradict expected utility theories and the rational preference hypothesis. In fact, preferences are unstable and irregular and do not respect the axioms of expected utility theory.

Specifically, in classical rational choice models the discount factor is a decreasing monotonic function; that is, events in the near future have greater importance which, therefore, have a lower discount rate in comparison to events further in the future. In reality, individuals in assessing inter-temporal choices use a much higher discount rate for shorter time horizons and a lower rate for more remote events. It follows therefore that households do not have time consistent preferences; they use a 'hyperbolic discount', that is to say they tend to systematically overestimate immediate costs and benefits and underestimate those in the future. In this way, individuals give greater importance to present events over those that will occur in the future (Kilborn, 2005).

As regards the decision to participate in the credit market, the hyperbolic discount factor pushes individuals in the moment when they have to decide whether to purchase on credit terms or not to opt for immediate purchase. This decision is made despite the fact that an individual is rationally able to judge that the level of debt taken on is unsustainable in comparison to future income receipts.

The hyperbolic discount explains why individuals choose 'buy now, pay later' solutions that bring immediate gratification at a future cost. Undoubtedly, there are forms of credit, such as revolving credit solutions, that encourage behaviours that respond to this psychological characteristic. The hyperbolic discount factor, in fact, means that individuals adopt impatient, short-sighted behaviour patterns which make it difficult for them to be fully aware of the consequences of their spending decisions on the sustainability of personal debt (Meier and Sprenger, 2007).

In psychology, the concept of hyperbolic discount has been generally linked to impulsivity (Zermatten et al., 2005; Franken et al., 2008; Strack et al., 2006). Results have shown a relationship between an altered sense of time and impulsivity; that is, impulsive subjects overestimate the duration of time intervals and, as a consequence, discount the value of delayed rewards more strongly than do self-controlled individuals (Wittmann and Paulus, 2008).

Impulsivity is 'a sudden and immediate purchase with no pre shopping intentions. The behaviour occurs after experiencing an urge to buy and it tends to be spontaneous and without a lot of reflection' (Beatty and Ferrel, 1998, §). Common elements of definitions of impulse buying in the consumer behaviour research literature include: a) little or no planning; b) making a decision too quickly or 'on the spot'; c) the presence of a heightened emotional state, which may be accompanied by the experience of compulsion; d) dissatisfaction and regret after purchase (Stern, 1962; Rook, 1987; Piron, 1991). The main implication is that the purchases result in less overall satisfaction and more buying mistakes.

Thus, impulsivity may drive consumption behaviour and, indirectly, affect debt decisions since consumptions may be financed partially by credit, rather than or in addition to current income or wealth.

The concept of hyperbolic discount has also been related to that of risk taking behaviours: consumers who engage in risk taking behaviours are more likely to have a present, rather than a future orientation.[3]

The impact of the hyperbolic discount factor and impulsive buying on consumer choices is heightened by the features of the social context in which an individual lives. Individuals, in fact, consume not only to satisfy basic needs, but also to have access to the power and prestige that ownership of certain goods represents and to compensate for individual personality problems such as low self-esteem. Owning particular goods is therefore a conduit for satisfaction and success within a particular social reference group.

Table 2.1 Behavioural variables influencing household debt demand

Behavioural factor	Effect on debt demand	Consequence
Availability heuristic	Underestimate the likelihood of adverse events	
Overconfidence	Overestimate ability to manage indebtedness	Increased risk of debt without control (financial vulnerability, over-indebtedness)
Time-inconsistent preferences/ Impulsivity	Buy now, pay later. Pushes individuals to hold debt	
Social comparison	Increases individual spending and tendency to fund consumption by borrowing	

Thus, social comparison becomes a crucial factor in the consumption decision as personal levels of satisfaction are evaluated in relation to the status of other individuals. As societies become increasingly more materialistic and consumerist, such competition clearly increases individuals' spending and their tendency to fund consumption by borrowing (Karlsson et al., 2004). The need to spend may in fact raise demand for credit without an individual's having a clear idea about what this involves. If the individual has a level of income below that of his or her social reference group, then the probability of overspending and ending up in debt increases (Watson, 2003).

Table 2.1 presents a summary of the behavioural factors influencing household debt demand and possible consequences. As will be analysed in depth in Chapter 4, one of the main consequences of the effect of behavioural variables on debt demand is an increased risk of debt without control, which, in turn, may cause financial fragility and over-indebtedness.

2.3 Credit instruments and the effect of behavioural factors

The effect of behavioural factors on household debt demand is likely to be different for secured and unsecured debt.

The underlying idea is that the effects of secured debt decisions last for a long time and will follow the life cycle. Conversely, unsecured debt decisions are largely determined by short run benefits since debt is used for shopping and are thus more subject to variables like impulsivity, materialism, social comparison and satisfaction or self-esteem.

In particular, there are concerns that some contract features in the consumer credit market may induce consumers to borrow too much and to make suboptimal contract and repayment choices. These concerns, in fact, are motivated in part by evidence suggesting that consumers have a time-inconsistent taste for immediate gratification, and often naively underestimate the extent of this taste.

In particular, among unsecured debt, a specific concern is related to the rapid growth in recent years in the use of revolving credit cards on the back of strong growth in payment systems and card usage. Such an increase in credit card holding is due to many factors, mainly innovations and market developments that have significantly changed the credit card industry. Advances in credit scoring, response modelling, solicitation technologies (issuers' aggressive mail and marketing efforts by telephone and Internet), product innovation, customer loyalty and lower interest rates have enabled easier access to the credit market, also for individuals with lower incomes. Competition has boosted the adoption of new pricing models, such as complex sets of Annual Percentage Rate(s) (APRs), new and increased fee structures, and sophisticated finance charge computation techniques. Further expansion is likely with the creation of SEPA – Single Euro Payment Area – and the shared infrastructure, standardised procedures and raised security levels it foresees.

Many academics differ on the question of whether this growth is detrimental to the consumer. Academic researchers have found that rapid credit growth signals rapid future consumption growth. Others have interpreted the growth in credit in a negative light, suggesting that it will create financial difficulties. The latter might be the case when credit cards are not used within a life cycle framework of 'rational choice'.

Meier and Sprengen (2007) document that low and middle income individuals who exhibit time inconsistency in experimental choices over monetary payments have more outstanding credit card debt; they are more likely to borrow and borrow more than dynamically consistent individuals. In fact, it is argued that present bias increases individuals' desire for instantaneous gratification and, as a result, increases borrowing.[4] The effect of present-bias preferences is different if individuals are sophisticated – they foresee the possibility of self-control problems (or naive); they do not foresee these self-control problems and believe that future preferences will be identical to those they have at the moment, not realising that as they get closer to executing decisions their tastes will have changed. This preference for immediate reward also has the consequence that people borrow more then they should and, to make matters worse, they underestimate the cost of credit and the possible penalties for falling behind the repayment schedule.

Laibson et al. (2003) estimate that to explain a typical household's simultaneous holding of substantial illiquid wealth and credit card debt, the household's short-term discount rate must be higher than the long-term discount rate. Because many households are calculated to be made worse off by owning credit cards, the fact that they possess these cards suggests some degree of naivety about future use. Consistent with this idea, consumers over-respond to the introductory 'teaser' rates in credit card solicitations relative to the length of the introductory period (Shui and Ausubel, 2004) and the post-introductory interest rate (Ausubel, 1999), suggesting that they end up borrowing more than they intended or expected. Caplin and Leahy (2004) also argue that credit cards lead to overspending because they provide absent-minded consumers with less information on spending flows than cash transactions do.

Norum (2008) finds that the a high score on the use of credit cards has a positive association with compulsive buying. Moreover, risk taking behaviours also extend to credit card use; the rise in consumer debt and bankruptcies is the result of increased levels of impulse or erratic buying and a decline in the individual's willingness to delay gratification by saving in the future.

Finally, using the 'accountant-shopper' model, Bertaut et al. (2008) find that the separation of purchase from payment made possible by credit cards creates the potential for a differential impatience, that is time preference, between the entities responsible for the two actions: the 'shopper' and the 'accountant'. The 'accountant' manages household assets and debts including the extent of debt repayment. The 'shopper' chooses consumption, taking as given the size of the unused credit card line as determined by the accountant; the shopper tends to overspend relative to what the accountant desires, because of differential time preference. Credit cards are special in allowing such a separation, and their potential for generating spending control problems is often stressed in household surveys. According to Durking (2002), about 40 per cent of card holders perceive control problems emanating from credit cards and the possibility of overspending.

The 'accountant-shopper' contributes to underlining the different effects of behavioural factors on household secured and unsecured debt demand. In fact, this model can be applied to issues involving consumer lines of credit in general, but it is not necessarily applicable to all types of loan purchases. For example, a house purchase backed by a mortgage is lumpy and important enough to induce coordination between accountants and shoppers in the decision making rather than separation of the accounting from the purchase decision. Thus, self-control problems occur when the benefits of consumption occur earlier and are dissociated from the costs, and this is typically the case of revolving consumer credit products.

Notes

1. These difficulties are due to two aspects:
   - Information relating to individuals' risk aversion levels is not readily available (this is not surprising, given the obvious problems in measuring risk preferences).
   - Many economists are sceptical about the use of information based upon subjective survey questions in general.
2. Rationality as a concept adopted in economic theory consists in a series of hypothetical, regularised preferences on the part of an individual described by their utility function.
3. 'They are more likely to desire immediate satisfaction rather than delay gratification; in economic terms they have a high discount rate for future utility' (Finke and Huston, 2003).
4. Present-bias preferences can be seen as the result of the interplay of two separate decision making systems: the affective system, which values immediate gratification and sharply discounts all factors; and the deliberative system, which makes long-run plans and displays higher discount factors.

3

The Traditional Approach to Risk Tolerance

Nicoletta Marinelli and Camilla Mazzoli

3.1 Risk tolerance in the MiFID suitability questionnaire

Assessing client risk tolerance is one of the most important, yet most nebulous, activities within the financial planning process. A person's level of risk tolerance impacts upon a diverse number of financial decisions, such as portfolio management, type of mortgage, insurance deductibles, estate planning, and so on (Roszkowski and Grable, 2005). For years, the need to understand the attitude of investors toward risk has led both academics and practitioners to find reliable tools to assess the risk tolerance of individuals.

On the one hand, a number of authors have called for the application of formal procedures and tests to the risk tolerance assessment process; however, there is no consensus on how to best conduct it (among others, Callan and Johnson, 2002; Yook and Everett, 2003; Hanna and Lindamood, 2004; Roszkowski et al., 2005). Techniques for measuring risk tolerance have been devised by economists, psychologists and decision scientists, but as Grable and Joo (2000) observed, the recommended procedures differ depending in part on the academic or professional background of the assessor.

On the other hand, supervisors and regulated firms across the banking, securities and insurance sectors have also dealt with the issue of accurately assessing the level of risk a client may tolerate, in order to provide a product or service that matches the client's characteristics and while avoiding the risks associated with mis-selling.

With specific reference to the European Union, the Market in Financial Instruments Directive (MiFID, henceforth) has formalised the need for financial firms to include their clients' risk tolerance in the set of information required to determine whether an investment is 'suitable' for a particular client. The legislative framework comprises the MiFID Level 1 Directive 2004/39/EC of the European Parliament and of the Council of 21 April 2004 and the MiFID Level 2 Commission Directive 2006/73/EC of 10 August 2006. The first legislative reference contains conduct of business obligations that apply to investment firms and credit institutions when providing investment services (art.19).[1] The second legislative reference specifically includes a section containing technical implementation measures on the assessment of suitability and appropriateness (art. 35 onwards). This Directive required Member States to adopt the laws, regulations and administrative provisions necessary to comply with it by 31 January 2007, and to apply these measures beginning 1 November 2007.

Within the MiFID framework, the client's risk tolerance assessment is included into the more general suitability evaluation process. Suitability is given a broad meaning:[2] 'the degree to which the product or service offered by the intermediary matches the retail client's financial situation, investment objectives, level of risk tolerance, financial need, knowledge and experience'. In essence, suitability is a process by which the firm *gets to know its customer.*

The general application of MiFID suitability obligations is in regard to investment services; nevertheless, the specific application of MiFID rules varies according to a number of conditions, summarised in Table 3.1.

Table 3.1 Modulation of MiFID suitability obligations

Influence of the financial firm upon the client's investment decision	Non-advised services (reception and transmission of orders, execution of orders, dealing on own account, placing of financial instruments)	• Less protection to the client • Smaller information exchange • No risk tolerance assessment
	Advised services (portfolio management, investment advice)	• Greater protection to the client • Wider information exchange • Risk tolerance assessment
Client's classification	Professional client	• Lower level of protection • Less information • Risk tolerance assessment
	Retail client	• Higher level of protection • More information • Risk tolerance assessment
Type of financial intermediary	Insurance sector	Partial application
	Banking and securities sector	Full application

First, the need for a deeper knowledge of the client depends upon the kind of investment service provided; the kind of investment service may be defined according to the influence that the investment firm exerts on the final investment decision of the client. In this perspective, investment services may be divided into two groups: a first group of services that entails an element of recommendation on the part of the firm upon the final investment decision of the client, as the firm advises some products or receives an explicit mandate from the client to manage his or her assets ('advised services', that is, investment advice and portfolio management); a second group of services that do not imply a recommendation by the financial intermediary, resulting in a mere execution of transactions autonomously decided by the client ('non-advised services', such as reception and transmission of orders, execution of orders, dealing on own account, placing of financial instruments). As we will outline below, the amount of information required to provide the first group of services is greater and includes the assessment of risk tolerance, according to the MiFID prescriptions.

Secondly, the MiFID suitability obligations vary also according to the type of customer the service is provided to. In this sense, the MiFID distinction between a 'retail customer' and a 'professional client' is important. In general, the term 'retail customer' is not defined. Instead, anyone who is not a 'professional' investor (for example, financial intermediaries authorised to operate in the financial markets, companies meeting specific size requirements, some public organisations and, on request, private individual investors meeting certain minimum net worth levels or experience standards) is generally treated as a retail customer.[3] Suitability requirements apply to both, but differently: for retail clients the sources of information are more numerous, while for professional clients the data requirements are more essential. Nevertheless, risk tolerance is required in both cases, as we will discuss later in more depth.

Finally, even if the notion of suitability is recognised in the regulatory requirements across all financial services sectors (banking, securities and insurance), there are some differences in its application in each sector. In particular, the application of MiFID suitability requirements is only partially mandatory among insurance intermediaries providing investment services, whereas they fully apply to banks and financial firms.

As we outlined before, suitability obligations are modulated first according to the kind of service provided and the underlying influence upon the client's investment decision. For the group of 'advised services', MiFID requires the assessment of suitability in the strict sense, while for the second group of 'non-advised services' the assessment of appropriateness is needed. Both suitability and appropriateness have to be assessed through the use of questionnaires that are commonly called the suitability questionnaire and the appropriateness questionnaire. The two questionnaires differ regarding three main points. The first, as we have just observed, is the different field of application: portfolio management and investment advice need the suitability questionnaire, whereas services other than financial advice or portfolio management (for example, where the client simply asks that an order be executed) require an appropriateness questionnaire. Under MiFID, in the case of execution-only services (but in non-complex products only) the appropriateness test is not applied, provided that the service is offered at the initiative of the client, that the client has been clearly informed that the firm is not required to assess the appropriateness of the instrument or service offered and accordingly that the client will not have the benefits that would otherwise be provided by appropriateness determinations; the investment firm also has to comply with its conflict of interests obligations. There are two further distinctions between the suitability and appropriateness questionnaires, even more relevant from an operational point of view (see Table 3.2).

Table 3.2 The suitability questionnaire and the appropriateness questionnaire: a comparison

	Suitability	**Appropriateness**
Application field	• Portfolio management • Investment advice	Investment services other than portfolio management and investment advice No test is required for execution-only service
Content	Three sections: • investment objectives • financial capacity • experience and knowledge	One section: • experience and knowledge
Operational effects	Compulsory questionnaire: if the questionnaire is not filled in by the client, portfolio management and investment advice services cannot be provided	Non-compulsory questionnaire: if the client refuses to give some information, the service may be provided all the same, but under a disclosure obligation by the firm

The suitability and appropriateness questionnaires require a different set of information from the client. The MiFID dictates that the suitability questionnaire should be deeper and organised in three sections containing different information about the client.

The first section is addressed to the investment objectives of the client; in this section, the client has to express his or her preferences about the time horizon and the risk profile of the investment he or she is going to make, in order to identify those investment products that matches his or her preferences about risk, return and length of time. The second section is focused on the financial capacity of the client; it relates to the client's financial ability to incur risk and is a function of some economic information, such as the amount and stability of his or her income, the amount of expenses relative to income, the diversification of assets, the amount, timeframe and structure of liabilities. The third section aims to investigate the experience and financial knowledge of the client, as clients who comprehend risk are more likely to make financial planning decisions consistent with accomplishment of their goals; typically, the types of service, transaction and financial instrument with which the client is familiar or that the client has used in the past are investigated. It is evident that the assessment of the client's level of risk tolerance is not a standalone section, but it is included as a supplementary piece of information into the 'investment objectives' section. With regard to the appropriateness questionnaire, the amount of information asked for from the client is lower; as far as 'non-advised services' are concerned, it follows that the only section to be assessed is the necessary experience and knowledge of the client, in order to understand if the client is able to recognise the risks involved in the product or investment service offered or demanded. As a consequence, no element about the risk tolerance of the client is recorded.

Finally, the suitability and appropriateness questionnaires differ with regard to the compulsoriness (or not) of their need to be filled in, resulting in different operational implications for the investment firm. The suitability questionnaire is compulsory: the firm cannot provide the advice or management service if the client has not completed the test and provided all the required information (therefore, also the assessment of risk tolerance); this means that the suitability questionnaire is a preliminary test of knowledge the firm cannot do without, as it works as a stopping step for the service provision. On the contrary, in cases where the client does not provide the information needed to perform the appropriateness questionnaire, or provides insufficient information, firms are required to warn the client that the firm does not have sufficient information to determine whether the service or product envisaged is appropriate; nevertheless, the service or product may be provided. Therefore, the appropriateness questionnaire is not a stopping step for the service provision, but it simply causes the rise of a disclosure obligation for the providing firm.[4]

Where an investment firm provides an investment service to a professional client, it shall be entitled to assume that, in relation to the products, transactions and services for which he or she is so classified, the client has the necessary level of experience and knowledge; moreover, where that investment service consists of the provision of investment advice, the investment firm shall be entitled to assume also that the professional client is able financially to bear any related investment risks consistent with his or her investment objectives.[5] This means that for professional clients the suitability questionnaire is reduced into two sections ('investment objectives' and 'financial capability'), when providing portfolio management, and even into one section ('investment objectives'), when providing financial advice, as the other information may be implicitly assumed by the firm. Nevertheless, in both cases the level of risk tolerance is investigated. In contrast, the appropriateness has no more need to be assessed, as the only set of information required for appropriateness ('financial experience and knowledge' of the client) is implicitly supposed to exist.[6]

The suitability and appropriateness obligations are explicitly provided only to investment firms providing investment services. Investment firms are defined as 'any legal person whose regular occupation or business is the provision of one or more investment services to third parties and/or the performance of one or more investment activities on a professional basis';[7] the reference is to the securities and banking sector, so that 'pure' investment firms and credit institutions that provide investment services are subject to the same rules. In the original MiFID prescription, nothing is specified as far as insurance companies providing investment products are concerned. As a consequence, each Member State is free to design a specific regime for the insurance sector, provided that the regime is compliant with the Directive 2002/92/EC of the European Parliament and of the Council of 9 December 2002 on Insurance Mediation (IMD, henceforth). For example, in Italy the Regulation n. 16190 of the 29 October 2007 (Reg. 16190/2007, henceforth), provided by the Italian regulatory authority for financial markets (Commissione Nazionale per le Società e la Borsa, CONSOB) and implementing MiFID prescriptions in the Italian legislation, extends the suitability and appropriateness obligations to the so-called Subjects Qualified to the Insurance Intermediation

(SQII, henceforth) (art. 85); Reg. 16190/2007 underlines that Italian and European investment firms, Italian and European banks, financial intermediaries belonging to the list ex art. 107 of the Legislative Decree n. 385 of 1 September 1993 and Poste Italiane are considered SQII, also when providing remote services (art. 83). When offering insurance products with an investment purpose,[8] they are asked to follow the same rule of suitability/appropriateness dictated to banks and investment firms. Art. 87 of the same regulation extends this prescription also to insurance firms that directly sell financial insurance products to the client, while no mention is made about insurance distributors, such as brokers and insurance agents, that continue to follow the general prescriptions dictated by the Italian regulatory authority for insurance firms, Istituto per la Vigilanza sulle Assicurazioni Private e di Interesse Collettivo-ISVAP ('Code of private insurance', Legislative Decree n. 209 of 7 September 2005 and ISVAP Regulation n. 5 of the 16 October 2006) and by the IMD cited above (see Table 3.3).

This lack of prescriptions for agents and brokers creates a gap between some distributors of investment linked insurance products and others: the same product may require a test of suitability/appropriateness or not according to the kind of subject responsible for the provision. If the product is provided by a SQII or directly by an insurance firm a suitability/appropriateness questionnaire must be done and it may work

Table 3.3 Normative framework about suitability/appropriateness applied to the Italian insurance sector

Intermediary	Financial insurance products	Non-financial insurance products
SQII	Suitability/ Appropriateness obligations ex MiFID (Art. 83ss. Reg. n. 16190/2007)	ISVAP rules (Code of private insurance and ISVAP Regulation n. 5 of the 16 October 2006)
Insurance firms (direct selling)	Suitability/ Appropriateness obligations ex MiFID (Art. 83ss. Reg. n. 16190/2007)	ISVAP rules (Code of private insurance and ISVAP Regulation n. 5 of the 16 October 2006)
Other 'traditional' distributors (agents, brokers...)	ISVAP rules (Code of private insurance and ISVAP Regulation n. 5 of the 16 October 2006)	ISVAP rules (Code of private insurance and ISVAP Regulation n. 5 of the 16 October 2006)

as a stopping step for the service provision, while if the same product is provided by an agent or a broker no questionnaire is needed and no stopping step occurs, apart from general rules of disclosure prescribed by ISVAP and IMD for selling insurance products.[9] The same considerations are true if we specifically consider the risk tolerance assessment, being a part of the suitability questionnaire.

This is evidently an inconsistency within the law, which should be considered and discussed at the institutional level, in order to avoid ambiguity in the provision of investment services and to effectively guarantee customer protection. From this perspective, the European Commission's Communication on Package Retail Investment Products (PRIPs, henceforth), which was published on 29 April 2009, points out a number of differences in the regulation of selling practices of PRIPs. In the Communication, the European Commission sets forth a horizontal approach in order to harmonise sales practices not only across different product classes, but also across various distribution channels. The work of the Commission, which has included a call for evidence and an open hearing, plans to revise the IMD and to make a legislative proposal at the end of 2010.[10]

From the above considerations, we derive that the MiFID suitability and appropriateness questionnaires are not strictly risk tolerance tests, as their general goal is wider and addressed to a global knowledge of the client in order to provide an investment service that is understood by the client in its risk profile and that matches the client's financial features. In this perspective, the client's risk tolerance assessment enters as just one component, among others, required to know the client. Nevertheless, even if the MiFID suitability questionnaires are not risk tolerance tests in the strict meaning of the term, it is important to discuss them, as they are actually the only tool that financial firms are obliged to provide by law to their clients before investment service provision. As the 'investment objectives' section contains questions about the client's risk profile, MiFID suitability questionnaires become also the only tool that financial firms are obliged to use by law for the assessment of risk tolerance.

3.2 The Italian experience: comparisons of MiFID questionnaires

The suitability determination and, within it, the risk tolerance assessment of individuals relies primarily on adequate information gathering by financial firms. From this standpoint, a key part of the analysis is to understand what firms actually do to meet their MiFID suitability obligations and to derive the risk profile of their clients. We analyse 14 suitability questionnaires provided by the first 14 Italian financial groups in terms of promoted assets[11] in the area of portfolio management; altogether, these groups share 90 per cent of the total market. Our analysis deals only with questionnaires in respect to *retail* customers and products with a significant *investment* component that require a suitability determination. Questionnaires for institutional investors and those addressed to the provision of services that require only an appropriateness evaluation are not part of this survey, as they may be considered a portion of the wider suitability questionnaire.

The aim of our analysis is twofold: on the one hand, we try to understand how the major Italian financial firms actually deal with their customer suitability obligations, in order to compare different approaches in developing the questionnaire and outline the main differences; on the other hand, a specific focus is addressed to investigate how these intermediaries specifically formulate questions to assess the risk tolerance of a client which will help to point out any possible gaps therein.

It is worth pointing out that the Italian regulatory authority for financial markets (CONSOB) has recently implemented the 'Level 3' (L3, henceforth) of MiFID, in order to homogenise the practices for fairness and transparency followed by Italian intermediaries towards retail clients, with a specific concern for illiquid and complex financial products.[12] In this perspective, CONSOB dictates further obligations that financial intermediaries have to follow when assessing the suitability/appropriateness of their customers. Specifically, CONSOB requires that in order to assess the suitability/appropriateness of a product, financial firms have to implement a set of controls, regarding the coherence between the complexity, the risk profile, the liquidity of the product and the characteristics of the client as derived from the suitability/appropriateness questionnaire. These obligations have led some Italian intermediaries to make adjustments to their suitability questionnaires and, most of all, in their algorithms for assessing the risk profile in order to be fully compliant to L3. For example, better specifications of illiquid and complex products inside the questionnaire have been sometimes needed, as well as some further specifications about the investment objectives and the time horizon desired. We collected suitability questionnaires from the 14 Italian financial groups after these regulatory adjustments.

At first glance, the 14 suitability questionnaires provided by the major Italian financial groups appear to be largely different. Some of them are very analytical, whereas some of the others are very short and essential. The number of questions asked to the client is a first proxy for the comparison: there are questionnaires where the maximum number of questions equals 37 and others with a minimum of 8; in our sample, the average number of questions asked to the client is approximately 19. Indeed, in our sample the range between the maximum and the minimum number of questions is quite high and also the dispersion around the average is not negligible, with a convergence towards the left side of the frequency distribution (see Figure 3.1).

In order to develop a deeper analysis of our sample of questionnaires and to derive a coherent basis for comparisons, we decided to use the information categories suggested by MiFID as an objective parameter. More specifically, as outlined in Section 3.1, MiFID asks firms to provide a suitability questionnaire made up of three sections, respectively in regard to: 'financial objectives'; 'financial capacity'; 'financial experience and knowledge'. These sections are compulsory and must be necessarily covered by each financial firm through the suitability assessment of its clients. At the same time, MiFID suggests a set of items that 'should' be included in each section, without formulating a legislative obligation for them directly.[13] This means that, even though MiFID stipulates some advisable questions to be included in the questionnaire, each financial firm is free to define the specific questions of its own suitability questionnaire, provided that the three main sections are covered. The set of items suggested by MiFID are summarised in

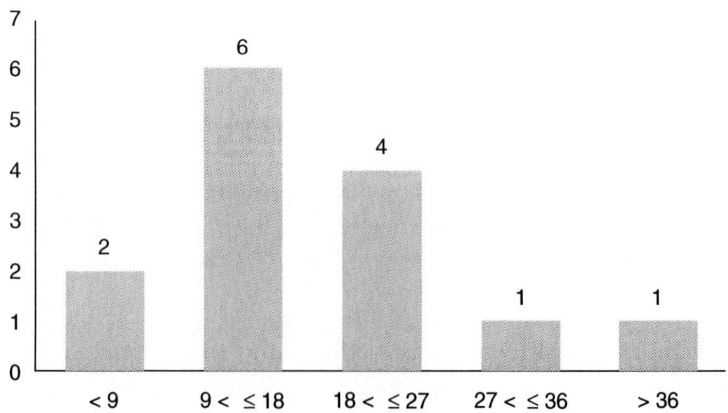

Figure 3.1 Number of questions in the suitability questionnaires (sample: the first 14 Italian financial groups in terms of promoted assets)

Table 3.4 Set of items suggested by MiFID for the suitability questionnaire

Section	Should include:
Investment objectives	• Information on the length of time for which the client wishes to hold the investment • The investors's preferences regarding risk taking • His or her risk profile • The purpose of the investment
Financial capacity	• Source and extent of his or her regular income • His or her assets (including liquid assets) • Investment and real property • His or her regular financial commitments
Experience and knowledge	• Types of service, transaction and financial instrument with which the client is familiar • The nature, volume and frequency of the client's transactions in financial instruments • The period over which the client's transactions have been carried out • The level of education of the client • Profession or relevant former profession of the client

Table 3.4 and we have decided to use them as a 'benchmark' to compare the completeness of various questionnaires provided by our sample of Italian financial firms.

The 'benchmark' questionnaire suggested by MiFID comprises 13 items, equally portioned among the three sections. All the items suggested by MiFID are clearly understandable; the only item that needs a specification is the one related to the risk assessment of the client. In this sense, MiFID makes a distinction between the preferences regarding risk taking and the client's risk profile; provided that the legislation does not explicit the specific meaning of each of them, we associated the 'preferences regarding risk taking' item with all the questions related to the risk and return characteristics of the investments the client is willing to undergo (objective risk), while we interpreted the 'risk profile' item as the one aimed to know the behaviour of the client in situations of riskiness and uncertainty (subjective risk).[14] This way, we are able to make a distinction between the assessment of the objective risk and the evaluation of the subjective aspect of risk.

With these premises, we try to analyse how much the 14 questionnaires under study verge on this 'benchmark' suggested by law and if

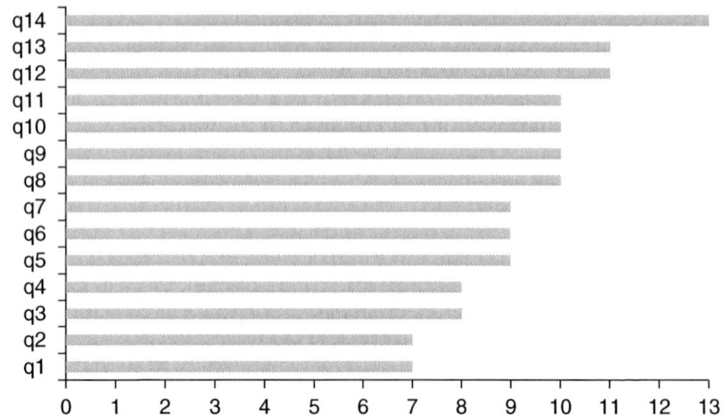

Figure 3.2 The completeness of the suitability questionnaires: number of MiFID suggested items covered

(sample: the first 14 Italian financial groups in terms of promoted assets)

the divergence among questionnaires is significant or not. A first synthesis of our findings is summarised in Figure 3.2.

If we evaluate the completeness of the suitability questionnaires in terms of how much they cover the set of items indicated by MiFID, only one questionnaire is complete, as the other ones leave one or even more suggested items uncovered. The largest element of our sample (nine questionnaires) includes a number of items between eight and ten. On the basis of this evidence, it is interesting to further identify what are the items generally covered in our sample and, conversely, what are the areas of questions generally overlooked. From the first point of view, the items covered by all the 14 questionnaires are those related to: the length of time for which the client wishes to hold the investment, preferences regarding risk taking, types of service, transaction and financial instrument with which the client is familiar, the nature, volume and frequency of the client's transactions in financial instruments.[15] On the contrary, the less investigated areas are those regarding: regular financial commitments (seven questionnaires), the asset composition (six questionnaires), the risk profile (four questionnaires), the period over which past investments have been carried out (one questionnaire). Some intermediaries provide 'extra' questions, not included in the 'benchmark' scheme suggested by MiFID. Nevertheless, generally these questions are introduced for insurance products, in order to be ISVAP compliant, or to acquire information useful for the firm providing the service rather than for the suitability assessment of the client.[16] The only 'extra' question, not suggested by MiFID, but useful to improve the knowledge of the client is the one related to the frequency to which the client brings himself or herself up to date about financial situation; in our sample, two financial firms include this question in their suitability questionnaires.

Shifting the analysis from the general scheme to the single compulsory sections of the questionnaire, we may provide a deeper insight about the specific questions asked and the different approaches followed by each intermediary. In this sense, as regards the 'investment objectives' section, the approach generally followed by our sample of Italian intermediaries is quite homogeneous (see Figure 3.3).

All the 14 suitability questionnaires under analysis include questions about the time horizon of investments and preferences regarding risk taking; moreover, the majority of questionnaires (85 per cent) ask the client to specify the purpose of the investment he or she is going to realise, in terms of capital conservation, capital growth, or strong capital growth. On the contrary, a generalised behaviour in our sample is to disregard questions about the risk profile of the client, as only four questionnaires include this item among the ones investigated. When the risk profile of the client is assessed, the firm asks the client to place himself or herself in a situation of financial risk or of a more common

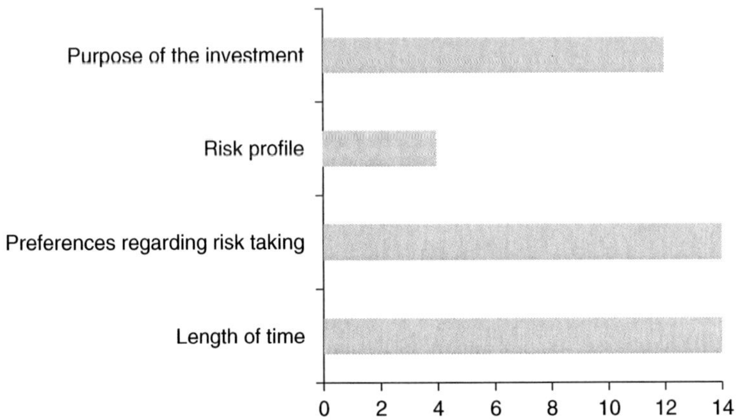

Figure 3.3 Investment objectives: coverage of MiFID suggested items (sample: the first 14 Italian financial groups in terms of promoted assets)

daily uncertainty and to choose the alternative that fits better his or her hypothetical behaviour in presence of that risk or uncertainty. From the perspective of our analysis, this is a critical point: our sample of Italian financial groups seems to take great care on the assessment of the objective financial risk, while less attention is given to the evaluation of the subjective component of risk. In other words, the client is always asked about his or her preferences in respect of the financial risk–return combination of future investments; conversely, the attitude of the client towards a general situation of riskiness or uncertainty is rarely comprised.

Further investigation of the 'financial capability' section of the suitability questionnaire reveals that more diversified choices are observed among Italian financial groups (see Figure 3.4).

There is not an item, among those suggested by MiFID for this section, that is covered by all the questionnaires. Nevertheless, the most frequent group of questions is the one related to the source and extent of regular income (13 questionnaires), followed by those questions regarding the overall property composition (11 questionnaires). The items concerning the evaluation of regular financial commitments and the financial portfolio composition are less investigated (respectively, only seven and six questionnaires). From the perspective of our study, this is another point worthy of note: on the one hand, regular financial commitments are a proxy of the risk capacity of an individual (that

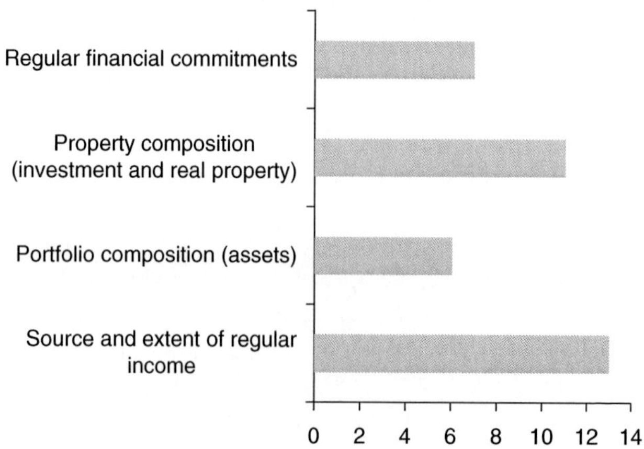

Figure 3.4 Financial capability: coverage of MiFID suggested items (sample: the first 14 Italian financial groups in terms of promoted assets)

is, how much risk he or she affords to take), as the presence of financial dependents reduces the client's ability to assume risk. On the other hand, the actual financial portfolio composition is another important proxy of the client's risk taking behaviour in real life, as it gives information about the financial decisions assumed in the past by the client. As a consequence, neglecting these two items means also that two important pieces of information in the general assessment of risk are overlooked.[17]

Finally, in respect to the 'financial experience and knowledge' section, all of the sample collects information about the type of service/products with which the client is familiar and the nature, volume and frequency of the client's transactions in financial instruments (see Figure 3.5). In contrast, almost none of the firms take the period over which past investments are carried out into account (only one questionnaire); respectively 12 and 10 questionnaires include the level of education and the profession among the set of questions to be filled in.

The 14 suitability questionnaires are very different not only with regard to the number of items globally asked and the adherence upon the MiFID 'benchmark', but also concerning the degree of investigation within each item. For example, even though the items of the length of time, preferences regarding risk taking, types of service/instrument with which the client is familiar and the nature/volume/frequency of the client's financial transactions are assessed by all of the 14 questionnaires, the number of questions included in each of them varies

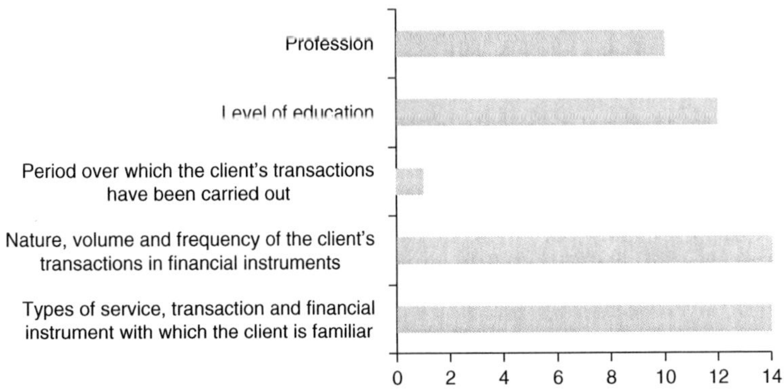

Figure 3.5 Financial experience and knowledge: coverage of MiFID suggested items
(sample: the first 14 Italian financial groups in terms of promoted assets)

consistently from one questionnaire to another: some questionnaires provide just one question for investigating each item, whereas other questionnaires are much more analytical and use more than five questions to analyse the same aspect.

In summary, a key finding of our analysis is that the implementation of the suitability assessment and, within it, of the level of risk tolerance, even though it is recognised as a common MiFID regulatory requirement, is applied in a highly variable manner by our sample of Italian financial firms. The differences that do exist may stem from the fact that supervisors give only general rules for the development of the suitability questionnaire without providing a unique and shared form, in adherence to a prudential regulation approach. As a consequence, each intermediary may develop its own suitability questions according to the:

- business model: the propensity to ask some information may vary depending on the kind of business that characterises each intermediary; the orientation toward a model of commercial banking or a prevalence of the investment business within the financial group, the penetration level in the market of investment services, the development of specific financial services, the diversification and sophistication in the offer of financial products, the characteristics of their prevalent client are all elements that may exert an influence
- compliance function: the specific questions included in the questionnaire may also depend upon how the compliance function of the firm interprets the regulatory recommendations and the relevance accorded to specific aspects in the application of the law
- competence level of front-offices: as front-offices are the bridge between the firm and the customer in the implementation of the suitability questionnaire, a different approach in the development of the questions may also depend upon the specific competence of the front-offices in terms of technical advice, ability to built a relationship, and commercial approach to the client
- a random component, that does not depend upon a strategic or rational motivation by the firm, but just upon erratic occurrences or behavioural biases in the people designed to the development of the questionnaire itself.

However, in spite of different constructions of the questionnaire, some common behaviours among our sample of Italian financial groups may be depicted. Specifically, the majority of our sample seems to derive the risk tolerance assessment of the client in a partial way: while the desirable objective risk–return characteristics of future investments are constantly investigated, the subjective risk profile of the client, as well as his or her past financial investments (risk taken in the real life) and his or her current financial constraints (risk capacity) are elements less frequently requested, even though they all exert an influence upon the suitability of suggested services/products and may work as a control for the chosen risk–return combination. Indeed, it seems that the suitability questionnaire provided by our sample of Italian intermediaries is drawn mainly with the aim of deriving objective parameters for the implementation of traditional asset allocation strategies (such as time horizon, purpose of investment, preferences regarding the objective risk) rather than with the purpose of making a deeper analysis of the subjective characteristics of the clients.

3.3 Consistency of clients' profiles across a sample of Italian MiFID questionnaires

In Section 3.2 we already underlined that with the introduction of the MiFID, the European Regulator has formalised the need for financial firms to *get to know their customers* before selling any financial service or product to them. Nevertheless, this practice was already consolidated among financial firms both in Italy and in the rest of Europe even before the introduction of the MiFID. Financial firms were already aware that the numerous contentions with their clients that took place in the last years could derive from a misunderstanding of the clients' preferences towards risk when subscribing an investment contract. The introduction of a questionnaire, whose function was to reveal the clients' needs and preferences towards the risk and return of the investment, was a tool to reduce possible misunderstandings. Moreover, as the risk preferences were written and subscribed by the client, it was a tool to protect financial firms against possible complaints from the client in the case of an unexpected loss of the investment. Therefore the MiFID has formalised a habit that was already widespread among financial firms and has also made it *compulsory*.

As already illustrated in Section 3.1 the Directive requires financial operators to submit their retail clients a suitability and appropriateness questionnaire when providing them with financial services and products. Depending on the result of the questionnaire, investors can be provided with products that are more or less risky according to their needs and profile. So, it is clear how important the information that is obtained from the questionnaire is in every step of the contract between the financial firm and the client:

(a) *before* the financial service or product is subscribed, in order to meet the preferences and need of the investors
(b) *during* the contract, in order to acquire any changes in the needs and preferences of the investor
(c) *after* the end of the contract, in order to protect the bank against any complaint that the client could make with reference to a loss that he or she did not expect but is physiological according to the level of risk that characterises the investment.

Unfortunately, the Directive only dictates general rules as far as the content of the questionnaire is concerned; thus, each financial firm makes use of its own questionnaire that is likely to be different from its competitors' as already demonstrated in Section 3.2. The aim of our analysis is to investigate how reliable MiFID questionnaires are, in terms of the consistency of profiles that come out from different questionnaires submitted to the same person. To do this, we collected a sample of MiFID questionnaires belonging to three Italian banks.[18] All three are suitability questionnaires addressed to retail clients. For each of them we also collected the scoring method used to calculate the profile of the clients answering the questions.[19] The three anonymous questionnaires (hereafter, A, B and C) were submitted to a sample of 100 potential investors in order to verify the consistency of their profiles.[20] The sample was chosen according to a totally random criterion; we did not face any sampling problems as each person represented a result by himself or herself through the comparison of the three different profiles.

Because each of the three banks provides a different structure of profiles, we were forced to subjectively match them according to the description of each classification offered. This way, before comparing the profiles, we made them comparable. In particular, Bank A classifies clients into conservative, balanced and enterprising; Bank B into safety, income, balanced, increase and dynamic; and Bank C distinguishes among cautious, moderate and dynamic. Each of the questionnaires provided a detailed explanation of the characteristics that feature each of the profiles as shown in Tables 3.5, 3.6 and 3.7. The way the profiles are described changes across the questionnaires; questionnaire A and B provide respectively three and five categories and describe in words the main features that investor must have to be included in each profile.

Table 3.5 Description of profiles for Bank A

Profile	Description of profile
Conservative	The portfolio suitable for this profile is addressed at realising a financial supply, without any expectation of capital increase and whose main goal is to allow the management of small expenses. It does not require any particular expertise in investing and is generally linked to a low risk propensity. Suitable products according to this risk profile are liquid assets, government bonds, financial insurance products with capital protection.
Balanced	The portfolio that is suitable for this profile is addressed at realising an increase in the invested capital through the acceptance and management of negative oscillations in the value of the capital. It requires a medium expertise in investing and is generally linked to a medium risk propensity. Suitable products according to this risk profile are diversified bond and stock investments and financial insurance products without capital protection.
Enterprising	The portfolio that is suitable for this profile is addressed at realising a relevant increase in the invested capital through the acceptance and management of huge negative oscillations in the value of the capital. It requires a good expertise in investing and is generally linked to a high-risk propensity. Suitable products according to this risk profile are sector stock investments and high-risk bonds and also derivatives.

Table 3.6 Description of profiles for Bank B

Profile	Description of profile
Safety	Capital conservation in the short term and slight increase in the medium term
Income	Capital conservation in the medium term and slight increase in the long term
Balanced	Increase of capital in the medium long term
Increase	Relevant increase of the capital in the medium long term
Dynamic	Relevant increase of the capital in the short medium term

Table 3.7 Description of profiles for Bank C

Profile	Description of profile
Cautious	35% in liquidity; 54% in bonds; 11% in stocks
Moderate	20% in liquidity; 47% in bonds; 11% in stocks
Dynamic	7% in liquidity; 33% in bonds; 68% in stocks

Table 3.8 Matching of profiles for Banks A, B and C

Questionnaire A	Questionnaire B	Questionnaire C
Conservative	Safety + Income	Cautious
Balanced	Balanced	Moderate
Enterprising	Increase + Dynamic	Dynamic

On the contrary, questionnaire C provides three risk profiles that are described in terms of the percentage of the capital that should be allocated among liquidity, bonds and stocks for each profile. In this way, any attempt of matching the profiles requires a high level of subjectivity. Table 3.8 illustrates how the different profiles are matched across the three banks in the following analysis.

In the experiment, each of the subjects was requested to fulfil all three questionnaires. Once this step was completed, the three profiles for each subject were calculated and compared in order to assess their consistency.

Table 3.9 illustrates the results; in particular, it shows the percentage of cases in which the profiles of single subjects are consistent throughout the sample.[21] The first column from the left informs that in 77 per cent of cases the same subject obtains profiles that are different across the three banks. In particular, in 14 per cent of cases the profiles are totally different as they range from the highest to the lowest profile across the three banks for the same subject. Moreover, in an attempt to understand if a questionnaire causes inconsistency of the profiles more than the other two, we provide the percentage of inconsistency of profiles for each couple of questionnaires. The analysis shows that the inconsistency is 51 per cent between questionnaires A and B, 60 per cent between A and C and 53 per cent between B and C.

In this sense, we cannot maintain that any of the three questionnaires is 'bad' because the couples of questionnaires show almost the same degree of inconsistency. More precisely, we should recognise that the questionnaires are strongly different as far as their structures and scoring methods are concerned. First of all, the range of questions that are asked to the client varies from eight in questionnaire A to 16 in questionnaire B and nine in questionnaire C, as shown in Table 3.10.

This evidence suggests that questionnaire B could be more precise and articulated that the others. Besides, by following the methodology that we already used in Section 3.2 we briefly analyse the

Table 3.9 Percentage of consistency of profiles across questionnaires

Across all 3 questionnaires	Between questionnaires A and B	Between questionnaires A and C	Between questionnaires B and C
23%	49%	40%	47%

Table 3.10 Number of questions in the questionnaires

Questionnaire	**Number of questions**
q_A	8
q_B	16
q_C	9

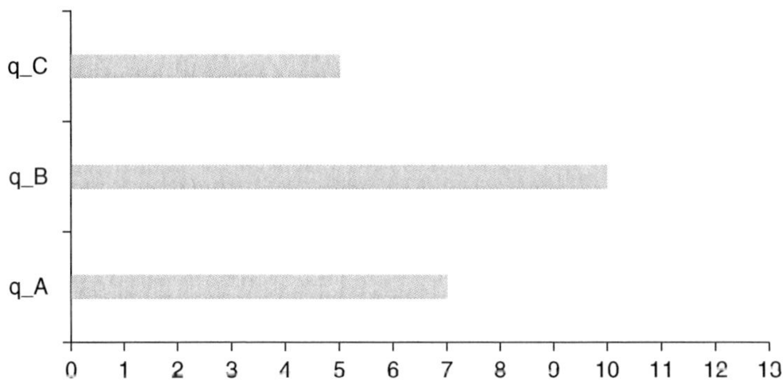

Figure 3.6 Number of MiFID suggested items covered

contents of the three questionnaires in order to catch any difference that could help explaining the relevant inconsistency of the profiles that a single person obtains when he or she is analysed by a bank or another. We first investigate the level of compliance to the MiFID suitability provisions in terms of the number of items that are included into the three questionnaires with respect to the 13 that are suggested in the Directive. Figure 3.6 shows that none of the three questionnaires is perfectly compliant to the number of items suggested (with B covering ten, A covering seven and C only five out of 13 items).

As for the similarities, the items present in all three questionnaires are those related to the purpose of the investment (within the 'investment objectives' section), the source and extent of regular income ('financial capability' section) and the types of services and products the client is familiar with ('financial experience and knowledge' section). This way, at least one of the items belonging to each of the main three sections is present in all of the questionnaires. As a further similarity, the period over which the investments were carried out is absent in all the questionnaires,[22] as Table 3.11 shows.

The main differences deal with the risk profile and risk preferences together with the level of education and profession. In fact, only questionnaire C investigates the investor's preferences for risk taking and only A includes a question on the risk profile. Moreover, questionnaire B is the only one interested in the level of education and current profession of the subject. All the other items are included by two banks out of three. Table 3.12 summarises the main findings in term of differences between the three questionnaires.

This analysis mainly confirms the results we already obtained in Section 3.2. In fact, by observing the information provided in Tables

Table 3.11 Similarities in the three questionnaires

Items included in all 3 questionnaires	**Items absent in all 3 questionnaires**
• Purpose of the investment • Source and extent of regular income • Services and product the investor is familiar with	• Period over which the investment was held

Table 3.12 Differences in the three questionnaires

Items included in one of the 3 questionnaires	**Items included in two of the 3 questionnaires**
• Preference for risk taking (q_C) • Risk profile (q_A) • Level of education (q_B) • Profession (q_B)	• Length of time of the investment (q_A and q_B) • Assets (q_A and q_B) • Regular financial commitments (q_B and q_C) • Nature, volume and frequency of transactions (q_A and q_B)

3.11 and 3.12, all three banks seem to be most interested in the *objective parameters* (purpose of the investment, source and extent of regular income, services and products the client is familiar with, length of time of the desired investment, regular financial commitments, and so on). On the contrary, very little is asked in terms of the level of education, profession, risk profile and also on the preferences of the investor. At the end of Section 3.2 we already focused attention on the possible reasons that could explain the huge differences in the contents of the questionnaires and in the scoring methods. The results of this analysis allowed us to maintain that those differences, together with the little attention to the *subjective characteristics* of the client, seem to provide good explanations for the variety and inconsistency of profiles that an investor can obtain by applying to different banks.

3.4 The post-MiFID Italian suitability assessment compared to the pre-MiFID and non-EU countries practice

We already discussed in Section 3.2 that the MiFID lists a series of information to be collected by banks and other intermediaries when submitting their suitability questionnaire to clients. The list only includes general items but there is no compulsory scheme to be followed by financial firms. As a consequence, the characteristics of the questionnaires, and also the profiles that come out, largely vary from one financial firm to another both within the same country and, even more, from one country to another. At the end of Section 3.2 we also discussed the possible explanations of the differences; in this section we propose another likely justification that is linked to past practice. In fact, the profiling of customers was a widespread habit even before the introduction of the MiFID both within and outside the European Union. As a consequence, many financial firms were already used to submitting their questionnaires and, after 2007, they may have only revised them in order to be as compliant as possible with the MiFID sections and items.

In order to understand to what degree the questionnaires might have changed with the introduction of the MiFID Directive, we compare a sample of *MiFID suitability questionnaires* (hereafter SQ) collected in 2010 with a sample of *profiling questionnaires*[23] (hereafter PQ) belonging both to European financial firms before the implementation of the Directive and also to non-EU financial firms. To do this we make use of the results of research that has been carried out by the Bank for International Settlement (hereafter BIS) in 2008 and also of the 14 Italian questionnaires already described in section 3.2.[24]

The BIS research was carried out among a sample of financial firms (belonging to both EU and non-EU countries) before the MiFID was implemented (between September 2006 and February 2007). Therefore, it offers a landscape of how clients were profiled before the introduction of the Mifid and in non-EU countries. By comparing the PQ in the BIS study with the 14 Italian SQ that we employed in Section 3.2 we should be able to testify how Italian intermediaries are now positioned in terms of clients' profiling and suitability assessment in respect to the average of the pre-MiFID European countries (and of the non-EU sample countries) with reference to:

- the completeness of the questionnaires in terms of the 13 items now suggested by the MiFID within the three sections
- the importance given to the risk tolerance and risk preference components.

The sample that has been used within the BIS research is made up of 90 financial firms belonging to different financial sectors and based in ten countries, as Table 3.13 shows.

It is worth a reminder that the Italian sample is made up of the major 14 groups as already explained in Section 3.2. Moreover, we were informed that all the firms belonging to the same group make use of the same questionnaire; this way, we need no distinction among sectors because each questionnaire is representative of the suitability assessment for the investment firms, the banks, the insurance companies and also the asset managers belonging to the group. As a consequence,

Table 3.13 Composition of BIS research sample

	Asset managers	Banks	Insurance companies	Investment firms	Financial advisers
Canada	2	–	–	1	–
France	3	2	4	2	–
Germany	3	-	2	-	–
Italy	3	5	–	2	–
Japan	4	3	4	3	–
Netherlands	1	5	-	–	–
Spain	–	5	1	–	–
Switzerland	–	6	3	–	–
United Kingdom	2	5	2	–	4
United States	1	1	1	10	–
Total	19	32	17	18	4

when comparing the contents of the PQ described into the BIS research with the Italian SQ we do not make any distinction among sectors and consider the results of the BIS research as a sum of the results coming from the different intermediaries included into the sample. The only exception deals with financial advisers that are not included in the 14 Italian groups. Moreover, even the BIS research sets apart this category

Table 3.14 MiFID suitability items included in the BIS profiling questionnaires

MiFID items included or excluded in BIS questionnaires			
MiFID sections	**MiFID items**	**MiFID items included or excluded in non-MiFID questionnaires**	
Investment objectives	Length of time to hold the investment	Time horizon	93%
	Risk preferences	Risk appetite	96%
	Risk profile	–	0%
	Purpose of investment	Purpose of investment	96%
Financial capability	Source and extent of income	Income	84%
	Assets	Diversity of portfolio	77%
	Investment and real property	Net worth	93%
	Financial commitments	Financed by credit	55%
Experience and knowledge	Products the investor is familiar with	Investment experience	94%
		Level of knowledge	89%
	Nature, volume, frequency of transactions	Type of assets held	82%
		Amount invested	93%
		Frequency of transactions	0%
	Length of the transactions carried out	–	0%
	Level of education	–	0%
	Profession	–	0%
Non-MiFID items present in BIS sample			
Age			100%
Family situation			81%
Tax status			77%
Guarantees needed			67%
Gearing strategy			43%

as the only four financial advisers included in the sample come from the UK. This peculiarity leads us to carry out two different analyses:

- First, we compare the contents of the PQ (before the MiFID) with the SQ (after the MiFID).
- Then, we focus on financial advisers by comparing non-MiFID practice with the current UK suitability assessment.

With reference to the first analysis, we compare the contents of the PQ and SQ by making use of the three sections requested by the MiFID.[25] The items that on average[26] are included in the PQ can be listed as in Table 3.14. The percentage on the right side indicates how many firms, out of the 90 that are considered, request that information in the questionnaire. Moreover, some of the questionnaires request extra information that is not included into the current 13 MiFID items; this information is illustrated at the bottom of Table 3.14.

It can be easily noticed that none of the 90 firms included in the BIS research asks questions about the risk profile or length of the transactions that have been carried out and they are also little interested in the education and professional level of the investor. Some interesting results emerge from the comparison of this evidence with the information about the 14 Italian MiFID suitability questionnaires.

With reference to the 'investment objectives' section, Table 3.15 shows the percentage of questionnaires that include the four MiFID requested items in the SQ and PQ samples.

In particular, the MiFID seems to have increased the attention of intermediaries towards the risk profile of the investors, as witnessed by an increase from 0 to 29 per cent; still, despite the fact that it is a sign of increased attention towards the investors' personal attitude

Table 3.15 Comparison of PQ and SQ with reference to 'investment objectives'

MiFID section	MiFID items	% in PQ	% in SQ
Investment objectives	Length of time to hold the investment	94%	100%
	Risk preferences	97%	100%
	Risk profile	0%	29%
	Purpose of investment	97%	86%

towards risk, it is too small, especially if compared to the 100 per cent of presence of the questions on risk preferences. Once again, as already outlined in Sections 3.2 and 3.3, the main focus of the financial firm seems to be on collecting the objective features of the desired investment rather than on understanding the real needs of the client according to his or her personal attitude and current financial situation.

Table 3.16 shows that the SQ sample, if compared to the PQ sample, seems to be less interested in the assets and liabilities of the client. All the percentages, apart from the source and extent of income, have fallen and the interest towards the assets has almost halved.

On the contrary, more attention is addressed to the education and professional level of the customer, as shown in Table 3.17. This information, that was never asked for before the MiFID and is not

Table 3.16 Comparison of PQ and SQ with reference to 'financial capability'

MiFID section	MiFID items	% in PQ	% in SQ
Financial capability	Source and extent of income	85%	93%
	Assets	78%	43%
	Investment and real property	94%	79%
	Financial commitments	56%	50%

Table 3.17 Comparison of PQ vs SQ with reference to 'financial experience and knowledge'

MiFID section	MiFID items	% in PQ		% in SQ
Experience and knowledge	Products the investor is familiar with	Investment experience	95%	100%
		Level of knowledge	90%	
	Nature, volume and frequency of transactions	Type of assets held	83%	
		Amount invested	94%	100%
		Frequency of transactions	0%	
	Length of the transactions carried out	–	0%	1%
	Level of education	–	0%	86%
	Profession	–	0%	71%

included in non-EU countries, is collected by the Italian sample in 86 per cent of cases for education and 71 per cent for the professional level.

Overall, we could say that, in respect to the pre-MiFID practice, the suitability questionnaires reveal an increased attention of the intermediary in assessing if an investment product is suitable or not to the customers, and this is perfectly adherent to the MiFID requests. Nevertheless, this practice leads the bank to ignore important information on the customer (risk profile, current financial situation and properties) that could be useful in deeply understanding the investment needs he or she is unaware of rather than only assessing whether an investment in suitable or not. In this sense, the MiFID has provided an opportunity to intermediaries to 'better understand their clients', but only a few of them seem to take advantage of this opportunity by using the information obtained through the questionnaire in a financial advisory perspective.

If this is true, the further step of the analysis, that focuses upon the financial advisers, should lead to different results. We already explained above that financial advisers are treated separately from all the other financial firms as the BIS research includes only UK advisers in the sample. For this reason, as they do not represent the international landscape in financial advisory but only the British one, we treat them with a separate analysis by comparing the customers' profiling practice before (PQ_FA) and after the MiFID (SQ_FA) in the UK. Once again, the comparison follows the scheme proposed above and we proceed by MiFID sections of information to be included into the questionnaire, as Tables 3.18, 3.19 and 3.20 demonstrate.

Table 3.18 Comparison of PQ_FA vs SQ_FA with reference to 'investment objectives'

MiFID section	MiFID Items	% in PQ_FA	% in SQ_FA
Investment objectives	Length of time to hold the investment	100%	25%
	Risk preferences	100%	100%
	Risk profile	–	25%
	Purpose of investment	100%	100%

Table 3.19 Comparison of PQ_FA vs SQ_FA with reference to 'financial capability'

MiFID section	**MiFID Items**	**% in PQ_FA**	**% in SQ_FA**
Financial capability	Source and extent of income	100%	100%
	Assets	100%	100%
	Investment and real property	100%	100%
	Financial commitments	100%	100%

Table 3.20 Comparison of PQ_FA vs SQ_FA with reference to 'financial experience and knowledge'

MiFID section	**MiFID Items**	**% in PQ_FA**		**% in SQ_FA**
Experience and knowledge	Products the investor is familiar with	Investment experience	100%	50%
		Level of knowledge	75%	
	Nature, volume and frequency of transactions	Type of assets held	100%	50%
		Amount invested	100%	
		Frequency of transactions	–	
	Length of the transactions carried out	–	–	25%
	Level of education	–	–	–
	Profession	–	–	75%

The information provided in Tables 3.18, 3.19 and 3.20 allows us to maintain that the introduction of the MiFID has not consistently changed the behaviour of financial advisers when profiling their clients. A high level of attention was given, and it still is, to the subjective characteristics of the client (such as the purpose of the investment, the risk preferences, the financial and properties situation, and so on) and this is consistent with the nature of the intermediary we are analysing, that is certainly more focused on collecting useful information for its advisory activity rather than on assessing the suitability of a product. Something unexpected comes from the 'experience and knowledge' section. In fact, the UK sample shows a decreased attention of financial advisers towards the experience and knowledge of the client (with the exception of the profession that is asked more for income knowledge reasons). This is consistent with the particular activity of the adviser, whose role is to help, and sometimes substitute, the client in his or her financial decisions and, in this sense, a deep understanding of the client's experience and knowledge is not vital.

Further developments of this study could be addressed to understand to what degree Italian questionnaires differ from those adopted in other European countries in the post-MiFID context. This analysis should involve a sample of intermediaries belonging to different EU countries and investigate to what degree the MiFID has really led intermediaries to a better knowledge of their customers; or, on the contrary, it may show that the Directive has mainly provided them with a tool to reduce the number of possible contentions with their clients.

Notes

Marinelli is the author of Sections 3.1 and 3.2 and Mazzoli is author of Sections 3.3 and 3.4.

1. Investment services and activities are defined in art. 4 of MiFID Level 1 Directive 2004/39/EC and refer in particular to a list of activities in MiFID Annex I-A (reception and transmission of orders, execution of orders, dealing on own account, portfolio management, investment advice, underwriting of financial instruments and/or placing of financial instruments on a firm commitment basis, placing of financial instruments without a firm commitment basis, operation of Multilateral Trading Facilities) related to financial instruments listed in MiFID Annex I-C.
2. See Bank for International Settlement (2008).
3. For a complete definition of 'professional client', see MiFID Level 1 Directive 2004/39/EC, Annex II.
4. This means that even if the MiFID Level 2 Commission Directive 2006/73/EC, art. 35 (5) does not allow intermediaries to recommend investment services or financial instruments to the client when the investment firm does not obtain the information needed, it could be possible for the investment firm to give other investment services which are subject only to the appropriateness test.
5. The MiFID Level 2 Commission Directive 2006/73/EC, art. 35 (2) – 36.
6. Note that a sub-group of 'professional clients' are the so-called 'eligible counterparties', who typically comprise those subjects professionally operating in the financial markets. When executing orders on behalf of an eligible counterparty and/or dealing on own account and/or receiving and transmitting orders with eligible counterparties, the investment firm may provide the service without being obliged to comply with the suitability and appropriateness obligations, as outlined in the art. 24, section 1 of the MiFID Level 1

Directive 2004/39/EC. For a deeper understanding of the inclusion into the 'eligible counterparty' category, we refer the reader to the art. 24 of the MiFID Level 1 Directive 2004/39/EC.

7. The MiFID Level 1 Directive 2004/39/EC, art. 4.
8. Art. 83 of the Reg. 16190/2007 defines as 'financial insurance products' life insurance policies under the class III and transactions under the class V, as indicated in the art. 2 of the Legislative Decree n. 209 of 7 September 2005, with the exclusion of individual retirement products.
9. Art. 183, section 1, letter b of the Code of private insurance generically prescribes that, before selling a product, insurance firms and insurance distributors acquire information from their clients in order to evaluate their insurance and retirement needs and operate so that their clients are always adequately informed. Art. 12, section 3 of IMD refers to the demands and the needs of that customer as well as the underlying reasons for any advice given to the customer. These are generic disclosure prescriptions, without any specific mention to suitability/appropriateness questionnaires.
10. In the debate which followed the work of the Commission, some interesting positions have emerged. With respect to selling practices, CEOIPS' report to the European Commission on PRIPs underlines that even if the IMD does not provide for a suitability/appropriateness test, the general provision on 'demands and needs' of the customer could be more protective for clients, as it applies to both advised and non-advised mediation and to both retail and professional clients (see CEOIPS' report to the European Commission on PRIPs, 2 November 2009). Moreover, the stopping step provided by suitability may apparently be more protective for the client compared to the regime dictated by IMD, where no stopping step exists; nevertheless, in the case of litigation, the protection of the client may be stronger within the IMD previsions, as the outcome of the suitability questionnaire creates a protection for the intermediary, while in the insurance regulation the insurance firm maintains a joint responsibility for the investment made. In essence, there is general support for the use of MiFID as a benchmark for the distribution of PRIPs; nevertheless, some encourage taking due account of provisions also in other legislation that might add value to the future PRIPs' framework.
11. See Assogestioni, 2009.
12. We refer to the CONSOB Communication n. 9019104 of 2 March 2009. This communication has been followed by interassociative guidelines for the application of L3 measures promoted by the category associations in 14 July 2009.
13. See the MiFID Level 2 Commission Directive 2006/73/EC, art. 35 and 37.
14. For the purpose of clarity, we classified questions of the form: *'Which of the following investment results fits better your preferences regarding risk taking? A- A low expected return with a low risk of loss; B- A medium expected return with a limited risk of loss; C- A high expected return accepting a high risk of loss'* as belonging to the 'preferences regarding risk taking' item, whereas questions like *'Suppose that you have made an investment in a long term stock fund. A month after your investment, the value of your fund drops by 15 per cent. What is your reaction? A- I sell my investment in order to avoid further panic if the market continues to go down; B- I try to keep a cool head and I wait until when my*

investment recoups its value over the planned time horizon; C- I buy some more in order to take advantage of low prices' as belonging to the 'risk profile' item.

15. This finding is coherent with the implementation of L3 that requires a set of controls for the complexity, the risk profile and the liquidity of the products.
16. For example, some questions are used to discover if all the financial assets of the client are deposited in that financial firm or not.
17. One may observe that each intermediary is able to know the portfolio composition of the client, without explicitly asking him or her, looking at their internal source of information and databases. Nevertheless, if this is true for the assets held at that intermediary, this is not possible for the part of the financial portfolio managed by other intermediaries. As a consequence, an explicit question is needed.
18. Names are not revealed for privacy reasons. Moreover, the questionnaires we employ in this study are different from those we used in Section 3.2.
19. Obtaining the scoring method was quite difficult because of the opposition of banks to reveal this information. This is the reason why we were able to collect only three questionnaires.
20. This way we submitted 300 questionnaires as a whole.
21. A full description of the results is provided on request.
22. See Table 3.4 for a description of sections and items suggested by the MiFID.
23. With profiling questionnaires we identify those that were used before the MiFID in order to profile a financial firm's clients.
24. We tried to enlarge the sample of MiFID questionnaires that are currently used to at least US and UK intermediaries but the only cooperation we were given comes from UK financial advisers. Banks, asset managers and financial firms did not give any answer to our request or clearly explained that they do not take part in university research studies.
25. According to the methodology already used in Sections 3.2 and 3.3.
26. As it is an average of the information requested across the five sectors analysed (banks, asset managers, insurance companies, financial advisers and investments firms).

4
Risk of Over-Indebtedness and Behavioural Factors

Luisa Anderloni and Daniela Vandone

4.1 'Non-rational' debt decisions and risk of over-indebtedness

Works in behavioural economics have made an important contribution in drawing attention to the role played not only by socio-demographic and economic variables, but also by behavioural factors as determinants of the demand for debt. As explained in Chapter 2, empirical analyses show that household debt demand seems less rational but more driven by emotional factors, such as overconfidence, impulsivity in consumption attitudes, social comparison and myopia; that is, the inability to perceive the long run consequences of today's debt decisions. Such behavioural factors may induce individuals to make 'non-rational' borrowing choices and this may lead them to hold a level of debt that is unsustainable in relation to their earnings. In turn, such a situation may cause over-indebtedness.

Although it is difficult to provide an exact definition of over-indebtedness, generally speaking this phenomenon occurs when an individual's level of debt cannot be sustained in relation to current earnings and any additional resources raised from the sale – at fair conditions – of real or financial assets.

It is reasonable to believe that over-indebtedness is more often than not the result of a combination of causes arising either from excessive levels of individual debt or unexpected events that make the debt contracted no longer sustainable. The literature (Banque de France, 1996; Anderloni, 1997) typically identifies two types of over-indebtedness on the basis of the causes that determine it: 'passive' and 'active'.[1] In the first case – passive over-indebtedness – financial difficulties are determined by unexpected factors beyond an individual's control, such as job loss, separation, death or illness, changes in macroeconomic variables (for example, interest rate hikes) or higher taxation. These factors can eliminate or reduce an income source and/or determine unexpected liabilities. In the second case, over-indebtedness is generated by excessive levels of debt held by households, following decisions to borrow up to a level that is unsustainable on the basis of present or future earnings. Such decisions may be due to lack of information transparency or individuals' inability to process effectively information available and, as a result, to evaluate the consequences of indebtedness. It can also be due to consumption and lifestyle behaviours which, either due to irresponsibility or short-sightedness, lead an individual to non-optimal consumption and indebtedness choices.

Thus, the distinction between active and passive over-indebtedness underlines the fact that over-indebtedness is not only determined by unexpected events that make the debt contracted no longer sustainable, but also by individual decision making behaviours, such as the inability to manage household finances effectively and to make consumption choices on the basis of available resources, spending and lifestyle habits that cannot be sustained by disposable financial and economic resources and which are therefore financed by debt (Waldron and Young, 2006; Rowlingson and Kempson, 1993; Elliott, 2005; Frade, 2004; DTI-MORI, 2004; Observatoire du Crédit et de l'Endettement, 2005; Gloukoviezoff, 2006; Koljonen and Romer-Paakkanen, 2000; Haas, 2006; Farinha, 2004; Johansson and Persson, 2006; Kish, 2006).

Such behaviour is often put down to social and psychological factors that reduce an individual's capacity to evaluate the consequences of his/her consumption and borrowing decisions, which may not be rational from an economic point of view. In fact individuals tend, on one hand, to overestimate their capacity to manage domestic financial resources and, on the other, to underestimate the possibility of being affected by negative events, such as illness or job loss (see Chapter 2).

As a result, these individuals systematically underestimate the risk of not being able to meet their financial commitments (Kilborn, 2002; Meier and Sprenger, 2007). Furthermore, they overestimate the immediate benefits and undervalue the future costs; such behaviour leads to the decision to purchase, using debt if necessary, regardless of the effect this choice may have on the sustainability of future debt levels (Meier and Sprenger, 2007).

The fact that over-indebtedness may be caused by individuals' irrational behaviour is significant and has to be taken into account when, first, choosing appropriate measures designed to prevent or manage situations of financial difficulties and, subsequently, evaluating such measures' effectiveness.

4.2 Over-indebtedness and its consequences

Developed countries are becoming increasingly concerned about the phenomenon of over-indebtedness, not only in terms of its extent, but also as regards its nature and impact on the welfare of society as a whole. In fact, it disproportionately affects persons who are weak from a social and economic point of view. In its most acute forms, over-indebtedness may also lead to financial exclusion. The relationship between the two conditions and also with social exclusion are complex and can be analysed from two different perspectives: the supply side and the demand side.

As far as the supply side is concerned, there are two main reasons why over-indebtedness may cause financial exclusion. First, there is the circumstance that banks consult both credit bureau registers and other special registers where payment incidents and dishonoured cheques are recorded not only when a credit application is submitted, but also when a request to open a bank account is made. In some countries, like France, banks can also consult files where persons involved in procedures concerning management of over-indebtedness situations are recorded. Clearly, over-indebted individuals, who have probably been included in these types of registers, face not only the risk of having their request turned down by banks but also ensuing financial exclusion. In some countries, basic banking accounts, with limited functions, have been introduced in order to avoid the risk of offering banking services such as payment facilities to those persons that are less trustworthy, while still allowing them some form of access to mainstream financial services providers.[2]

Secondly, when a situation of financial distress is not already clear, though the applicant is already characterised by elements of economic and financial weakness (low income, unstable job, poor financial management ability, family relationship problems, and so on), commercial banks have few incentives in serving them. Consequently, this kind of customer is induced to resort to alternative financial providers that offer credit services at unfavourable terms in the form of high interest rates and charges, limited amounts advanced that often multiply the number of different contracts signed, and short reimbursement times. This feeds a vicious circle where the sequence of over-indebtedness, payment difficulties, insolvency and financial exclusion is often found.[3]

On the demand side, those who experience over-indebtedness conditions may be induced to quit the financial market, i.e. become financially excluded, for various reasons. Negative experience in managing debts and dealing with banks may generate fear of loss of control, and a preference to manage the family budget only by cash[4] and, when incomes are low, to forsake a relationship with a deposit institution. In other cases, as mentioned regarding the supply side above, sometimes banks refuse to open a full transaction bank account to certain groups of people such as those with a poor credit history or those who failed credit scoring systems because their characteristics meant they were assessed as high risk. However, there is evidence that people may be deterred from opening an account if it does not offer overdraft facilities to ease access to money paid into it. Furthermore, delays in clearing cheques paid into an account mean that people may not have instant access to any money paid in. Consequently, considering the offer inadequate to their needs, some persons may develop a negative attitude towards the banking system and refuse a relationship limited solely to basic banking services. In other words, they show a lack of interest in opening a savings account.

Alternatively, also the risk of seizure of the so-called 'guaranteed minimum income' where paid on a bank account can cause self-exclusion, i.e. a preference to go without a bank relationship. Nonetheless, in most countries nowadays a bank account is needed to receive a salary and social benefits, and even occasional work payments; without this banking channel, financial self-exclusion can lead to social exclusion.

Besides its links with financial exclusion in general, the issue of over-indebtedness of households has given rise to two particular concerns at EU level. The first is the impact on consumers of the enlargement of the credit market, and increased competition and innovation. This is in the context of European Union moves towards a single harmonised market for financial services, progress with the Financial Service Action Plan[5] and the new Directive on consumer credit.[6] The priority is to find a balance between the goals of maintaining accessible and affordable credit together with the promotion of the internal market, while ensuring at the same time a high degree of protection for consumers throughout the European Union.

This debate highlights a discrepancy between the objective of offering financial service providers legislation to allow them to operate in the same way in all the Member States, through full harmonisation of key legislation and, at the same time, the goal of not reducing levels of consumer protection, leaving space for regional problems and combating the increase in over-indebtedness. A major concern is that, in some contexts, aggressive policies to promote the use of credit via revolving cards could lead to an intolerable increase in indebtedness, including over-indebtedness among those who are most economically and culturally fragile and who would be most exposed to the risk of taking on excessively onerous commitments too quickly. The increase in card based payments undeniably presents a number of policy problems, the most serious of which is the likelihood that the use of cards will contribute to an unjustifiable level of consumer credit and that borrowing on the cards will contribute to an increase in the level of consumer bankruptcy.[7]

Secondly, preventing and dealing with different forms of over-indebtedness represents, in some countries, an important part of the common objective to fight against poverty and social exclusion. The Lisbon European Council has established a political framework, including the fight against exclusion in the Union's overall strategy.[8] This is to be achieved through an open method of coordination combining national action plans and a Commission's initiative for cooperation in that field. In accordance with its mandate, the Treaty of Nice endorsed the fight against social exclusion and all forms of discrimination, within its European social agenda.[9] Furthermore, it has included the fight against exclusion within art. 137 of the Treaty establishing the European Community. Based on this, the Council has invited the Member States to elaborate a common approach by preparing two-year National Action Plans on Social Inclusion.[10] In this context it should be pointed out that, among initiatives aimed at preventing the risk of exclusion, several national plans have included specific initiatives to confront over-indebtedness and financial exclusion.

4.3 Measures to tackle over-indebtedness

The measures adopted so far in Europe to tackle over-indebtedness, despite the considerable cross-country differences that exist, are typically either preventive or curative. The former seek to influence behaviour on both the demand side (that is responsible borrowing) and on the supply side (that is responsible lending). Responsible borrowing measures mainly consist of financial education and debt counselling services designed to raise awareness about the implications of debt and to help individuals fix levels of debt that do not lead to financial difficulties. Penalties for late or non-payment if made clear before entering the credit market can also act as an effective deterrent. Responsible lending includes a raft of measures such as: mandatory disclosure and transparency requirements on the part of financial intermediaries regarding the terms and conditions of loans; appropriate scoring procedures of the applicant's creditworthiness and total level of exposure; flexible approach to early warning signs of indebted households in difficulty; the fixing within certain limits of interest rate ceilings on lending to customers.

Curative measures are various *ex post* responses to default, such as debt management and restructuring schemes in the form of debt settlement procedures, which in some cases offer the possibility of cancelling part of the debt. Both sets of measures have dual aims: on the one hand, to avoid active over-indebtedness; on the other, to prevent or reduce the seriousness of passive over-indebtedness by offering advice and solutions that allow households to manage more effectively the effects of adverse shocks that can negatively impact their financial situation.

In this analysis we focus only on *ex ante* measures, since we believe that their appropriate adoption can modify individuals' behaviour, bearing in mind the fact that, as seen above, individuals' debt demand may be partly due to behavioural factors (Table 4.1).

Our attention here on preventive measures does not imply the lesser importance of curative measures. Indeed, we believe that the effectiveness of these measures depends crucially on their capacity to mediate between, on the one hand, the need to resolve the situation of difficulty in a way that takes into account the interests of all parties involved while, on the other, not conveying *ex post* distorted signals that may induce superficial behaviours that disincentivise responsible *ex ante* commitments.

Among preventive measures that seek to achieve more responsible borrowing by individuals, financial education plays an important role in the prevention of over-indebtedness both by increasing an individual's ability to understand financial information relating to the state of his or her financial assets and liabilities and by helping raise awareness about the effects consumption and lifestyle behaviour has on a household's finances. More specifically, financial education addresses three causes of over-indebtedness.[11] First, financial education seeks to improve individuals' capacity to understand financial information, raise awareness about the risks and consequences of their borrowing

Table 4.1 Relations between possible causes of over-indebtedness and measures for its prevention and management

DETERMINANTS	PREVENTIVE MEASURES			
	Responsible borrowing		**Responsible lending**	
	instrument	*Objective*	*instrument*	*objective*
Excess debt ('Active' over-indebtedness)				
Inability to understand information	Financial education	To improve individuals' capabilities in understanding information available so as to evaluate the sustainability of borrowing decisions	Credit bureaus	The use of positive information supplied by credit bureaus allows lenders to have a more complete picture of an individual's total debt exposure. This information may lead to a rejected application for credit if the individual is not able to understand correctly the information available and therefore is not in a position to assess the sustainability of the debt requested
	Debt counselling	To provide individuals with advice concerning the management of household finances and decisions regarding consumption, savings and borrowing	Interest rate ceilings	With ceilings in place, financial intermediaries do not lend to high risk customers because if they did, the rate applied would be higher than the maximum amount established by law

Continued

Table 4.1 Continued

DETERMINANTS	PREVENTIVE MEASURES			
	Responsible borrowing		**Responsible lending**	
	instrument	*Objective*	*instrument*	*objective*
Limited transparency of information	*Transparency and completeness of information*	To give individuals the essential informational tools necessary for an informed and responsible borrowing decision	*Transparency and completeness of information*	Mandatory market disclosure requirements entail the provision on the part of financial intermediaries of complete and correct information
Non-rational consumption choices	Financial education	To create greater awareness on the part of individuals of the financial consequences of their spending decisions	Credit bureaus	Also in this case, positive information supplied by credit bureaus allows intermediaries to have a more informed picture of an individual's overall debt exposure, thereby avoiding over-indebtedness due to an inability to evaluate the consequences of spending, savings and indebtedness choices

	Debt counselling	To improve the capability of individuals to evaluate the consequences of consumption and lifestyle habits by raising knowledge levels regarding the management of household finances	Interest rate ceilings	With ceilings in place, financial intermediaries do not lend to high risk customers because if they did, the rate applied would be higher than the maximum amount established by law
	Penalties for late payment	To use clear and transparent information regarding the penalties that will be incurred for late payment so as to reduce the influence of psychological factors, such as hyperbolic discount and availability heuristic, which tend to induce individuals to underestimate the consequences of their actions		
Strategic default	Credit bureaus	To deter individuals from strategically defaulting by making them aware of the negative consequences such behaviour will have on future applications for credit	Credit bureaus	The negative information supplied by credit bureaus allows intermediaries to have a more informed picture of an individual's repayment behaviour, thereby reducing the risk of granting credit to delinquent borrowers

Continued

Table 4.1 Continued

DETERMINANTS	PREVENTIVE MEASURES			
	Responsible borrowing		Responsible lending	
	instrument	*Objective*	*instrument*	*objective*
	Penalties for late payment	To deter individuals from strategically defaulting by making them aware of the penalties they will incur during debt settlement procedures		
Unexpected events ('Passive' over-indebtedness)				
Unexpected events such as job loss, divorce or separation, negative changes in interest rates, cost of living, taxes	Financial education	To improve individuals' capabilities in understanding and using instruments designed to reduce the impact of unexpected events	Arrears management	Flexible and prompt arrears management solutions applied at the early warning stage of temporary indebtedness can increase the likelihood that a loan returns to a performing status rather than degenerating into insolvency
	Debt counselling	To help individuals choose the right instruments to address the effects of unexpected events by planning and managing household finances more effectively		

decisions and to help them choose the right financial products for their needs. Secondly, financial education targets behaviour patterns due to inability, irresponsibility or short-sightedness that lead individuals into excess debt. By helping individuals understand the difference between what they want and what they need and what they can afford, and between essential items and those that can be purchased at a later date, significant inroads into the behavioural causes of over-indebtedness can be made. Thirdly, financial education sets out to limit the negative impact that unexpected events can have on household finances. Increased financial knowledge in fact helps individuals to manage their finances more effectively, to better understand, for instance, the consequences of their debt decision and put into place savings or insurance solutions designed to safeguard their financial future.[12]

Within the European Union, financial education is viewed as a key factor in helping individuals make informed choices regarding savings or borrowing.[13] It can help citizens make better financial provision for unforeseen situations, invest wisely and save for their retirement. It can help people to avoid the pitfalls of payment fraud. People who understand financial issues make better choices of financial services for their particular needs and are more inclined to heed regulatory risk warnings. They are less likely to purchase products they do not need, or be tied into products that they do not understand, or take risks that could drive them into financial difficulties.

However, as will be seen later, financial education is not a panacea and behavioural experiments have highlighted that the results of financial advice are not leading to better financial decisions when behavioural factors prevail.

Although financial education acts on the demand side, it also involves the supply side as financial education is also strictly related to information transparency. In order for an individual to make a responsible borrowing decision on the basis of the product description available, the information describing the loan has to be clear, transparent, correct and comprehensive in addition to being expressed in such a way that makes it fully and correctly understandable. Consequently, financial intermediaries have to provide information – product description, terms and economic conditions applied, measures adopted in the event of payment arrears, terms and conditions relating to variations in instalments – which allows individuals to make a responsible and informed borrowing decision and to compare products easily.[14]

It is essential that such transparency provisions should also apply to instalment payment plans signed directly between retailers and customers: dealers, having strong incentives to sell consumer credit products, on the one hand, tend to use aggressive marketing strategies, such as rapid no hassle loans, discounts for consumer credit purchases, etc., and, on the other, are not always able to provide complete and exact information about the loan agreements their customers are signing. The transparency and completeness of information is generally guaranteed by legal safeguards aimed to protect the consumer both during the promotion of the financial products and at the moment of concluding the contract.

As far as debt counselling services are concerned as a tool to promote responsible borrowing, networks of counselling agencies are well established in many European countries, particularly in the north and Scandinavia.[15] These agencies offer preventive solutions by promoting awareness of the importance of the commitments taken on when signing a contract and the compatibility of these commitments with household finances. *Ex post* support is also commonly offered for the management of situations of difficulty when these emerge. Measures range from simple advice services to more complex help with out of court agreements and formal debt settlement procedures, as well as access to special rate consolidation loans.

Finally, the existence of penalties that vary in amount and method of application in the case of late payment, default or other contractual breaches can deter individuals from underestimating the extent of the commitments agreed to or from adopting forms of superficial or incorrect behaviour. As well as acting as deterrents, penalties can also raise awareness among more responsible borrowers about their situation, working as a stimulus to negotiate debt restructuring terms or to proactively search for other conditions. The effectiveness of penalties is crucially linked to their being fair, i.e. sustainable, in that they do not push debtors into critical situations from which there is little chance of escape, and to their being transparent, i.e. in that they are clearly stated both in the credit information form and in the subsequent credit agreement.[16]

Together with responsible borrowing measures, responsible lending measures are of the utmost importance. Primarily, the transparency and fairness of the conditions mentioned above represent the basis for responsible lending behaviour. Mandatory disclosure of terms and conditions such as those contained in Europe in the Consumer Credit Directive and in the United States in the Truth in Lending Act (TILA) or in Regulation Z seek to promote this type of behaviour. Responsible lending measures depend also on financial institutions having the resources to assess the overall financial situation of the prospective borrower in order to evaluate correctly their customers' level of indebtedness and repayment ability. Clearly, the quantity and quality of information the lender can access regarding the applicant's socio-demographic and economic profile, repayment history and overall debt exposure will be vitally important.

As widely discussed in the literature, banks try to overcome moral hazard and adverse selection problems by the screening and monitoring of customers' credit risk profiles.[17] In particular, with regard to personal loans, the total amount of which does not justify individual detailed credit risk evaluations, lenders use credit scoring procedures that identify counterpart risk profiles and as a result reject or accept applications on the basis of insolvency projections generated by the model.[18]

Credit scoring models have been developed in order to identify default risk by companies granting consumer credit. Scoring is typically constructed from a sample of applicants who have already been granted credit. For each of these individuals the credit history is needed to see whether they turned out to be a 'good' risk or a 'bad' risk. Discriminant analysis, multiple linear regression, probit, logit or some other types of classificatory procedure are the techniques applied in order to construct these models. Two more recently adopted methods in estimating default probabilities include options pricing theory models and neural networks.

Due to their proprietary nature little is known about the specific content and structure of credit scoring models in order to predict the probability of personal default; however, a relatively large number of studies have been published on such models. The models utilise both socio-demographic characteristics,[19] economic features of the borrower and historical data on credit performance. These data are then used to calculate the predicted probability of default for each new applicant by combining the estimates coefficients from the probability of default regression with the applicant's values of the explanatory variables, or in dividing borrowers into high and low default risk classes.

The most common socio-demographic variables are: age, gender,[20] education, marital status and number of children or other dependants. To evaluate economic characteristics, the most important variables used are income (measured and considered in various dimensions), employment, labour agreement, housing tenure and other indicators such as time at address and time in employment (that is, stability), telephone and postcode of the applicants and of his/her employer (in order to access economic indicators) and credit insurance. Credit history takes into account not only the experience of defaults and of delinquencies and of dishonoured payment instruments or other non-payments, but also the number of credits, guarantors (and use of), credit card use, savings and other financial assets, and the number of requests for information regarding the applicant received by the credit agency in previous months. Indirectly, transparency regarding an individual's scoring assigned by the credit bureau in addition to information regarding speedy credit repair[21] plays an important role in helping participants in the credit market to adopt responsible borrowing practices.

Credit scoring, however, is not without its pitfalls, especially if scorecards are inadequately constructed or irregularly integrated.

The main problems that have been the subject of considerable debate in the literature are:

- the reject inference
- the population drift
- the unobserved effects.

In particular, we should point out in this context that among those unobserved effects, psychological factors and individual behaviours may play a significant role. Indeed, as already highlighted in Chapter 2, individuals may have a different level of overconfidence in their ability to manage resources or may have less impulsive behaviours; all these heterogeneous features may be reflected in different consumption attitudes and saving and debt decisions and, in turn, in a different level of exposure to the risk of over-indebtedness.

As regards a flexible approach to early warning signs of indebted households in difficulty, the rapid awareness of these signs is significant, as we have seen, not only on the demand side, but also on the supply side. The assessment of supply side developments should be *ex ante* so as to identify changes in the economy (labour market, housing market, the economic situation in general) and in society as a whole (changes in lifestyles, values and behavioural patterns) and the impacts these changes will have on loan repayments; assessment should also be ongoing throughout the life of the credit agreement thereby enabling a rapid corrective response to situations of difficulty.[22]

As far as interest rate caps, legal interest rate restrictions have been a controversial issue among economists for centuries. Usury and interest rate restrictions practices historically have often been linked to moral, social and religious beliefs. In practice, several countries have imposed different rules on interest rate ceilings as well as the cost of credit.

More generally, intervention can take the form of law and regulations, code of conduct or simply moral suasion of financial authorities. The Member States of the European Union have heterogeneous legislation on this issue and recently two elements have provided new fuel to the debate: first, the economic and financial crisis and the difficulties faced in 2007–2008 by households and microenterprises to repay debts incorporating high interest rates have sharply risen following the market; secondly, the need for 'levelling the field' in the European internal market in order to promote fair competition, innovation, efficiency and cross-border transactions.

Within the confines of the problems we are discussing, limits or regulation of interest rates may prevent lenders from exploiting less informed, or fragile and riskier individuals while at the same time forcing financial providers to adopt responsible lending policies, i.e. to provide credit only to debtors with acceptable levels of risk, in which case the application of the correct risk premium to each customer does not push interest rates above the threshold. Responsible lending structured in this way can also play a role in preventing active over-indebtedness.

The rationing effects of interest rate caps is a major issue analysed by a body of theoretical and empirical literature. Depending on the hypothesis adopted, the effect may be positive or negative with respect to single individuals or to society as a whole. Among the negatives with potential impacts on over-indebtedness, exclusion from access to mainstream financial providers may push individuals to resort to illegal market solutions that make the vicious circle of their financial difficulties more acute. Furthermore, interest rate caps may not only limit product innovation, since the incentive to satisfy the diversified and complex credit needs generated by freedom of pricing effectively vanish, but also represent an impediment to cross-border activity of lenders.

4.4 The importance of behavioural factors in the effectiveness of measures to prevent over-indebtedness

The creation and implementation of measures targeted at preventing and managing the risk of over-indebtedness cannot ignore the role behavioural variables has as determinants of irrational borrowing decisions. As outlined in Poppe (2008), 'An adequate understanding of the debt problem phenomenon presupposes a more comprehensive perspective rather than an economic perspective and any set of remedial steps to solve, ease and prevent serious instances of over-indebtedness must be based on knowledge about how social orientations or psychological behaviours impact financial decisions'.

Furthermore, the empirical literature has shown how psychological factors have an impact on the effectiveness of policies adopted to prevent and manage financial difficulties arising from over-indebtedness. Studies carried out within behavioural economics have also shown that individuals have little awareness of the existence and consequences these psychological mechanisms have. Indeed, individuals in financial difficulties tend to lay the blame on exogenous factors such as family or work-related problems which reduce income levels below those expected. Rarely do individuals recognise that the causes for their difficulties lie principally, or at least also, with their inability to manage money and the decisions made regarding spending and indebtedness. Furthermore, many studies have shown how deviant behaviour patterns persist even when individuals are aware of the risks they face. Individuals' incapacity to take corrective steps despite knowing of the dangers of over-indebtedness may have significant repercussions in designing effective policies for the management of situations of indebtedness that are already or are at risk of becoming pathological (Kilborn, 2002; Watson, 2003; Lea et al., 1995).

Thus, a correct analysis of the link between psychological factors and debt demand is of utmost importance for the effectiveness of policy measures to tackle households' financial fragility.

Financial education initiatives and the services provided by debt counselling agencies certainly help to improve individuals' abilities to borrow responsibly. However, these measures on their own cannot be realistically expected to prevent over-indebtedness. Individuals, in fact, may continue to have difficulties understanding correctly the financial information made available to them or may not be able to alter significantly those behaviour patterns that lead them to over-borrow, as suggested by the above mentioned literature on psychological factors.

On the basis of the financial education received, individuals may also overrate their ability to evaluate correctly the risk and subsequent impact, for instance, of taking out a loan. Willis (2008b) makes the telling point that 'turning cognitive literacy into positive action requires a well calibrated degree of confidence – neither underconfidence nor overconfidence. Consumers' belief about the efficacy of their own financial decision making must match the actual and perceived difficulty of the decision at hand. Overconfident consumers are unlikely to ask for help when they need it and will spend too little time and effort on financial decisions. Underconfident consumers tend to shy away from engaging in the information search, planning, and calculations that good financial decisions require'.

Many research studies on biases in judgement and decision making have shown that individuals tend to display overconfidence about their ability to manage resources but also overconfidence about their knowledge (Kahneman and Tversky, 1996). Due to overconfidence, people often believe that they know more than they actually do, and this can have negative consequences since it affects decision making because individuals overweight their own judgements relative to other input; that is, for example, all the technical information provided by banks on credit.

As for debt counselling services designed to raise awareness about the implications of debt, Hung and Yoong (2010) find that expanding access to advice can have positive effects, particularly for the less financially literate. At the same time, more extensive compulsory programmes of financial counselling may be ultimately ineffective if the target population, despite lacking the necessary skills, is not inherently prepared to take advice.

Summarising, policy makers involved in financial education and debt counselling should investigate what kind of financial knowledge has most impact on financial behaviours, also taking into account individuals' bias and heuristics.

As far as responsible lending is concerned, credit rating models do not take into account individual behaviours and behavioural variables. Although it is hard to imagine how a credit scoring system, typically with a high level of standardisation, could also include behavioural data, the fact that there might be a link between psychological factors and risk of over-indebtedness is relevant since these are unobserved events that may significantly explain heterogeneity among individuals and the reason why measures to tackle over-indebtedness may be not effective.

This is particularly important since credit scores affect many aspects of consumers' lives: they can influence lenders' decisions to grant credit and can affect a consumers' ability to get a job, rent an apartment or buy a car or a home. Given the growing importance that credit scores play in the lives of consumers, it is particularly relevant that consumers understand what is in their reports, how reports and scores are used and the potential impacts of both. Indeed, Perry (2008) finds that people tend to overestimate their creditworthiness and this may negatively affect responsible financial decision making. In particular, individuals who have mistaken beliefs about their credit ratings are less likely to budget, save or invest; behaviours that may exacerbate credit problems.

Moreover, studies carried out in the field of psychology (Brockett and Golden, 2007) have also highlighted a link between credit scores and biochemical factors (testosterone, dopamine, cortisol, and so on) and psychological personality types (sensation seeking) are found to occur in studies of everyday financial decision making affecting one's credit score. This may have direct implications for both credit counselling and financial behaviour control mechanisms.

Notes

1. For a detailed analysis of the causes of over-indebtedness see Vandone (2009).
2. In some countries the decision to introduce such accounts is left to the banks, while in others the introduction of these accounts is mandatory.
3. In France many people are denied access to an account (Gallou and Le Queau, 1999).
4. A survey conducted in Italy, France and Spain on access to banking accounts and payment services, credit and savings by low-income individuals at risk of financial exclusion revealed that in Italy and France it is not infrequent the case of persons who decide to return to the bank their credit card as a way to avoid spending more than they can afford (Anderloni et al., 2007).
5. See http://ec.europa.eu/internal_market/finances/policy/index_en.htm
6. See the new Consumer Credit Directive (2008/48/EC).
7. Because increasing financial distress imposes externalities on the economies in which it occurs, the global rise of the credit card poses serious policy questions.
8. See Lisbon European Council, Presidency Conclusion, 23 and 24 March, issue 'Promoting social inclusion'.
9. See Nice European Council Meeting, 7, 8 and 9 December 2000, Presidency conclusions, Annex I, European Social Agenda, III Fighting Poverty and all forms of exclusion and discrimination in order to promote social integration.
10. See NAPS/Inclusion 2003–2005 and updated reports on 2004–2006 NAPs/Inclusion.
11. The principal instruments of promoting financial literacy by means of financial education include teaching programmes for schoolchildren and adults, government campaigns through the mass media, consumer associations, banking associations, web-based initiatives and interactive games as well as what is learned from other individuals. For details regarding the objectives, instruments, users and providers of financial education, see among many others FSA (2005), FSA (2006), Molyneux (2006), Anderloni et al. (2006), GAO (2006). Financial education is a multifaceted question which, however, for the purposes of this paper is analysed exclusively in relation to the problem of over-indebtedness.

12. With reference to debtors see, for instance, the use of Payment Protection Insurance.
13. The question of financial education is the subject of wider debate outside the European Union, in particular in the United States, Canada and Australia. See OECD (2005), Consumer and Financial Literacy Task Force (2004), World Bank (2005). We should, however, be wary of the risk of viewing financial education as a convenient panacea. Indeed, the model that posits the sequence *'financial education → financial literacy → good financial decision and behaviour'* may be flawed. For an interesting recent critique of financial education, see Willis (2008a), Tatom and Godsted (2006) and Hathaway and Khatiwada (2008).
14. To this end, the new Consumer Credit Directive (2008/48/EC) sets out informational requirements across four distinct stages: information to be included in advertising; pre-contractual information; information to be included in credit agreements; information to be provided after the signing of the credit agreement.
15. In the UK there are many agencies, some of which operating on a regional basis, in addition to government websites promoting financial knowledge and information regarding access to credit in general; in Ireland the Money Advice and Budgeting Service was created in 1992; in Germany, debt counselling is a municipal task explicitly mentioned in section 11 of Book XII of the German Social Security Code (SGB XII). Both laws provide that debt counselling shall mainly be carried out by third parties. According to section 17 of Book II SBG (SGB II), independent charities shall be entrusted with the implementation of debt counselling. According to the regulations of Book XII SGB (SGB XII), municipalities shall cooperate with independent charity organisations and shall not establish own advice agencies as long as the offering of the charities is sufficient (section 5, paragraphs 2 and 4 of SGB XII). In Sweden, countrywide advice offices were established with the Debt Rehabilitation Act in 1994; § 1 of the law obliges every municipality to offer free advice for indebted or over-indebted individuals. Only a few years after the law came into force, debt counselling has turned into a countrywide, highly specialised and professionalised advice service. In Finland debt counselling is structured in a uniform hierarchical way. While the Finnish Ministry for Commerce and Industry and the subordinated department for consumer issues are responsible for the whole country, six provincial administrations have been ensuring debt advice for the municipalities of the individual provinces since 2001.
16. The Directive provides that the Standard European Consumer Credit Information format shall provide pre-contractual information. At section 3 of pre-contractual information (costs of the credit), the lender shall clearly state that the customer will be charged with default charges or additional interest rate for missing payments.
17. Asymmetric information, deriving from the fact that borrowers have more information regarding the probability of default in comparison to lenders, gives rise to problems of adverse selection and moral hazard. The first, which occurs during the evaluation of the borrower's financial position aimed at deciding whether to grant the loan and if so at what price, refers to

situations in which those borrowers prepared to pay higher rates of interest presumably represent a higher level of risk as they know that the probability of repaying the loan is low. Moral hazard occurs after the loan has been granted; the higher the rate of interest, the greater the probability is that borrowers will embark on high risk projects and consequently lenders will apply a price beyond which the loan application will be rejected (Stiglitz and Weiss, 1981; Freixas and Rochet, 1997). This information may already be available in an intermediary's own customer records, gleaned directly from the customer or acquired from a credit bureau.

18. For an overview of the literature of credit scoring and the personal characteristics associated with insolvency risk see Thomas, Edelman and Crook (2002) and a dedicated edition of the *Journal of Operational Research Society* (January 2001).
19. The information that can be used to build a score model is often subject to regulation. In the US, for example, the Equal Credit Opportunities Act (1974 and 1976) stipulates that score-models cannot include variables such as race, gender or marital status. Similarly, in the UK the Sex Discrimination Act (1975) and the Race Relations Act (1976) makes it illegal to discriminate on grounds of gender and race when granting credit.
20. In countries where there are no restrictions regarding the elements that can feed the credit scoring models.
21. Examples are: pay down credit cards, use cards lightly, update credit limits, dust off an old credit card, negotiate for having erased old delinquencies.
22. These situations have become ever more common in the wake of the property market crisis, economic recession and the sub-prime mortgage crisis that exploded in 2008.

5

Decision Making: Psychological Perspective

Gianni Brighetti, Cristina Ottaviani, Valeria Nucifora and Rosita Borlimi

5.1 Risk perception, sensitivity and tolerance

In general, *risk perception* is the subjective judgement that people make about the characteristics and severity of a risk. In physiology, *perception* is a detectable change in the internal or external environment. But what is *risk*? The concept is highly complex. There are many definitions of risk, which vary by specific application and situational context. Fear is a clear example of what we think about risk in terms of our intuitive feelings. In all the definitions, the emphasis is on the negative nature of the consequences. Risk is any situation where negative or adverse outcomes cannot be ruled out. Neither do we know that they will happen, nor can we guarantee that they won't.

Several studies described the *characteristics of risk* that influence perception. Results show that the greatest influence on the way risks are perceived is played by:

- control: risk appears lower if people feel that they have some control over the process that determines it
- choice: a risk that we choose to take seems less hazardous than one imposed upon us by another person
- possibility of personal impact: any risk seems greater to us if we ourselves or someone close to us are the victims
- cost–benefit ratio: if there is a perceived benefit in a specific behaviour or choice, the risk associated with that behaviour or choice will seem smaller than when no such benefit is perceived

- memory of risks: a person's experience will determine whether he or she gives greater importance to one particular risk than to another
- effects on personal safety and personal properties: an event is perceived as more risky when it affects basic interests and values; for example, health, housing, the value of property and the future.

Besides the characteristics of risk, risk perception is strongly influenced by human subjectivity (background, experience, personal preference, self-interest). A number of studies (for example, Johnson and Tversky, 1983; Wright and Bower, 1992) have found that risk perception is also highly influenced by *affective states*. For example, people in a positive affective state report a higher subjective probability for positive events and a lower subjective probability for negative events. A possible explanation could be that people more easily retrieve mood congruent memories and focus their attention more on mood congruent information when assessing subjective probabilities (Wright and Bower, 1992). Intuitively, this optimism should translate into more risk taking. Accordingly, Arkes et al. (1988) found that subjects in a positive affective state were willing to pay more than controls for lottery tickets. On the other hand, Leith and Baumeister (1996) exposed participants to a mood manipulation, showing that those who were made to feel high arousal negative emotions, such as anger and embarrassment, were more likely to shift toward foolish risky choices (for example, high risk lotteries) compared to those in whom neutral emotions were elicited. The elucidation for contradictory findings comes from a number of studies that further specified that the association between positive states and risk seeking exists only when the stakes are low and it is possible to benefit from the gain without losing too much (Mano, 1994). Whenever the stakes become high, risk aversion arises, according with a view of avoiding large losses (Isen and Patrick, 1983; Isen and Geva, 1987; Isen, Nygren and Ashby, 1988). To account for these findings, Leith and Baumeister (1996) called into question 'affect regulation goals'; that is, the motivation of people in positive affective states to maintain their positive state and to avoid substantial losses. According to the authors, current emotional state does not necessarily damage the ability of people to engage in thoughtful decision making, rather they merely shift people's priorities to engage in immediate mood reparation instead of maximising long term gains.

Generally, people's risk perception appears to be described by two more general factors; that is, the *uncertainty/ambiguity* and the *dread* of the risk. The uncertainty involves factors such as the novelty and scientific uncertainty surrounding the risk. The dread, which is the strongest determinant of risk acceptability, relates in part to how involuntary and uncontrollable the risk is. Interestingly, these two dimensions of risk perception, uncertainty and dread, also correspond roughly to different evaluation systems in the brain. Feelings of dread, which stimulate a desire to control outcomes, appear to activate the neural structures termed the 'pain matrix' that are also activated in the actual physical experience (Berns et al., 2006). In addition, the type of uncertainty matters, since responses to ambiguity differ from responses to risk. Although the precise correlates depend on the task, the striatum often has prominent activations in the presence of risk, while the orbitofrontal cortex and the amygdale are the brain regions most prominently activated by ambiguity and are the structures associated with the concept of somatic marker that has been developed by Antonio Damasio (1996) and constitutes the focus of the following section.

5.2 Risk sensitivity as the ground for adaptive risk taking

Until very recently, scholars and practitioners alike agreed that wise decision making was understood to occur under only the most rational conditions (Simon, 1957). Most theoretical models of risk taking assumed that risky decision making is largely a cognitive process of integrating the desirability of different possible outcomes with their probabilities. The use of formal logic was believed to result in the best available solution for any problems facing us in any circumstance. Indeed, the rational theory of decision making assumed that the decision maker possesses and uses a logical strategy for producing valid inferences upon which an appropriate response option is made (see Loewenstein and Lerner, 2003 for a review). As Damasio (1994) points out, 'An important aspect of the rationalist conception is that to obtain the best results, emotions must be kept out' (p. 171). The ideal decision maker was understood to be acting from a 'cool head'. Put another way, emotions only served to impede good decision making.

This early literature on decision making can be classified as being part of the *normative approach*. As the term 'normative' itself shows, the approach implies that the suggested rule is the best one under certain conditions and tells people how to make good choices under risk.

There are two main normative rules for choice under risk: the *expected value* rule and the *expected utility* rule. According to the idea of the expected value, when faced with a number of actions, the rational procedure is to identify all possible outcomes, determine their positive or negative values and the probabilities that could result from each course of action and then multiply the two to give an expected value. The action to be chosen should be the one that gives rise to the highest total expected value. The expected utility theory assumes that people choose between alternative courses of action by assessing the desirability or utility of each action's possible outcomes and weighting those utilities by their probability of occurring. The expected utility rule is a simple transformation of the expected value rule. It is still a summation of probabilities times their respective value, except that the values are subjective values called utilities, rather than the actual monetary values. The utility function of a person serves as a measure of that person's risk tendencies. In general, a linear function describes a risk neutral person; a concave function a risk averse person; and a convex function a risk-seeking person. It should be noted that, in many decision making situations, precise objective probabilities are not available. That is the reason why the *descriptive approach* started to take a different route; that is, it looked at the ways in which people make decisions in situations involving risk, instead of telling decision makers how they should make choices, then tried to come up with models which describe what people actually do. The descriptive research has identified a number of expected utility anomalies patterns of behaviour, contradicting the axioms and violating the model's predictions. People often do not behave according to the normative models' rules.

In the late 1960s, under the heading of *'behavioural decision theory'*, a formalised critique of the traditional view emerged. The main belief of this theory was to identify: 1) cognitive errors that people make when they judge the likelihood of future consequences; and 2) simplified heuristics that people use to cope with the complexity of decision making (Tversky and Kahneman's *'Prospect theory'* (1974)). Kahneman and Tversky (1979) developed a model of choice under risk, demonstrating that that a non-linear probability weighting function describes behaviour. Specifically, people overweight small probabilities and underweight moderate and high probabilities, while they are insensitive to variations of probability in the mid-range. This perspective, however, still largely ignored the role played by emotions in decision making.

So, beginning around 1970, evidence has been growing of the incompatibility of the two approaches and a number of scientists demonstrated that, contrary to popular belief, emotions play a central role in decision making. Since their conceptualisation, emotions are now considered the primary constituent of the perception of a decision, to the point that if no emotionally oriented value motivates the decision, it will simply not appear if a decision needs to be made. Paradoxically, in any plausibly emotion free situation that involves a decision, the decision is likely to be neglected.

In order to gain a better understanding of the different roles played by emotions in decision making, it is necessary to distinguish between two different ways in which emotions can enter into decision making (Loewenstein and Lerner, 2003). The first influence of emotions consists of predictions about the emotional consequences of decision outcomes. *Expected emotions* are not experienced as emotions at the time of decision making, but they are expectations about emotions that will be experienced in the future. The second kind of affective influence on decision making consists of *immediate emotions*, that are experienced at the time of decision making and that influence decision making through a direct or indirect impact. Immediate emotions reflect the combined effects of emotions arising from contemplating the consequences of the decision itself (*anticipatory influences*), as well as emotions arising from factors unrelated to the decision (*incidental influences*). Incidental emotions do not arise from considering the consequences of decisions; their influence on decision making is typically considered non normative. According to Loewenstein and Lerner's conceptualisation (2003), immediate emotions can have both direct and indirect effects (changes in the prediction of consequences, selective processing of information and changes in the quality and depth of processing) and are produced by two types of inputs. Considering that expected affect is fundamentally a cognition (about future utilities), while anticipatory affect is fundamentally an emotion (about future utilities), they indeed proceed along distinct neural pathways and they have different potential to shape behaviour (Panksepp, 1998).

An influential attempt to disentangle these processes comes from Damasio's Somatic Marker Hypothesis (SMH; Damasio, 1994, 1996). As explained by Damasio in 1994, 'somatic markers are a special instance of feelings generated from secondary emotions. Those emotions and feelings have been connected by learning to predict future outcomes of certain scenarios. When a negative somatic marker is juxtaposed to a particular future outcome, the combination functions as an alarm bell. When a positive somatic marker is juxtaposed instead, it becomes a beacon of incentive'. According to this hypothesis, each behavioural option is specifically associated with unconscious somatic responses, including neural responses, evoked by its previous consequences that either encourage or discourage a certain choice. Damasio postulates that the somatovisceral signals from the body (affective reactions) ordinarily guide individuals' decision making and risk engagement processes. During decision making, somatic signals (for example heart rate, skin conductance, tonicity), the so-called 'somatic markers', arise from the periphery and indicate an emotional reaction to the response option. Accordingly, for each response option a somatic state is generated and stored in memory. The SMH proposes that the somatic markers are represented and regulated in the emotion circuitry of the brain, particularly in the ventromedial prefrontal cortex. When a particular situation that is similar to a previously experienced situation arises, information regarding the possible response options and their likely outcomes is reactivated. This information is associated with the somatic responses to the given situation and assists decisions by encouraging the rejection of disadvantageous choices and endorsement of advantageous ones. According to the SMH, the reactivation of the somatic responses is evoked on two different pathways. First, these somatic responses can actually be elicited and projected to the somatosensory cortex (the so-called 'body loop'). Secondly, the representation of the somatic affective response can be directly activated in somatosensory brain regions without eliciting peripheral bodily responses (the so-called 'as if body loop'). The vagal route seems to be especially critical in this process (Bechara, 2004). Somatic markers are held to be particularly important in situations of uncertainty and complexity and are thought to enable a faster and experience driven integration of decision making. Since somatic markers can be represented overtly and covertly, this process can operate both with and without conscious awareness. The somatic marker hypothesis is consistent with the idea of a 'hot' decision making. Specifically, Damasio (1994) hypothesised that the somatic marker's role in 'hot' decision making is to assist the 'cold' decision making process by unconsciously biasing the available response selections in a complex decision making task. 'Cold' decision making is associated with rational and cognitive determinations of risks and benefits associated with options and requires the knowledge of the risk–benefit ratio, the ability to retrieve them from memory and the ability hold them in mind while comparing and contrasting them (working memory), whereas 'hot' decision making involves emotional and affective responses to the options (Seguin et al., 2007).

The Iowa Gambling Task (IGT; Bechara et al., 1996; see Section 6.3 for a detailed description) was originally developed to explain decision making deficits in people with specific frontal lobe damage. These patients seem unable to learn from previous mistakes, as reflected by repeated engagement in decisions that lead to negative consequences. In striking contrast to this real life decision making impairment, these patients' intellect and problem solving abilities are largely normal, thus their decision making deficits cannot be explained by attention, working memory, or other cognitive impairments (Damasio, 1994). In addition to their inability to make advantageous decisions in real life, patients evince a generally flat affect and their ability to react to emotional situations is somewhat impaired. This led Damasio to hypothesise that the primary dysfunction of these patients was an inability to use emotions to aid in decision making, particularly decision making in the personal, financial and moral realms. To test this hypothesis, Bechara and colleagues coupled their gambling task with the measurement of skin conductance response (SCR), an autonomic index of emotional arousal. In a series of experiments, it was shown that normal subjects elicited SCRs that were larger before choosing from the disadvantageous decks than before choosing from the advantageous decks. Furthermore, it was found that this anticipatory emotional response preceded explicit knowledge of the correct strategy. Patients with vmPFC damage did not show such anticipatory emotional responses showing that this region is necessary for anticipating the emotional impact of future rewards and punishment.

The IGT has successively proven to be effective in exploring the implications of the Somatic Marker Hypothesis in a variety of psychiatric populations (Viswanath et al., 2009; Miu et al., 2008) and healthy subjects (Franken et al., 2008).

The somatic marker hypothesis provides neurobiological evidence in support of the notion that people often make judgements based on 'hunches', 'gut feelings' and subjective evaluation of the consequences (Damasio, 1994; Loewenstein et al., 2001; Schwartz and Clore, 1983; Tversky and Kahneman, 1981; Zajonc, 1984). In Overskeid's terms, they help select the *solution* that *feels* the best.

In agreement with Damasio's conceptualisation, Zeelenberg and colleagues developed the 'feeling is for doing' approach, where emotions are conceptualised as motivational processes (Zeelenberg et al., 2007; Zeelenberg and Pieters, 2006). The authors propose that 'emotions commit decision makers to certain courses of action by providing control precedence (Frijda, 1986), which means that the experience of an emotion brings forward an associated goal that may overrule other goals'. For example, when one is fearful, running away from the fear evoking stimulus (for example, a big, hairy eight-legged friend) has priority. Because different emotions are associated with different goals (Nelissen et al., 2007), it follows that different emotions have their idiosyncratic impact on decision making. For example, anger will motivate us to move against the source of our anger, whereas fear motivates us to move away. In addition, we expect that the same specific emotion in different situations may activate different behaviours, depending on the overarching goal that people strive to. Put differently, emotions do not automatically call for a specific action, but rather they reflect a concern of the decision maker that is potentially threatened (in the case of negative emotions) or served (in the case of positive emotions). The emotion then facilitates behaviour that is in line with our concerns and that is aimed at closing the gap between the current situation and the goal strived for. Depending on the situation one is in, different behaviours can fulfil this role ('many roads lead to Rome'), but the authors believe that which behaviour will be implemented is based on their accessibility, acceptability and their instrumentality to the current overarching goal. Thus, because of the specific meaning that they convey to the decision maker, specific emotions may help us to better understand the goals and motivations of the decision makers and hence better predict the specific behaviours the decision makers engage in or refrain from. The feeling is for doing approach puts emphasis on the forward looking, motivational function of emotions (see also, Nelissen and Zeelenberg, 2007; Zeelenberg et al., 2007). It explains how emotions may be instrumental in achieving the goal one is striving for.

5.3 The dark and bright sides of emotions in decision making: is it just a matter of rationality?

There are indeed opposing views regarding the role of emotions in decisions. In fact, we know that human emotions have evolved for survival purposes to either increase one's tolerance for risk or lead to risk avoidance in a decision making situation (Hasselton and Ketelaar, 2006; Ketelaar, 2004). The automatic emotions triggered by a given situation prioritise certain goals and thereby mobilise energy and give direction to behaviour (Bagozzi et al., 2000; Frijda, 1986, 2006). They help the normal decision making process by narrowing down the options for action, either by discarding those that are dangerous or endorsing those that are advantageous, thus speeding up the decision making process. On this point, LeDoux (1996, p.176) provides a telling example: 'If you were a small animal faced with a bobcat and had to make a deliberate decision about what to do, you would have to consider the likelihood of each possible choice succeeding or failing and could get so bogged down in decision making that you would be eaten before you made the choice.' In this view, emotions are a kind of radar and rapid response system, constructing and carrying meaning across the flow of experience. Some recent research is consistent with the idea that emotions play a necessary and beneficial role in decision making that can even be undermined by conscious reasoning. A clear example is provided by researches which have found that the individuals who were instructed to pause and calculatedly consider the pros and cons of their prize options rationally enjoyed their prize item less later and thus tended to regret their choice compared to those who were instructed either to make an immediate 'gut' decisions (Carmon et al., 2003). Moreover, individuals who have difficulty in connecting their emotions with decisions make very poor decisions in some contexts and take risks even when they result in catastrophic losses (Bechara et al., 1997; Damasio, 1994; Rogers et al., 1999; Shiv et al., 2005). Monkeys who have damage to the amygdala, an emotion centre, become passive regarding important choices, displaying lack of preference for their caretaker and lack of avoidance of snakes and potentially hostile primates (Bauman et al., 2004; Kalin et al., 2004). Individuals with normally functioning emotion systems can attempt to suppress their emotions, but this often impairs their thinking in multiple ways (Butler and Gross, 2004; Richards et al., 2003). Fenton-O'Creevy et al. (2008) suggest that the most important lesson to take away from these new developments is that the widespread view of emotions as an inhibiting influence on cognition is both incorrect and misleading and that affective engagement with self and the environment is key to successful decision making.

There are, however, circumstances in which a naturally occurring emotional response must be inhibited, so that a deliberate and potentially wiser decision can be made. In fact, despite the fact that when we take a risk the somatic states signal the possible negative consequences of the outcome, it is possible for the individual to override these biases by higher cognitive processes. Without any doubt, most of us learn from early on in life that emotion can only cloud the mind and interfere with good rational decisions, a good example is given by the fact that strong negative emotions such as jealousy and anger can lead to destructive patterns of behaviour such as crimes of passion and road rage (Loewenstein, 1996).

These opposing views of emotion, as adaptive or disadaptive, have received strong support: on the one hand there is a rich body of research in neuroscience and psychology that has highlighted the positive roles played by emotions in decision making (Bechara et al., 1997; Damasio, 1994; Davidson et al., 2000; Dolan, 2002; LeDoux, 1996; Loewenstein and Lerner, 2003; Rahman et al., 2001), and on the other, there is evidence of the biasing effect of non-relevant emotions on decision making (Benartzi and Thaler, 1995; Loewenstein and Lerner, 2003) and recent studies demonstrated that there are specific circumstances under which individuals who lost the capacity to process emotional information might actually make better decisions than normal individuals (Damasio, 1994; Shiv et al., 2005). Specifically, whenever risk taking is rewarded, dysfunctions leading to reduced levels of risk aversion have more advantageous decisions as a consequence (Gneezy, 1997). For example, Damasio (1994) described the case of a patient with damage to the orbitofrontal region of the prefrontal cortex whose lack of fear allowed him to perform optimally during a drive under hazardous road conditions. On the contrary, whenever risk taking is not rewarded, the tendency to strongly experience affective states would be associated with superior decision making performance. For example, highly anxious individuals, who choose safe options more often in tasks involving risk evaluation, would perform better under these circumstances (Werner et al., 2009; Hockey et al., 2000; Maner and Schmidt, 2006; Mitte, 2007; Maner et al., 2007). To summarise, studies that demonstrated a positive role of emotion in decision making involved tasks of decisions under ambiguity (that is, the outcome is unknown) while studies in which even relatively mild negative emotions played a counterproductive role used tasks of decisions under risk (that is, the outcome is risky but it is defined by some probability distribution). Thus, taking a risk is not the same as having poor judgement and impaired decision making.

To conclude, depending on the circumstances, moods and emotions can play useful as well as disruptive roles in the process of making advantageous decisions. Emotions can either increase one's tolerance for risk or lead to risk avoidance in a decision making situation. As Shiv et al. (2005) suggested, it could be possible that emotion is disruptive to decisions under risk, but not to decisions under ambiguity; that is, risk taking behaviour and impaired decision making are not synonymous.

Another line of research responds to the observation that people often compare the consequences of their decisions to what could have happened under different circumstances (Gilbert et al., 2004). This results in counterfactual emotions, such as regret, as well as from a comparison between the outcome one experiences as a consequence of a decision and the outcome one would have experienced if one had chosen differently. The major advance from this field includes the acknowledgment that people respond emotionally to relative changes in their situations, rather than to the absolute consequences of their decisions. That is, they compare what happened against counterfactual scenarios and derive utility not only from concrete outcomes, but also from the outcomes' implications for everyone.

5.4 Emotionality, rationality and another odd thought process: the mind wandering

Each of us has experience of rational processes of thought and certainly of emotional experiences, as, just using introspection, everyone admits the obvious tendency of humans to daydream. We all experience the journeys that our minds take moving away from the task on which it was focused on to pursue thoughts, fantasies, pleasurable sensations and other more or less pleasant activities of thought. The mind wandering theme, though pervasive in our mental life, was not a focus for psychological research until a few years ago.

In recent years, however, we have seen a revival of interest for such a pervasive phenomenon in human life.

Several lines of research have developed that link all the phenomenal features of mind wandering to a shift of attention away from a primary task.

In an important work, Smallwood and Schooler (2006) propose 'that mind wandering is a situation in which executive control shifts away from a primary task to the processing of personal goals'. In this way, mind wandering can be well represented by those situations in which people temporarily stop doing the task in which they were engaged to care about something else. Obviously, the amount of mind wandering is much lower when the primary task is challenging, and occurs much more frequently and with greater intensity when the task is easy or automatic. Also, when the process of wandering mind is activated, it is associated with simultaneous deficits in performance because fewer resources are available to complete the primary task. Of great interest are the conclusions of Smallwood et al. (2003), who suggest that mind wandering is a state where information processing is decoupled from the primary task.

When the mind wanders, attention may become split between internal and external information. For Smallwood and Schooler (2006), mind wandering can be viewed as a state of decoupled attention because, instead of monitoring online sensory information, attention shifts inward and focuses on one's thoughts and feelings. This interpretation of the mind wandering process belongs to a long tradition that attributes the general function of organising the stimuli that come from different sensory and perceptual pathways to the standard notion of executive control. This concept is in contrast with fMRI techniques with the now more accepted notion of a networking process, claimed in a recent paper by Mason et al. (2007), who analysed the activation of brain areas during tasks in which mind wandering could be evoked, thus demonstrating the presence of a default neural network in those conditions that were linked to stimulus independent thoughts.

These two interpretations are in contrast for the fact that the process of mind wandering, conceived as a splitting of attention, is unable to account for the simultaneity of states represented by oscillatory neuronal networks capable of parallel tasks in dependence on the external or internal conditions of each subject. The difference is likely to be crucial because the shift of attention in a network model not only undermines, albeit in a very limited way, the performance, especially when this is largely automated, but also affects it, especially when the task is based on such choices as alternatives on complex motor tasks, reading comprehension, film viewing and novel reading. As we stated in the previous section, it is known that emotional arousal of different intensities can produce varying degrees of inhibition of cognitive responses, resulting in lower levels of accuracy and speed of response, as the mechanism of aversive conditioning induced by the different forms of punishments associated with different types of stimulation has been abundantly studied. Less explored, however, is the mechanism by which the activity of mind wandering affects cognitive performance, penetrating into it and in some cases determining its outcome. According to Smallwood et al. (2008), the effect of mind wandering, analysed by the psycho-physiological technique of cortical event related potentials with the measurement of the P300 response, cannot be attributed to changes in motor activity or in conjunction with general arousal, but when the mind is engaged in tasks of sustained attention, it will naturally ebb and flow in the depth of cognitive analysis applied to events in the external environment.

Smallwood et al. (2008) describe in a particularly effective way the two forms of mind wandering, as follows:

- TUNING OUT: Sometimes when your mind wanders, you are aware that your mind has drifted, but for whatever reason you still continue to perform the task. This is what we refer to as 'tuning out', when your mind wanders and you know it all along.
- ZONING OUT: Other times when your mind wanders, you don't realise that your thoughts have drifted away from the text until you catch yourself. This is what we refer to as 'zoning out', when your mind wanders, but you don't realise this until you catch it.

These phenomena of mind wandering have been observed not only in non-clinical subjects (Shaw and Giambra, 1993) but also in attention deficit hyperactivity disorder children (Castellanos et al., 2005) and in this case attributed to a transient 'catecholaminergic deficit in the ability to appropriately modulate such oscillations in neuronal activity'.

Similarly, Fox et al. (2005) and Fransson (2005), using physiological and fMRI techniques, showed that the default activity during a resting state shows a systematic fluctuation between two brain networks: one largely involving default network structures, the other involving the engagement of task relevant structures.

As postulated by Fox et al. (2005), the fluctuations recorded by the BOLD activity level can be interpreted as 'a dynamic interplay within and between large spatially distributed systems representing opposing components of our mental lives' (p. 9677).

Of particular interest are the findings of Smallwood et al. (2008), who conclude as follows: 'During task performance, attention is often strongly coupled to the external world, presumably affording fast and effective responses to events in the immediate environment. But at the same time, attention can be, either intentionally or unintentionally, decoupled from the immediate environment and directed instead to the internal or private experiences of the individual. Among other things, this state allows the individual to entertain goals and thoughts which extend well beyond their immediate circumstance' (p. 467).

Several researchers described the phenomenon as 'mental time travel' (Addis et al., 2007; Buckner and Vincent, 2007; Mason et al., 2007; Suddendorf and Busby, 2005), thus well capturing the dynamism of the process.

Of these definitions, we feel that the aspect that should be particularly pointed out is the simultaneity of the two processes, attentional task oriented and mind wandering oriented to the internal or private experiences of the individual. Simultaneity means availability in the direction of wandering even without the presence of an external stimulus that works as an attentional engagement and goal oriented means the copresence of multiple conscious or unconscious purposes, in the unconscious case, triggered by internal signals from physiological systems (cardiovascular, immune, endocrine), but also by the flow of thoughts in terms of the rumination or worry that accompany all our waking life. Regarding the latter, Smallwood et al. (2005) developed an interesting study highlighting how the task unrelated thinking (TUT) could be amplified by the association between a ruminative style and a negative mood in the form of dysphoria, thus introducing the fruitful field of research of mind wandering associated with more or less negative characteristics of our personality.

In this brief overview on the neural basis of the experience of mind wandering, we can legitimately conclude that the phenomenon inevitably accompanies our usual daily experience and it has the power to influence many of our behaviours. Furthermore, it has been shown that wandering has the characteristic of being domain specific (Weber et al., 2002) but also to express itself phenomenologically in the shape of the reverse image of the different tasks we are doing in everyday life.

We could say that the mind wandering network may be activated frequently turning a real problematic or negative experience in an illusory fantastic solution of the experience itself, thus creating also a kind of protective factor for our many daily defeats. This example reflects the opinion of Baars (2010), who, starting from the simple observation of the large amount of time spent by each of us in spontaneous daydreaming, concluded that it is reasonable to think that such a large allocation of mental resources must have an adaptive function.

It must also be considered that the spontaneous activity of the brain during rest breaks from an experimental task was initially called 'default' or 'resting state', when it is in fact an extremely active state and plausibly in pursuance of fundamental life tasks (Dehaene and Changeux, 2005; Delamillieure et al., 2009).

In the cognitive neuroscience literature another line of research exists that deals with the same theme, especially in terms of the logic of language and thought and it is the one that extends the theme of mind wandering to the 'counterfactual logic', based on the conditional 'If only P (or I)...then...' (Byrne, 2002; Byrne and Johnson-Laird, 2009; Egan et al., 2009; Hofstadter, 1985; McMullen and Markman, 2002; Thompson and Byrne, 2002).

Counterfactual thoughts are pervasive throughout our everyday lives. They are connected to thoughts based on causal relationships and help us to learn from experience affecting at the same time many cognitive activities, from creativity to probability judgements.

They give rise to emotions and social ascriptions, such as guilt, regret and blame. People show remarkable regularities in those aspects of the past they mentally 'undo' in their counterfactual thoughts. These regularities provide clues about their mental representations and cognitive processes, such as keeping in mind true possibilities and situations that are false but temporarily supposed to be true (Byrne, 2002).

However paradoxical it may seem, this way of working that characterises human thinking can also be associated in the psychology field with the definition of 'subjective probability'. People, even when they are perfectly able to calculate the probability of an event to happen, tend to evaluate this probability in a 'personalised' way, especially after adverse events or when they have to choose an undesirable behaviour, such as stopping smoking or drinking alcohol, in anticipation of an immediate or future benefit for their health. In these cases, the assessment of risk, statistically proven, is often hidden or changed and individual cases that constitute exceptions may be taken as examples. Counterfactual thinking is common to all peoples and it is independent from the structure of the language in which you learned to speak, to the point that it is present also in Chinese native speakers who have no specific linguistic markers (Au, 1983). The ability to generate counterfactual thoughts can be lost, however, following impairments to the frontal cortex (Knight and Grabowecky, 1995).

Counterfactual thoughts provide the building blocks for generating imaginary possibilities in creative and insightful cognition (Hofstadter, 1985; Sternberg and Gastel, 1989; Thomas, 1999). Many studies that have focused on the antecedents of counterfactual thoughts have shown that they are often generated by poor outcomes of behaviour that could be modified, for example, *'If I'd studied I would have got an A'*, serve a preparatory function, helping people to learn from mistakes. These are 'upward' types of counterfactual thoughts, but there are also 'downward' ones, for example: *'If I hadn't crammed last night I would only have got a C'*, serve an affective function, helping people to feel better. People generate more upward counterfactual thoughts although they generate downward ones when they are in a good mood. Their counterfactuals may be filtered by their motivations, for example, to console a victim or to assign blame (Byrne, 2002).

People show remarkable regularities in focusing on the same things from an infinite set of possibilities (Kahneman and Miller, 1986), even if the counterfactual thinking normally tends not to alter the fundamental physical laws to be goal driven and strongly influenced by the availability of alternatives. They make minimal mutations, perhaps corresponding to core categories of thought: space, time, cause and intentionality (Byrne, 1997).

Again, as Byrne (2007) says: 'The human imagination remains one of the last uncharted terrains of the mind. People often imagine how events might have turned out "if only" something had been different. The "fault lines" of reality, those aspects more readily changed, indicate that counterfactual thoughts are guided by the same principles as rational thoughts. In the past, rationality and imagination have been viewed as opposites.'

The focus of counterfactual thinking is that counterfactual thoughts are organised along the same principles as rational thought. The idea that the counterfactual imagination is rational depends on three steps: (1) humans are capable of rational thought; (2) they make inferences by thinking about possibilities; and (3) their counterfactual thoughts rely on thinking about possibilities, just as rational thoughts do.

If, in the research mentioned above, the counterfactual thinking appears as a process carried on by events that have already happened from which we can learn or by upcoming events that we imagine could or should happen in a certain way, the next step is to connect the counterfactual logic to the mind wandering process and, in agreement with a neural network model, to consider plausible the simultaneity of the two processes, the first linked to the task we have to do and the second that shifts the attention, in the language of Smallwood and Schooler (2006) on the universe of our aspirations, desires and motivations.

The result of this simultaneity is a kind of personality that is split without being pathological, most likely developed with that level of inconsistency that everyone finds within himself with a minimum of honest introspection. This interpretation basically originates from the pioneering work of Kahneman, who, in the essay that he has written with Tversky (1982) posed the key question for cognitive scientists, that is: 'How do people mentally "undo" reality?' This is a crucial issue, particularly when the domain of analysis concerns the economic facts. This leads us directly to the themes examined in the next section.

5.5 The need for an interdisciplinary approach: the case of Neuroeconomics

Given that emotional responses, counterfactual thoughts and also the continuous activity of the parallel process of mind wandering, rather than rational forces per se, have recently started to be considered as major factors in financial decision making processes, it seems plausible to export Damasio's hypothesis, linked to the above mentioned models of functioning, in the field of economics. In fact, the patients on whom Antonio Damasio developed his hypothesis often engaged in behaviours that led to diverse kinds of losses, including financial losses. Economists have long recognised that decision makers often deviate from rational choices, despite prior knowledge that could lead them in a different direction. In fact, the somatic marker hypothesis can explain why 'hunches' and 'gut feelings' are often better predictors than market data and fact sheets.

Accordingly, many scholars have postulated a relationship between psychological processes, how investors buy and sell and financial market price movements (Barberis et al., 1998; Daniel et al., 1998; Dremen and Lufkin, 2000). The trader practitioner literature is full of references to emotion and 'market sentiment'. Kamstra et al. (2003) presented international evidence that seasonal depression, which correlates with the length of the day, has a negative effect on stock returns. The role of emotion and its impact on trading performance has been extensively analysed and reported by Fenton-O'Creevy et al. (2008). They found that successful expert traders are more likely to engage in self-monitoring and emotion regulation and this carries important benefits in terms of trading performance. It is now evident that although humans are definitely capable of conscious deliberation, many if not most economically relevant decision processes are characterised by certain other features. First, they rely on automatic, fast and effective cognitive processes, which are not under direct volitional control. Secondly, they are under the influence of unrecognised and finely tuned affective mechanisms, which often play a decisive role in action (see Walter et al. (2005) for a review).

Given these premises, economics, psychology and neuroscience started to converge into a single field under the label of *neuroeconomics*, aiming at employing recent neuroscientific methods in order to analyse economically relevant brain processes (Kenning and Plassmann, 2005). This innovative field has repeatedly revealed deviations from the classical theory of economists, highlighting that subjects show dysfunctional behaviours that are not explicable with the traditional concept (Weber et al., 2007). Applying diverse methods, including the lesion method (for example, using brain damages that occur as a result of stroke to examine how different brain areas contribute to various mental functions), functional imaging and other physiological techniques, neuroscientists began to elucidate the neural process underlying the execution of successful and unsuccessful decisions. This effort has converged with the field of behavioural economics to show that decision making involves not only the cold-hearted calculation of expected utility based upon explicit knowledge of outcomes but depends critically on prior emotional processing (see, for example, Rustichini, 2005). Neuroscientists explain that emotions and feelings arise as a subcortical process in the brain and as they are inextricably tied to the body, emotions come first in development (before cognition and rationality) and thus retain a primacy that permeates *all* of our mental functioning. Research in the neural processing of decision making reveals that a collection of neural systems dedicated to functions of reasoning and decision making (particularly decisions in personal and social domains) is the same collection of systems involved in emotion and feelings (Bechara et al., 2000).

The aspect of uncertainty most commonly considered by both economists and neuroscientists is risk, which refers to situations with a known distribution of possible outcomes. An important area of ongoing research is the study of individual differences. To address this issue, some researchers have evaluated whether risk attitudes constitute a personality trait as it seems plausible to think that some individuals are inherently risk seeking, while others are consistently risk averse. On the contrary, risk taking seems to be highly domain specific, such that one might find very different attitudes toward risk taking in financial versus health versus social situations (Hanoch et al., 2006). The same person can therefore behave as both risk averse and risk seeking in different situations. As a consequence of the fact that neither psychologists nor economists have been particularly successful in developing a single psychological questionnaire to predict risk taking behaviour across multiple domains (Nicholson et al., 2002), this topic has started to be addressed from a biological point of view. Neuroimaging techniques proved to be a powerful approach to track the neural changes associated with decision making under uncertainty. Specifically, the proposed neural circuitry underlying the somatic marker hypothesis departs from the limbic system in an anatomical sense and it incorporates a variety of brain regions outside of the classic limbic system structures (MacLean, 1949), including ventromedial prefrontal cortex (VMPFC), somatosensory cortices, insula and basal ganglia (Damasio, 1998).

In a series of case studies, Steenbarger (2002) specifically presents evidence linking emotion with trading performance. Shiv et al. (2005) used a decision making instrument known as the investment task, which simulates real life investment decisions in terms of uncertainties, rewards and punishments. The task was closely modelled after a paradigm developed in previous research to demonstrate myopic loss aversion; that is, an extreme level of risk aversion towards gambles that involve some possible loss (Thaler et al., 1997). The investment task was specifically designed in such a way that the rational choice of participants would be to invest in every single round because the expected value on each round was higher if one invested than if one did not. Results revealed that patients with abnormal emotional circuitry experienced less myopic loss aversion and made more advantageous decisions. In other words, they earned more money by investing in more rounds than individuals with an intact emotional circuitry. Myopic loss aversion has been proposed as an explanation for the large number of individuals who prefer to invest in bonds, even though stocks have historically provided a much higher rate of return, a pattern that economists refer to as the equity premium puzzle (for example, Choi et al., 2009). These findings on pathological patients suggest that affective states can interfere with efficient trading performance.

Up to now, only one study examined the relation between financial risk measures and emotional states and dynamics by measuring traders' psychophysiological responses (for example, skin conductance, blood volume pulse, and so on) during live trading sessions (Lo and Repin, 2002). Significant differences in mean electrodermal responses during transient market events relative to no event control periods and significant mean changes in cardiovascular variables during periods of heightened market volatility relative to normal volatility control periods were highlighted. Although Lo and Repin (2002) documented significant emotional responses among the most experienced traders, they subsequently showed that being emotionally affected by one's own daily profits and losses is counterproductive from the perspective of trading performance. Specifically, subjects whose emotional reactions to monetary gains and losses were more intense on both the positive and negative sides exhibited significantly worse trading performance, therefore supporting the common wisdom (Lo et al., 2005). It has to be noted that the Lo et al. (2005) study consisted of survey data, such as daily emotional state questionnaires and trading reports, while the Lo and Repin (2002) study included psychophysiological measures.

However, many real world decisions have a more complex form of uncertainty compared to risk, because the distribution of outcomes is itself unknown. When the outcomes of a decision cannot be specified, even probabilistically, the decision is said to be made under ambiguity. In most circumstances, people are even more averse to ambiguity than to risk alone. Economists and psychologists have studied how these different aspects of uncertainty influence decision making showing that expected value is often a poor predictor of choice. In fact, although expected utility models provide a simple and powerful theoretical framework for choice under uncertainty, they often fail to describe real world decision making. Across a wide range of situations – from investment choices to the allocation of effort – uncertainty leads to systematic violations of expected utility models. This research indicates that people are generally uncertainty averse when making decisions about monetary gains, but uncertainty seeking when faced with potential losses. However, when either probabilities or values get very small, these tendencies reverse. Given the pervasiveness of uncertainty, only through explicit interdisciplinary, multimethodological and theoretically integrative research it was and it will be possible to addressed some key questions.

Fundamental advances in the study of decision making will only arise from the reciprocal integration of expertise and techniques across traditionally independent fields.

6
The Layout of the Empirical Analysis

Caterina Lucarelli, Cristina Ottaviani and Daniela Vandone

6.1 The sample

The research relies on an innovative cross-disciplinary approach, mixing financial competences with others, related to psychology and affective neuroscience. The analysis involves an assorted sample of individuals, with different levels of financial education/competences: customers of banks, traders and asset managers. More than 600 individuals were asked to take part in the experiments, and 445 of them actually did it.[1]

The organisation of the experiments took place with the cooperation of some financial intermediaries, in relation to specific subjects to analyse. We received the cooperation of an Italian investment company, Twice SIM, which hosted our experiments during two Italian national meetings of traders (the Trading Expo held in Borsa Italiana in Milan in October 2008 and the Italian Trading Forum in Rimini in May 2009). Then we obtained the cooperation of a medium-sized bank, Banca Popolare di Ancona (BPA), belonging to the UBI Group, which involved 11 of its branches spread over small and medium towns in central Italy. Finally, we obtained the cooperation of the Italian Association of Asset Managers, Assogestioni, which allowed the participation of seven asset managers running all or part of their activity in Italy: Eurizon Capital sgr; ARCA sgr; PRIMA sgr; UBI Pramerica sgr; Azimut sgr; JPMorgan Asset Management sgr and Pioneer sgr.

The research team asked hosting partners to get randomly in touch with a list of people who may have been assuming financial decisions. Each person was assigned an Identification Number (ID).[2] The overall number of people asked to take part to the experiment was 619; only 445 of them (71.9 per cent) accepted, while the residual 28.1 per cent refused (174 individuals).

We asked our hosting partners to write down some basic information (age, gender, marital status, financial activism, income) about those individuals they had contacted for the experiment. In this way we collected some general features of those accepting the experiment and of those refusing it. Some of these characteristics will be presented in detail in Chapter 8. We need to point out that the information presented in this section was provided by the hosting partner, while that of Chapter 8 was provided directly by the interviewees.[3] Here we try to give a basic idea of the main differences, if any, between those willing to take part in the experiment and those refusing it, in order to manage the so-called *self-selection bias.*

Mean values between Group 0 (refusals) and Group 1 (acceptance) are statistically different, as shown in Table 6.1. Specifically, the sample of people willing to take part in the experiment is younger than the sample who refused it. Comparing the gender feature, Figure 6.1 shows that a higher percentage of females (33.3 per cent) refused to take part in the experiment rather than accepting it (21.6 per cent).

Furthermore, Figure 6.2 shows that people more willing to be involved in the experiment were more likely to be those characterised by a higher average number of contract/financial operations managed in their daily life.

Table 6.1 Acceptance and refusals of the experiment by age

Two-sample t test with equal variances

Group	Obs	Mean	Std. Err.	Std. Dev.	[95% Conf.	Interval]
0	174	47.44253	.9629528	12.70222	45.54188	49.34318
1	445	42.70562	.5561335	11.73165	41.61264	43.7986
combined	619	44.03716	.4899461	12.18972	43.075	44.99932
diff		4.736911	1.073978		2.627816	6.846005

diff = mean(0) - mean(1) t = 4.4106
Ho: diff = 0 degrees of freedom = 617

Ha: diff < 0	Ha: diff != 0	Ha: diff > 0
pr(T < t) = 1.0000	pr(|T| > |t|) = 0.0000	Pr(T > t) = 0.0000

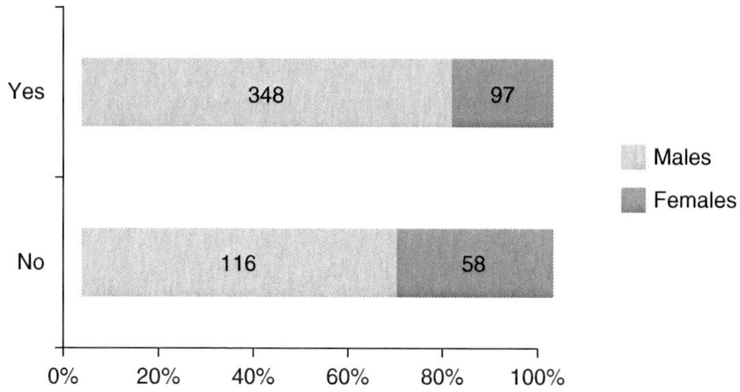

Figure 6.1 Acceptance and refusals of the experiment by gender

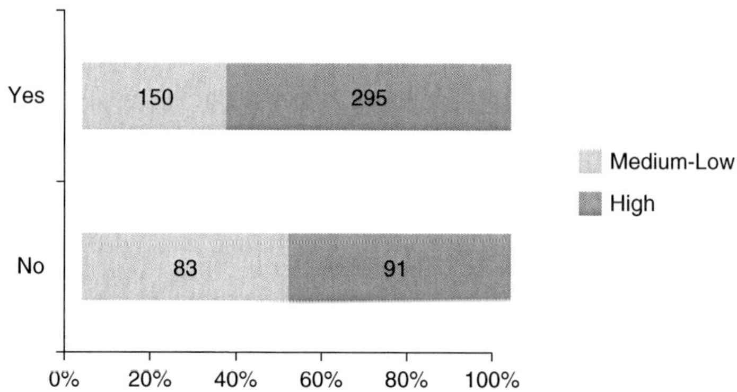

Figure 6.2 Acceptance and refusals of the experiment by financial activity

No relevant difference is related to the marital status, with a little higher presence of singles and people divorced or widowed accepting the experiment, than the others (maybe because they have more spare time available, than people with a family). Finally, the income variable is not crucial to draw a distinction between the 'yes' and 'no' sub-samples of individuals.

Table 6.2 offers an overall list of the number of interviewees by hosting partner. The involvement of various intermediaries located in different

Table 6.2 Individuals by hosting partners

Hosting partner	Number of interviewees
BPA Ancona	30
BPA Civitanova Marche	19
BPA Fabriano	19
BPA Forlì	14
BPA Jesi	31
BPA Macerata	23
BPA Pesaro	14
BPA Ravenna	16
BPA Rimini	13
BPA Senigallia	27
BPA Urbino	16
Eurizon Capital sgr	19
ARCA sgr	21
PRIMA sgr	7
UBI Pramerica Sgr	10
Azimut Sgr	20
JP Morgan Asset Management sgr	10
Pioneer sgr	27
ITForum 2009	63
Trading Online Expo 2008	46
Total	445

Italian regions allow us also to take into consideration an effect due to the general 'environment' experienced/faced by subjects (in particular, we will compare people living in metropolitan areas with those living in little towns/provinces).

6.2 The questionnaire

One of the two instruments used during the experiment was a traditional questionnaire, made up of three sections (an example of this questionnaire is offered in Appendix 1). The first one is the Grable and Lytton (1999 and 2003) questionnaire, used to measure the biased risk tolerance (BR); the second section holds an impulsivity test; the third one permits the collection of socio-demographic and economic information, together with personal financial choices, as far as both past investments and debts are concerned.

6.2.1 The Grable and Lytton financial risk tolerance questionnaire

At the beginning of the research, we looked deeply in the literature for an instrument capable of measuring the risk tolerance of individuals, according to a self-evaluation procedure. As already anticipated in Chapter 3, assessing a client's risk tolerance is one of the most important and difficult activities within the financial planning process. Several contributors proposed procedures and tests to the risk tolerance assessment process, reaching no consensus. We also considered the possibility of creating a financial risk tolerance test that was completely new and specifically suited to the Italian situation.

The essential attributes of a risk tolerance test, useful for our empirical goals, are first that it must have been already validated as a financial risk tolerance self-assessment tool. This brought us to exclude the idea of a new questionnaire 'of our own', because the time for its validation would have been unfeasible with the limits and the goals of our research. The second condition is that the test allowed the computation of an overall score able to synthesise if the interviewee is risk averse or a risk lover, according to his or her self-evaluation. This induced us to exclude many financial risk tolerance tools (such as, for example, the FinaMetrica's Risk Profiling System[4]) which are covered by copyright and do not allow an autonomous risk scoring computation.

These considerations brought us to select the financial risk tolerance questionnaire proposed by Grable and Lytton (1999), who provide a validated questionnaire together with a decoding description which allowed us to replicated their results in our sample.

6.2.2 The Barratt Impulsiveness Scale (BIS)

Impulsivity has been included as a variable in the present study in light of the link between this psychological concept and the economic notion of hyperbolic discount, which has been borrowed by psychologists to explain impaired decision making in psychopathological subjects (for example, addiction). Although its detrimental effects have been mainly studied on clinical populations, however, the few studies on healthy subjects suggest a link between impulsivity and impaired decision making (Franken et al., 2008; Zermatten et al., 2005). Moreover, Wittmann and Paulus (2008) showed a relationship between an altered sense of time and impulsivity; that is, impulsive subjects overestimate the duration of time intervals and, as a consequence, discount the value of delayed rewards more strongly than do self-controlled individuals. In general, highly impulsive individuals are biased towards immediate rewards during option evaluation and are less sensitive to the negative consequences of their choices (Martin and Potts, 2009; Potts et al., 2006). More specifically, Franken et al. (2008) and Sweitzer et al. (2008) demonstrated that the decreased ability to alter behaviour in response to fluctuations in emotional significance of stimuli showed by highly impulsive subjects was associated with poorer performance at the Iowa Gambling Task (IGT; Bechara et al., 1996).

In the present study we used a validated and widely used questionnaire, such as the Barratt Impulsiveness Scale (BIS-11; Patton et al., 1995), as a measure of impulsivity. The BIS-11 is a 30 item self-report questionnaire designed to assess general impulsiveness taking into account the multi-factorial nature of the construct. The questionnaire provides a total score and separate scores for the three subscales measuring different aspects of impulsiveness: 1) motor impulsiveness, which reflects the tendency to act without forethought; 2) non-planning impulsiveness, which reflects a lack of planning for the future; and 3) attentional impulsiveness, which is characterised mainly by having difficulty in maintaining attention and concentrating. The items are scored on a four point scale (Rarely/Never [1], Occasionally [2], Often [3], Almost always/Always [4]). The validity and reliability of the Italian version of the BIS has been previously demonstrated (Fossati et al., 2001).

6.2.3 The economic section

The questionnaire used in the survey of section three of Appendix 1 was designed according to the aim of the research project and the existing economic literature. It allows the collection of socio-demographic and economical information, together with data on personal financial choices related to investment and debt decisions.

In particular, the questionnaire includes questions designed to capture the socio-demographic profile of individuals, such as age, gender, marital status, composition of the household, width of the place of residence and geographic area. Such questions are typically used in national and international surveys in order to investigate, at different levels and with different aims, characteristics and behaviours of individuals and families.

It also includes questions traditionally designed to capture the economic and financial profile of the family, including working conditions, amount of income, amount and composition of financial and real wealth, and presence of secured and unsecured debt. Such questions are accompanied by other questions designed to investigate the adequacy of monthly income over expenditure; that is, whether the family manages to make ends meet, whether it manages to save or whether it has to borrow.

The questionnaire also includes questions to investigate the level of individual education and culture and the ability to correctly interpret financial information, as well as questions related to the ways in which individuals take investing and debt decisions; for example, by oneself, with the family, with the advice of the salesperson or bank employee, or with advice from friends and colleagues.

Finally, there are questions designed to investigate the risk aversion or appetite of individuals, such as insurance coverage, reaction to recent financial crises, the maximum loss the individual is willing to bear before deciding to withdrawal an investment, and so on.

6.3 The Iowa Gambling Task

Although originally intended to explain decision making deficits in people with specific frontal lobe damage, the Iowa Gambling Task (IGT) has been successively proven to be effective in exploring the implications of the Somatic Marker Hypothesis (Damasio, 1994) in a variety of psychiatric populations (for example, Viswanath et al., 2009) and healthy subjects (for example, Franken et al., 2008).

The IGT simulates real life decisions in conditions of reward and punishment and of uncertainty. Independent from its value for the SMH, the IGT is a well-validated paradigm which has been widely used to assess decision making performance (for example, Werner et al., 2009). The performance at the IGT involves the progression from decision making with unknown probabilities (decision making under ambiguity) to, at the limit, decision making with known probabilities (risky decision making). For the majority of healthy subjects the IGT consists of two phases: (1) an early or initial phase (approximately the first 40 trials) where subjects learn to make choices, but without having any explicit knowledge about the contingencies that guide their decision. At this stage, the decisions are largely guided by implicit information; (2) a latter phase (after the first 40 trials, but this probably differs from person to person), where subjects acquire some conceptual knowledge about the contingencies in the task, and the decisions become more influenced by explicit knowledge about the risks associated with each deck (Brand et al., 2007). Thus decisions under ambiguity are assumed to be characteristic of the earlier phase (or trials) of the IGT; that is, before the rules for gains and losses are figured out and become explicit to the subject. In contrast, decisions under risk are most likely characteristic of the latter phase (or trials) of the IGT; that is, after the risks associated with each deck become more explicit. The main criticism of the task is that the influence of conscious explicit knowledge about wins and losses in the IGT rather than unconscious signals could account for the observed results (for a review, see Dunn et al., 2006).

In the present study, a computerised version of the task based on the original as described in Bechara et al. (1994) was used. In detail, participants saw four decks of cards labelled A, B, C and D, and a starting amount of fiches on a computer screen. The subjects were instructed to maximise gains and minimise losses when playing the game. Using the corresponding key on the keyboard, subjects could select a card from any of the four decks. Each card carried an immediate reward (100 euros in decks A and B and 50 euros in decks C and D). However, the ultimate future yield of each deck varies because the penalty amounts are higher in the high-paying decks (A and B), leading to a negative balance, and lower in the low-paying decks (C and D), leading to a final gain. Thus, decks A and B are 'disadvantageous', whereas decks C and D are 'advantageous'.

So that they can perform the task, the subjects are given the following instructions: 'In front of you on the screen, there are four decks of cards A, B, C and D. I want you to select one card at a time, by clicking on the card, from any deck you choose. Each time you select a card from a deck, the computer will tell you that you won or lost some money. You are absolutely free to switch from one deck to another any time you wish. The goal of the game is to win as much money as possible and, if you find yourself unable to win, make sure you avoid losing money as much as possible. I won't tell you for how long the game will continue. You must keep on playing until the computer stops. You will get 2,000 euros credit to start the game.'

The players cannot predict when a penalty will occur, nor calculate with precision the net gain or loss from each deck. They also do not know how many cards must be turned before the end of the game (the game in fact ends after 100 card selections). The task duration was about 30 minutes for each participant. The computer tracked the sequence of the cards selected from the various decks.

As each subject performed the task, Skin Conductance Response (SCR) activity was recorded continuously by the Biopac MP150 system (Biopac Systems, CA, USA) and collected simultaneously on a personal computer. SCR is measured by the voltage drop between two electrodes placed on the skin surface of the second phalanx of the index and middle fingers of the non-dominant hand. Changes in SCR occur when eccrine sweat glands, innervated by the sympathetic autonomic nervous system fibres, receive a signal from a certain part of the brain. Sample rate was set at 1 Hertz. Each time the subject clicked the mouse and selected a card, the action was recorded as a 'mark' on the polygram of SCR activity. Each click was registered as a selection from the specific deck that had been chosen. Thus, SCRs generated in association with a specific deck could be identified precisely on the polygram. Although the inter-trial interval was set at 6 seconds, to allow for psycho-physiological recordings, in reality the time interval between two card selections was longer, because it took a few additional seconds for the subject to decide which card to pick next. This time interval varied from trial to trial (10 seconds on average). During the 6 second inter-trial interval the decks were displayed continuously on the screen, and the subject could ponder which deck to choose next. The time windows for the reward and punishment SCRs were the 5 seconds immediately *after* the click of a card. SCRs generated during the end of the reward/punishment window and *before* the next click of a card are considered anticipatory SCRs. For each subject we obtained two dependent variables of anticipatory SCRs (one from the good decks and one from the bad decks).

From SCR recordings, the area under the curve (AuC; mS/s) of SCRs was extracted in the intervals of interest. The intervals of interest were of two kinds, comprising a) 5 second intervals after each card was turned, which, depending on the type of the card, were of the reward or punishment type; and b) 'anticipatory' intervals between the end of each 5 second reward or punishment interval and before the next card selection (see Bechara et al., 1997).

To score the performance of the subject on the gambling task, the total number of cards picked from decks C and D were added and subtracted to the total number of cards picked from decks A and B (see Bechara et al., 1997). To obtain an index of the temporal dynamic of the test, the same calculation was repeated separately in each block of 20 cards.

Notes

Lucarelli is the author of Sections 6.1 and 6.2.1; Ottaviani is the author of Sections 6.2.2 and 6.3; and Vandone is the author of Section 6.2.3.

1. This is the largest sample ever studied at an international level with psycho-physiological tests.
2. The research team never knew the names of the interviewees and each subject was identified uniquely through his or her ID. Anonymity was guaranteed as a condition for taking part in the experiment.
3. The hosting partner may be not completely informed, for example, of the updated marital status or income level of individuals.
4. See www.finametrica.com/Login.aspx.

7
The Indicators of Risk

Caterina Lucarelli and Giulio Palomba

7.1 Sources of information and theoretical assumptions

Theoretically, financial risk tolerance depends upon different dimensions of risk. Some commentators (Cordell, 2002) have defined the term 'risk tolerance' to mean a combination of both *'risk attitude'* (how much risk I *choose to take)* and *'risk capacity'* (how much risk I *can afford to take*) (Roszkowski et al.). The first empirical goal of this study is to compare levels of financial risk tolerance which are obtained through alternative measurements: a traditional financial risk tolerance test, a psycho-physiological test and the analysis of real life financial decisions. When using the financial risk tolerance test, we rely upon the self-evaluation of individuals; the computation from this test returns a biased risk tolerance level (BR). The second tool should provide a more objective evaluation of risk tolerance, given the fact that it relies on risky choices influenced by spontaneous somatic responses; it should return an unbiased risk tolerance level (UR). Finally, we considered the real life financial decisions of individuals obtaining a measure of the risk tolerance effectively assumed (the real life risk, RLR). Therefore we have the chance to compare how coherent RLR is in relation to both BR and UR.

The sources of information available for the empirical computation of the different indicators of risk tolerance are:

- For the BR, the global score from the financial risk tolerance test (Grable and Lytton, 1999) located in section 1 of our questionnaire. The empirical work of Grable and Lytton also provides the lowest and the highest score (maximum and minimum risk aversion, respectively), together with the average score of their empirical distribution.

- For the UR, the IGT provides us with information about the preference of each subject for advantageous (not risky) or disadvantageous (risky) decks. Moreover, we have a whole information set of the particular strategy employed during the game and the valuable somatic response data before and after each choice. All this information is available both in terms of an overall score/average for the test of each subject and also as a disaggregated time series data set within the 100 choices undertaken.
- For the RLR we use the responses given by each subject in section 3 of our questionnaire in relation to the financial decisions assumed in his or her real life.

The need to put UR, BR and RLR side by side required having them metrically comparable. To accomplish this, two alternative options exist from which we could choose: the first was to impose two extreme behaviours (the maximum and the minimum risk aversion), being symmetric in relation to a midpoint corresponding to indifference towards risk; the second choice was to figure out the two extreme behaviours without a theoretical assumption of indifference towards risk.

The first choice, which we considered briefly (Brighetti and Lucarelli, 2010), involves the statement of a top extreme (equal to +1) for the maximum risk propensity and a bottom extreme (equal to -1) for the maximum risk aversion. The hypothetical value of the indicator equal to 0 should reveal the behaviour of indifference toward risk. This last point is crucial and is related to the true meaning of 'indifference' towards risk. Let us take, for example, the computation of the BR indicator. It is indeed the easiest one to calculate, precisely because it is based upon previous empirical research (Grable and Lytton, 1999). This in turn correspondingly sets the top and bottom scores which indicates the extreme risk propensity and aversion of individuals. The empirical computation also offers an average score value, between the two extremes. At first sight it could be assumed that this alludes to an 'indifference' towards risk: however, those individuals showing this average score may not necessarily be risk seekers or risk averters. Furthermore, this does not mean that they are indifferent towards risk. Rather, they have only a moderated (average) behaviour between the two extremes of maximum or minimum risk aversion.

The relevant limitation of the theoretical (and empirical) meaning of indifference towards risk is revealed best by the UR indicator. This computation is the most daring of all since we have to take into consideration information from several sources (the preference for advantageous/disadvantageous decks, the anticipatory and reward/punishment SCR in relation to the choices, any game strategy and the dynamic interconnection of all these variables as the 100 test choices are made ...). In addition to this, we are aware of the fact that any previous research on non-pathological subjects provides us with neither theoretical nor empirical framework to set reliable behavioural extremes for the individual skin conductance response. In fact, the computation of the preference for advantageous/disadvantageous decks allows us to set the extreme behaviours of risk lovers or risk averters because the number of choices is limited (100) and the features of advantageous/disadvantageous decks is well known. Nevertheless, no indication is available for bounds of anticipated and post SCR. Each individual has his or her personal level of SCR and no objective parameters can set what can be considered, for a human being, to be either 'extreme' or 'normal'. Previous empirical research (Bechara et al., 1996) has only confirmed that, on average, people who 'feel' the risk more strongly demonstrate a higher anticipatory SCR before the choice from a disadvantageous deck is made. But neither theory nor empirical studies set a top value of anticipatory SCR because of the various peculiarities of human behaviour.

More precisely, we are unable to correctly specify the top SCR extreme primarily because the bottom extreme is well known for the way SCR is computed: it is always positive (Fowles et al., 1981). So this evidently entails that the lowest SCR value is equal to 0. Let us consider a subject revealing no somatic response to a risky deck. It is obvious that this behaviour is not related to risk aversion and we might then assume as such that the subject is indifferent towards risk. However, this statement could induce us into a tremendous fault. A person who fails to 'feel' the risk is paradoxically the most dangerous subject, in terms of both financial and other behaviours (for example, driving a car). We might state that the more you feel the risk (either because you love it or because you are scared of it) the more likelihood there is of undertaking responsible behaviours (assuming or refusing risky actions); the less you feel it, the higher the probability is of making irresponsible choices (Damasio, 1994). The final deduction is that, on the one hand, neither theoretical nor empirical support indicates a highest SCR value; on the other hand, the lowest SCR value (0) is not completely appropriate as the bottom extreme. So there is no basis to compute a reasonable range for our unbiased risk indicator (UR), which is strongly affected by SCR. Moreover, the theoretical concept of 'indifference towards risk', for the UR computation, does not correspond to an 'average behaviour' or a behaviour that can be deemed to be not overly that of a risk lover or risk averter in nature, as for the BR computation. It is a proxy of not feeling the risk, with all the related concern about responsible actions. The same considerations are applicable to the RLR indicator.

That is why the alternatives we have available in setting the range for our indicators of risk have to avoid the concept of indifference toward risk. We can only consider the two extremes (highest aversion and propensity) without a midpoint. Hence the preference goes to the choice of a range between 0 and 1. People revealing a risk indicator (either BR, UR or RLR) equal to 0 are considered risk averters, whereas those exhibiting a score equal to 1, are judged to be risk lovers.

Finally, it is essential to underline that, excluding the BR, both the psycho-physiological test and the analysis of real life financial decisions should observe precisely the same theoretical concept of risk tolerance. This means that what is essentially required is something which embraces both the risk attitude and the risk capacity dimension. The point is clear for real life risk, RLR, which has two determinants: the real life attitude (RLA) and the real life capacity (RLC), as shown in Section 7.4. Nevertheless, the UR computation also relies upon the assumption that risk tolerance is a mix of attitude and capacity. In fact, UR is computed after modelling in a multivariate framework the drivers of a binomial choice between a risky and a non-risky asset in the IGT test. As shown in Section 7.2., UR is a risk tolerance indicator because it is characterised as having both a risk attitude dimension (the rational choice, together with the somatic compulsion aspect) and a risk capacity dimension (how rich or poor you believe yourself to be in relation to past negative/positive monetary wins).

7.2 The unbiased risk indicator (UR)

Given that the available sample contains N=445 individuals who play the game in the experimental setting by choosing from T=100 decks, the data can be represented using a panel data structure. In particular, we try to model the deck selection given a set of explanatory variables which can influence individual decisions; hence, we use an Arellano and Bond (1991) estimator for the following model:

$$deck_{i,t} = \mu + \beta_1 deck_{i,t-1} + \beta_2 y_{i,t} + \beta_3 pre_{i,t} + \beta_4 post_{i,t-1} + \sum_{j=1}^{k} \theta_j dwin_{i,t-j} + \epsilon_{i,t} \quad (7.1)$$

where:

- $deck_{i,t}$: dummy variable for the risky deck;
- $y_{i,t}$: variable which approximates the game strategies. It is defined as:

$$y_{i,t} = \frac{1}{k}\left[y_{i,t-1} + \sum_{j=1}^{k} j^{-1} x_{i,t-j} \right] \tag{7.2}$$

where $x_{i,t} = -2B_{i,t} - A_{i,t} + D_{i,t}$ represents a proxy of any game strategy calculated by assigning negative weights to risky decks A and B (maximum risk), and a unit weight to the 'regular' deck D. According to this assumption the score corresponding to decks B, A, C and D are –2, –1, 0 and 1 respectively.

- $pre_{i,t}$: SCR collected 5 seconds before the deck selection;
- $post_{i,t-1}$: SCR collected 5 seconds after the previous deck selection. Obviously, in the model the lagged value is used because the individual strategy could be influenced by the somatic reaction to the previous choice.
- $dwin_{i,t}$: first difference of the variable $win_{i,t}$ which represents the game payoffs;
- $K = 5$ derived from the assumption that players involved in the game reasonably can remember only the last 5 payoffs;
- $\varepsilon_{i,t} \sim$ i.i.d.$(0,\sigma_{\varepsilon}^{2})$ is the model disturbance.

The time series dimension is reduced to T=80 because we assume that the first 20 decks chosen by each individual correspond to a game learning period.

The use of the Arellano and Bond (1991) framework is primarily motivated by three different aspects. First, it allows us to model the individual choices from a dynamic perspective. Secondly, the fitted values could represent a good proxy of the deck selection process via a linear combination of some explanatory variables related to the game strategy and to the somatic responses. Finally, it permits us to be able to obtain an estimate of the individual UR: once estimated by the dynamic panel model, the UR indicator is obtained via the computation of the individual median calculated on the fitted observations. The individuals who show values greater than the median are those who adopt the more risky strategies during the game.

Table 7.1 1-step Arellano-Bond, using 33,075 observations Included 441 cross-sectional units Dependent variable: $deck_{i,t}$

	coefficient	std error	t-ratio	p-value
$deck_{i,t}$	0.129558	0.020668	6.27	3.65e-10***
const	0.017063	0.002167	7.87	3.47e-15***
$y_{i,t}$	0.000615	6.32e-05	9.74	2.03e-22***
$pre_{i,t}$	0.057428	0.012213	4.70	2.58e-06***
$post_{i,t-1}$	0.078020	0.011092	7.03	2.01e-12***
$dwin_{i,t-1}$	0.000154	1.30e-05	11.89	1.36e-32***
$dwin_{i,t-2}$	0.000120	1.15e-05	10.46	1.30e-25***
$dwin_{i,t-3}$	0.000106	1.24e-05	8.56	1.12e-17***
$dwin_{i,t-4}$	5.94e-05	1.23e-05	4.84	1.31e-06***
$dwin_{i,t-5}$	1.34e-05	1.72	0.0859*	2.31e-05

Sum squared resid 13638.36 S.E. of regression 0.642239
Test for AR(1) errors: z = – 19.8081 [0.0000]
Test for AR(2) errors: z = 1.50081 [0.1334]
Sargan over-identification test: Chi-square(71) = 79.664 [0.2252]
Wald (joint) test: Chi-square(9) = 396.311 [0.0000]

The model (7.1) estimation is presented in Table 7.1; before the estimation took place, four players were dropped because they always selected the same type of deck (exhibiting outlier behaviour), hence the number of individuals in the sample is restricted to N=441.

The Arellano and Bond (1991) estimation shows that all the variables used in model (7.1) play a key role in determining the deck selection with the only exception of variable $y_{i,t}$; the autoregressive coefficient is positive which means that people usually select a risky deck after selecting a risky deck. The variables related to SCR also have an impact on the dependent variable. In particular, the individuals seem to emotionally react before their choice ($pre_{i,t}$ augments when a disadvantageous deck has to be preferred), while if they reacted to the previous deck they tend to prefer advantageous ones in the following choice (the coefficient related to $post_{i,t-1}$ has a negative sign). The game strategy variables also seem to influence the individual decisions made, because they positively impact in relation to the selection of risky decks. Finally, the choice of using k=5 lags for variable $dwin_{i,t}$ seems to be appropriate and confirms the relevance of game payoffs which influence the risky choices. It is relevant to point out that the payoffs are significant as flows (if individuals are richer or poorer between two sequential choices) while stocks (levels of wealth obtained during the game) result in being insignificant and have therefore been omitted in model (7.1).

7.3 The cases of 'alphas'

The $pre_{i,t}$ variable is significant and positive when running model (7.1) in panel structure form, confirming an overall behaviour already proven in the literature (Bechara and Damasio, 2002): when shifting from an advantageous to a disadvantageous deck (moving from *deck* 0 to 1), the whole sample of individuals generate a stronger anticipatory SCR. In spite of the fact that they 'feel the risk' they choose to shift from advantageous to disadvantageous choices, either because they love the risk (Bechara and Damasio, 2002), refers to high risk takers, thrill seekers, or gamblers), or because they are scared of it.

In order to understand the behaviour of *each* subject during the 100 choices of the test, we check this result running an estimation of model (7.1) as 411 separate time series regressions. Results[1] show that not all the individuals show the $pre_{i,t}$ variable to be significant and positive when considered separately, as theory would induce us to expect. We add notation of those acting coherently with the 'theoretical normal decision making system' and we also categorise them as 'alphas'. Surprisingly, 'alphas' cover only a small part of the sample (82 from the overall 411 individuals; that is to say, 20 per cent are deemed to be 'alphas'). It is relevant to notice that the 'alphas' performed the IGT task better than the 'non-alphas', preferring advantageous (not risky) decks. They are distributed between males and females with the same percentage of the overall sample; there is no distinction to be made regarding financial knowledge (half of the 'alphas' declare a high level of financial of education, half the opposite). No link with age, profession or other socio-economical variables is proved either. Alphas appear randomly distributed in our sample. This allows us to conclude that most of the individual time series estimations appear to be based on an information set inferior to the panel estimation, confirming that our methodology in computing UR is the most effective. Nonetheless, the sub-sample of 'alphas' is used as a robustness check in order to control and ascertain as to whether some relevant relationships (correlations among risk indicators, multivariate analysis) change when considering the different typologies of individuals.

7.4 The biased risk indicator (BR)

As far as BR is concerned, the measure was obtained from the global score (S) and from the Grable and Lytton test (GLT) in which each subject i participated (Grable and Lytton, 1999). We evaluated the possibility of customising the GLT, but the final choice was to keep the original version of the questionnaire, in order make a comparison of our results with their previous findings possible. Specifically, we find it convenient to exploit the mean, minimum and maximum score of the GLT in order to set the extreme values of our biased risk indicator. Grable and Lytton (1999) tested their questionnaire on more than 600 individuals, and from the test results they set a score of 37 for the mean, 20 for the minimum and 63 for the maximum values. In our empirical distribution the average score was 44, the minimum 27 and the maximum 58. Our sample appears to be mainly based on people with a higher risk tolerance (self-declared) than those studied by Grable and Lytton (1999), mainly because we included individuals with different levels of financial competencies (normal clients together with asset managers and traders).

To set BR within the 0–1 range (0 signalling the highest aversion and 1 indicating the highest propensity) we have to apply this formula for each subject i:

$$BR_i = \frac{(S_i - S_{min})}{(S_{max} - S_{min})} \tag{7.3}$$

where:
S_i is the score obtained by the subject i in the GLT;
S_{max} is the maximum score obtained by GLT (63);
S_{min} is the minum score obtained by GLT (20).

7.5 The real life risk indicator (RLR)

The construction of the real life risk indicator should be strictly coherent with a risk tolerance meaning. This implies a full understanding of the investor's circumstances (risk capacity) and risk preferences (attitude towards risk) (Yook and Everett, 2003). For example the RiskPACK approach (Cordell, 2002) asserts that an analysis of the client risk tolerance involves an evaluation of four risk concepts: propensity, attitude, capacity and knowledge. Nevertheless, the author proposes that from a planner's perspective, we should set aside risk propensity and risk knowledge, and analyse risk tolerance in two dimensions only: risk attitude and risk capacity. Moreover we can dispense with risk propensity because it is essentially encompassed by these two factors (Cordell, 2002).

Given the wide range of information we obtained in regard to the real life risk behaviour of individuals, from section 3 of our questionnaire (see Appendix 1), we can obtain both a precise computation of the real life risk tolerance indicator (RLT) and an interesting set of control variables (gender, education, financial knowledge, profession).

The coherence with the theoretical fundamentals of risk tolerance causes us to assume that RLR is a function of the real life risk attitude (the risk the individual chooses to assume – RLA) and of the real life risk capacity (the risk the individual can afford to hold – RLC).

$$\mathrm{RLR} = f(RLA, RLC) \tag{7.4}$$

For the purpose of this study the nature of function *f*, seen above in equation (7.4), is not relevant and thus the two drivers of RLR will be kept separate.

7.5.1 The real life attitude indicator (RLA)

Each component of RLR has a precise computation. The RLA corresponds to the average score obtained by each individual in relation to seven items of our questionnaire, in section 3. The RLA drivers were: 1) the risk weighed asset allocation of his or her investments (rla_1); 2) if he/she ever invested a considerable amount of money only for the thrill (rla_2); 3) the level of risk of past investment decisions (rla_3); 4) the level of risk of present investment decisions (rla_4); 5) the highest level of tolerated financial losses (rla_5); 6) the degree of insurance coverage (rla_6); 7) the actions undertaken after the 2008 crisis (rla_7).

The entire set of drivers (seven) for RLA enables us to compute the overall indicator for each subject *i*:

$$RLA_i = \sum_{d=1}^{7} \frac{rla_{d,i}}{7} \tag{7.5}$$

The first driver for the computation of RLA (rla1) arises from the risk weighed asset allocation of his or her investments. Question 18 of section 3 of the questionnaire asked for the percentage of the personal global portfolio invested in a list of asset classes (see Table 7.2). A weight

Table 7.2 The real life asset allocation of individuals

Code	Asset class	Weight for the asset class risk
Ac_1	Current account	0
Ac_2	Bank deposit, Certificate of deposit, Repo contract	0.05
Ac_3	Postal deposit	0.05
Ac_4	Treasury bills and bonds	0.25
Ac_5	Financial management, Mutual funds and ETF shares	0.5
Ac_6	Stocks	0.75
Ac_7	Foreign financial products	0.75
Ac_8	Structured products and derivatives	1
Ac_9	Hedge funds	1
Ac_{10}	Financial insurance policies	0.4

for the relative likely risk is associated to each asset class (w_c). This weight evolves from the subjective judgement of the authors, but it is grounded in both the empirical evidence of financial markets and by asset class risk scoring used for MIFID purposes.[2] The score used to weight the associated risk goes from 0 (the current account is considered the risk free asset) to 1 (structured products, derivatives and hedge funds are considered the most risky asset classes).

The overall rla_1 indicator is obtained as follows:

$$rla_1 = \sum_{ac=1}^{10} \frac{p_{ac} * w_{ac}}{10} \tag{7.6}$$

where:

p_c is the percentage the subject invested in the asset class *ac*;
w_c is the weight for risk associated to the asset class *c* from Table 7.2;

The normalisation of the weights for risk (w_{ac}) allowed us to obtain the rla_1 component moving within a 0–1 range.

The further four determinants for the RLA indicators are derived from the scores we assigned to the answers provided by individuals to questions 20 to 23 in section 3 of our questionnaire, as shown by Table 7.3.

The sixth RLA component, shown in Table 7.4, is obtained considering the insurance coverage of the subject as revealed by question

Table 7.3 Scores for drivers of RLA

Question	Items	Scores	Driver
20) Have you ever invested a huge amount of money in a risky asset just to feel the thrilling sensation of knowing its return?	1. No	0	rla_2
	2. Rarely	0.5	
	3. Yes	1	
21) What level of risk did you bear in the past when taking financial decisions?	1. I never took financial decisions	0	rla_3
	2. Very low	0.20	
	3. Low	0.40	
	4. Medium	0.60	
	5. High	0.80	
	6. Very High	1	
22) What level of risk are you now willing to bear when taking financial decisions?	1. I never take financial decisions	0	rla_4
	2. Very low	0.20	
	3. Low	0.40	
	4. Medium	0.60	
	5. High	0.80	
	6. Very High	1	
23) What is the maximum financial loss you bore in the past before deciding to withdraw your investments?	1. I never bore financial losses	0	rla_5
	2. Very little	0.25	
	3. Up to 1/4	0.50	
	4. Half	1	
	5. More than half	1	
	6. I kept the investment even if it was in a loss	1	

Table 7.4 Score for drivers of insurance behaviours

Code	Insurance coverage combination	Weight for the insurance combination risk (*rla_6*)
Ic_1	All of the five alternatives (four alternatives plus pension fund)	0
Ic_2	A four alternatives combination	0.20
Ic_3	A three alternatives combination	0.40
Ic_4	A two alternatives combination	0.60
Ic_5	The subject holds only one among the five alternatives	0.80
Ic_6	The subject has no insurance coverage	1

24. We asked which insurance contracts were held, apart from car accident policies which are obligatory in Italy, among: life insurance (death, index/unit linked), disease or disability insurance, burglary and fire insurance and civil liability insurance (four different insurance alternatives, in multiple choice). We included also the pension fund alternative, as well as the possibility of not holding any insurance coverage. Even if the pension fund may not be considered an insurance contract in the proper meaning, we are convinced that those willing to underwrite a pension fund in the Italian financial environment[3] exhibit a point of view which could be considered to be akin to risk aversion. We assigned a weight to each level of real life risk attitude acquired from the declared insurance coverage combination (*ic* from 1 to 6, shown in Table 7.4). We set a 0–1 range for these weights; 0 for the lowest and 1 for the highest risk tolerance revealed by the insurance behaviour of the subject. This weight is the value of rla_6 for each subject.

The major rule followed in the assignment of this weight was first to set which insurance behaviour corresponded to the extremes. We thought it reasonable to consider the most risk averse subject as being (rla_6 =0) one who holds the whole set of insurance contracts we proposed (four alternatives plus a pension fund). On the contrary, we assumed the subjects least afraid of risk to be those who do not hold any insurance coverage (rla_6 =1). Then, considering the lack of further details available for each insurance coverage, we assigned a progressively higher value to rla_6 in relation to how many insurances the subject declared to hold (lower contracts, higher value). We are aware that this specific driver for risk attitude may be strongly influenced by the risk capacity of each individual: it is reasonable to assume that the preference to widen the insurance coverage may be due to the increase of one's wealth. The real life risk capacity indicator (RLC) is calculated to control and address for such a situation as this.

The last driver of RLA (rla_7) refers to the behaviour shown in reaction to the 2008 financial markets (Question 25: How did you react financially to the recent financial crisis?). The subject had multiple choice among the alternatives, namely: buying undervalued stocks; selling part of his or her financial assets; selling the majority of his or her financial assets; doing nothing. The combination of the multiple choice is particularly relevant, because naturally the risk attitude of a subject is completely different when he or she only sold the assets, on the one hand, from when he or she sold the asset together

Table 7.5 Score for behaviours after the sub-prime crisis

Combination of answers	rla_7
Selling the majority of financial assets	0
Selling part of financial assets	0.20
Doing nothing	0.50
Buying undervalued stocks	0.80
Selling part of financial assets + Buying undervalued stocks	0.90
Selling the majority of financial assets + Buying undervalued stocks	1

with the (we may argue, in order to) buying of undervalued stocks, on the other.

We set the extremes of rla_7 giving the lowest level of risk attitude (rla_6 =0) to those answering that they have sold the main part of their investment; the highest level of risk attitude is given to those who sold the majority of their financial assets and then bought undervalued stocks (rla_6 =1). Those who did nothing are considered neither risk lovers nor risk averters. The other behaviours were scored according to the values of tr_7 shown by Table 7.5.

7.5.2 The real life capacity indicator (RLC)

In addition, the real life capacity indicator (RLC) corresponds to the average score obtained by each individual in relation to a series of items in our questionnaire, in section 3. The RLC drivers were: 1) the relevance of familiar weight (rlc_1); 2) the nature of the professional contract (rlc_2); 3) the composition of family income (degree of diversification) (rlc_3); 4) the monthly income of the family (rlc_4); 5) the real estate wealth (rlc_5 and rlc_6); 6) the financial wealth (rlc_7); 7) the economic stress due to debt repayment (rlc_8). The main rule adhered to in setting the RLC drivers was to establish each indicator within the 0–1 range, giving a value of 0 to the situation revealing the lowest capacity and a value of 1 to the situation indicating the highest capacity.

The whole set of all of the (eight) drivers for RLC, shown in Table 7.6, allows us to compute the overall indicator for each subject i :

$$RLC_i = \sum_{d=1}^{8} \frac{rlc_{di}}{8} \tag{7.7}$$

Table 7.6 Score for the drivers of RLC

Question	Items	Scores	Driver
5) People belonging to your family that are dependent on you (multiple choice):	Given the three options for familiar weight (Wife/Husband; Children; Elderly), we assign the highest capacity (1) to those having nobody and a progressively lower level to the others, up to the 0 for those having all the three typologies). 1. All of the 3 typologies 2. 2 of the 3 typologies 3. 1 of the 3 typologies 4. Nobody	0 0.33 0.66 1	rlc_1
8) Type of working contract:	1. Open-ended 2. Fixed term 3. Other	0 1 0	rlc_2
9) Composition of family income: (multiple choice)	Given the six options (Work income; Retirement income; Real estate income; Financial income; Financial support from parents; Other) the situation with more diversification obtains the level of having four types of income. So we set 1 for this highest diversification, 0 for only one source of income and finally proportional scores therein for the other combinations. 1. One source of income 2. 2 sources of income 3. 3 sources of income 4. 4 sources of income	0 0.33 0.66 1	rlc_3
10) Total amount of family income (monthly net income)	1. < 500 euros 2. between 500 and 1,000 euros 3. between 1,000 and 2,000 euros 4. between 2,000 and 3,000 euros 5. between 3,000 and 4,000 euros 6. between 4,000 and 5,000 euros 7. between 5,000 and 6,000 euros 8. more than 6,000 euros	0 0.14 0.28 0.42 0.56 0.70 0.85 1	rlc_4
14) Number of real estate properties	1. 0 2. 1 3. 2 4. 3 5. more than 3	0 0.25 0.50 0.75 1	rlc_5

Continued

Table 7.6 Continued

Question	Items	Scores	Driver
15) What is the global estimated value of your real estate properties?	1. I do not have any real estate property 2. less than 200,000 euros 3. between 200,000 and 500,000 euros 4. between 500,000 and 1,000,000 euros 5. more than 1,000,000 euros	0 0.10 0.35 0.75 1	rlc_6
16) What is the global estimated value of your financial properties?	1. I do not have any financial property 2. below 50,000 euros 3. between 50,000 and 100,000 euros 4. between 100,000 and 200,000 euros 5. between 200,000 and 500,000 euros 6. beyond 500,000 euros	0 0.10 0.15 0.30 0.70 1	rlc_7
27) Amount of the global monthly instalment for all the debts you are paying at the moment:	Given the alternatives (in absolute values) offered for the answer to this question, we compute this indicator as a 1 minus the ratio between the midpoint of the monthly payments due for debts and the midpoint of total amount of family income declared by the subject in question 10. The range of this ratio goes from 0, for people absorbing (theoretically) the whole monthly income to repay debts, to 1, for people holding to debt (and relative monthly charge)		rlc_8

We specify that the scores assigned to each indicator increase proportionally (for rlc_1, rlc_3, rlc_5) when the alternatives show a regular growth of capability (for example from 0 to 1; from 1 to 2; from 2 to 3, and so on). On the contrary, the scores increase progressively (for rlc_4, rlc_6, rlc_7) because the items show a different degree of scale.

As a robustness check, we also ran a principal component analysis to deal with the high number of drivers; this applies to both the RLA and the RLC. Nevertheless, results show that the resulting components where not effective to contribute in explaining, shortly and precisely, the real life attitude and capacity. Therefore we use the average function of (7.6) and (7.7).

7.6 Correlations among BR, UR and RLR indicators

The summary statistics for our indicators of risk are shown in Table 7.7 as far as the overall sample of 441 individuals is concerned. The unbiased risk indicator (UR) shows the highest average value, among the others, with the highest standard deviation as well. For the UR, the minimum and maximum values are slightly below and above 0 and 1 respectively, because we considered *estimated* values of a binomial choice 0 or 1. On the contrary, the lowest average level is shown in relation to the real life risk attitude (with the lowest standard deviation also): individuals seem to assume risk at a level even lower than their relative risk capacity. The overall sample shows that people tend to be strongly emotionally attracted towards risk, with an unbiased risk tolerance noticeably higher than the levels of risk they assume in real life. Additionally the biased risk (the self-evaluated risk tolerance) is higher, on average, than the financial riskiness held in real life, but a level slightly lower than the emotionally driven unbiased risk.

Figure 7.1 shows the main relationship among our risk tolerance indicators, for all of the 441 individuals in the sample, while Figure 7.2 presents a sub-sample that is restricted to the 'alphas' only (82 individuals).

The analysis of the relationships between the risk indicators, two by two, informs us that when considering the whole sample (441 individuals) the biased risk is positively correlated with the real life risk, both as far as attitude (Figure 7.1c) and capacity (Figure 7.1d) are concerned. That is to say, the higher the risk attraction one has, the riskier

Table 7.7 Summary statistics for risk tolerance drivers

Variable	Mean	Std dev.	Min	Max
br	0.562	0.138	0.163	0.884
ur	0.580	0.458	–0.036	1.015
rla	0.495	0.151	0.129	0.886
rlc	0.521	0.137	0.204	1.000

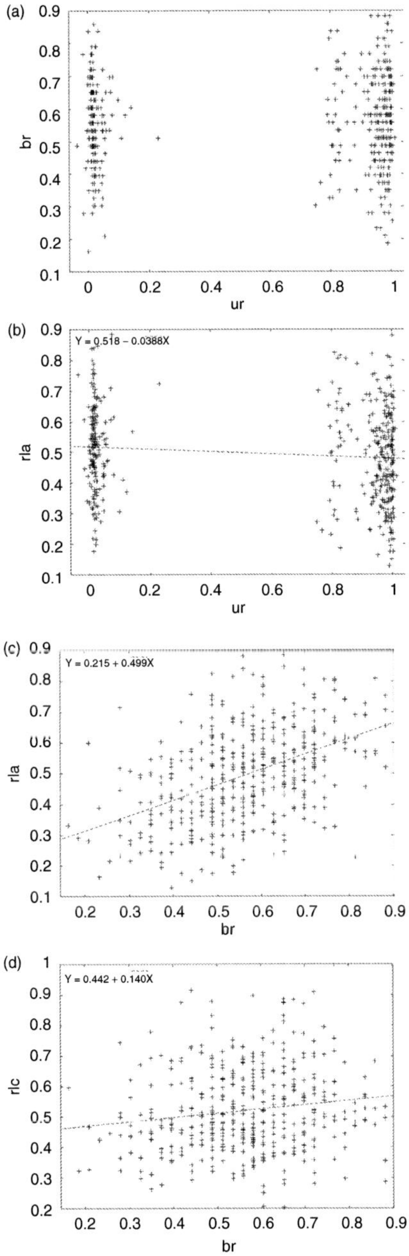

Figure 7.1 Relationships between risk tolerance indicators (overall sample)

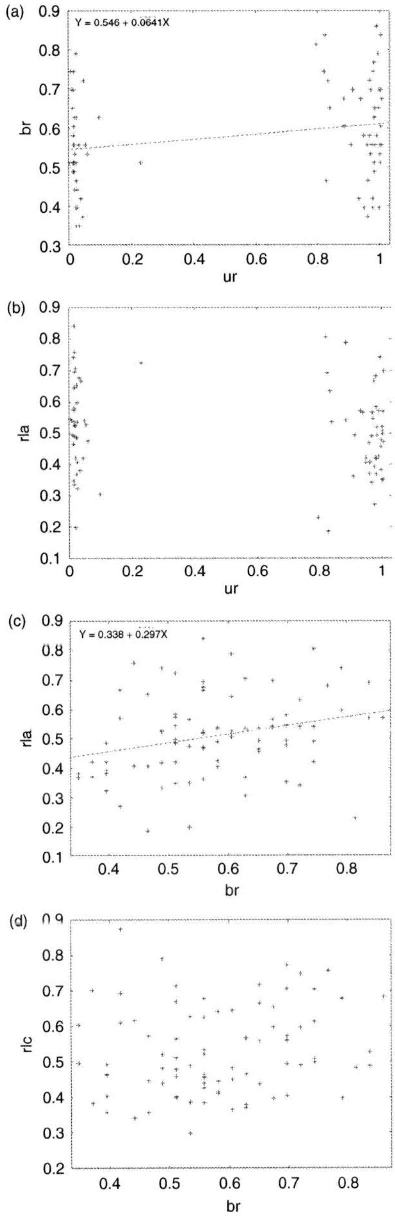

Figure 7.2 Relationships between risk tolerance indicators (sub-samples of 'alphas')

one's investment/debt choices will be. What is more, the higher an individual's economic capability is, the higher the self-evaluation of their risk attraction will be. Surprisingly, the unbiased risk is negatively correlated with the real life attitude (consider Figure 7.1b). This should mean that people showing a low real life risk attitude (low RLA) experienced a strong unbiased attraction towards risk (high UR). This point is crucial and will be duly developed in Chapter 8.

This preliminary evidence could testify to something anomalous in the behaviour of individuals from to our sample, when running the IGT test, and when testing the basis of the UR computation. We might think that a moral hazard behaviour could have taken place to some extent or another. Those less willing to take risks in real life assume high levels of risk during the experiments. Nevertheless, when selecting only the 'alphas' who supposedly rely upon a 'theoretically normal decision making system' when making choices, we find no linear correlation between UR and RLA (see Figure 7.2b). Moreover, in the 'alpha' sub-sample another relationship is of importance: the positive correlation between BR and UR (Figure 7.2a). This should testify to the fact that the higher the self-evaluation of risk attraction (BR) is, the higher the unbiased attraction towards risk (UR) will be; nevertheless, UR continues not having significant relationship with the real life risk attitude (Figure 7.1c). Keeping in mind that 'alphas' are randomly distributed in our sample, it will be relevant to look for the socio-demographical and cultural reasons which could explain such kinds of differences in relation to both the levels of risk tolerance indicators and also regarding the main relationships between the major factors involved. An important impact of these findings is that they induce us to think that the best perspective to employ in our analysis should be one that is founded in a multivariate frame.

Notes

Palomba is the author of Section 7.2 and Lucarelli of the remaining sections.

1. We skip the presentation of the tables, because they would take several pages. They are available upon request.
2. See Chapter 3.
3. In Italy pension funds are not compulsory. Even when a pension plan is working for a specific sector/industry according to an agreement between social parties, each subject is free to decide whether to participate to the plan or not (in the former case, some rules for contributions are provided). Art. 1, comma 2, Dlgs. n.252/ 2005.

8
Results on the Investment Side

Caterina Lucarelli

8.1 Risk indicators and explanatory variables

One of the most valuable goals of our research is to understand whether we act financially as we are or as we are supposed to be. We aim to find some coherence, if any, among our real life financial choices, our biased risk tolerance (the one we declare both to ourselves and to others) and the risk attraction we emotionally and somatically possess.

The last section of Chapter 7 shows that the real life risk attitude (RLA), for the overall sample, is positively related with the biased risk (BR) and, surprisingly, negatively related with the unbiased risk (UR). People in real life on average assume decisions at a level of risk much lower than the one they emotionally would prefer. Moreover, their unbiased attraction towards risk is generally even higher than the level indicated via the self-evaluation process (see Figure 8.1).

We might suggest that a strong component of unconscious and unaware risk attraction is proven to exist in the sample of individuals we observed. Again, one might think that a moral hazard type behaviour could have driven the actions of our subjects during the IGT/SCR experiment. Nevertheless, restricting the sample to those subjects whose behaviour is proven to be more coherent with a gambler attitude (the 'alphas'), we found that these individuals were not the ones who have exhibited the higher levels of UR. In other words, in our sample we have many subjects revealing a strong risk attraction without any psycho-physiological signal of being gamblers. In this work, when the unbiased risk (UR) is much higher than the risk assumed in real life (RLA) but, at the same time, higher than the self-evaluation (BR), we suggest the presence of an 'unconscious sleeping factor'.

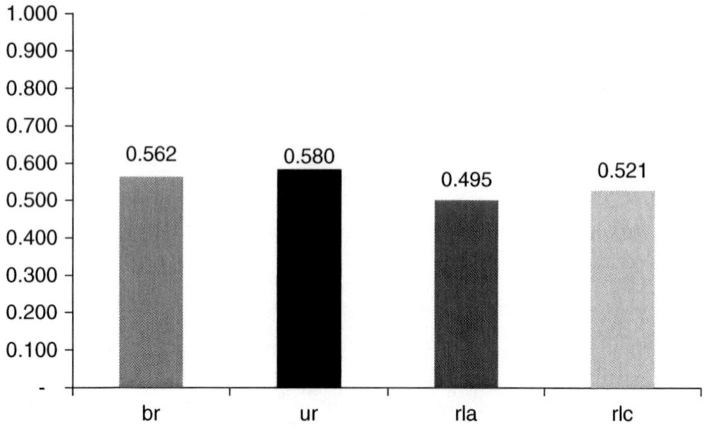

Figure 8.1 The average values for risk indicators: overall sample

That is why it is even more interesting to unearth some important characteristics of our sample, in order to understand when the coherence among indicators is proven to exist or not (how we *are* or, even better, at which level of phase synchrony the neural populations that guide our choices oscillate (UR); how we *think we are*, or better which representation we have of ourselves (BR); and how we *act* (RLA), given our restrictions, RLC). Specifically, we want to understand whether our biased self-representation, on the one hand, or our unbiased emotional risk attraction, on the other hand, *differently* affect our real life attitude in relation to a set of socio-demographical and cultural variables.

Section 3 of our questionnaire has been largely used to provide information essential to compute both the real life attitude and real life capacity indicators. Many further questions have also been included to deal with this part of the analysis. Specifically, we consider five main sets of variables relevant to explaining differences in both the levels and relationships of our risk tolerance indicators. We included information related to: a) the socio-demographical conditions (age, residence, gender and marital status); b) the knowledge of individuals (educational qualification, knowledge of financial products, profession); c) the information generally used to take financial decisions (economic/financial magazines, degree of information for past financial results, degree of information for debt evolution); d) the organisation of the decision process (how frequently decisions are taken, updated and with whom they are shared); e) some proxy of conditions of vulnerability and trust (income forecasts, occurrence of odds, self-trust and trust in the future).

It is relevant to point out that the two risk tolerance dimensions (UR and BR) strictly belong to a *personal inside* perspective and that the horizon of this perspective is made up of three dimensions: rational capacities, emotional experiences, and a third dimension constituted by the daydreaming or wandering minds that accompany every moment of our lives and are uniquely referred to each individual (we call it the restless mind). On the contrary, RLA and RLC refer to the overall family unit to which the subject belongs. RLA and RLC are, in non-clinical subjects, the constraints of reality. We are aware that in real life the level of risk assumed (for example, the asset allocation or the insurance coverage) is the result of an overall decision process in which the whole capacity of the family is considered and the personal inside perspective of each subject is balanced with a set of internal and external strengths (knowledge, information, organisation of decision process, role of financial advisers, and so on). That is why a proper study of any relationship among UR, BR, RLA and RLC would require a multivariate statistical approach.

Nevertheless, being aware of limitations of the following univariate analysis, we provide evidence of average values of risk tolerance indicators grouped by some relevant internal and external variables presumably affecting the financial behaviour of individuals. In fact, some of these basic statistics appear particularly effective in explaining the unexpected levels of risk attraction.

8.2 The socio-demographic drivers

Before any further considerations, we have to keep in mind that our sample was built with the aim of selecting people who take financial decisions. The bank (Banca Popolare di Ancona, UBI Group), the investment company (Twice SIM) and the asset managers who took part in the empirical process were kindly asked to select randomly a list of individuals (customers or personnel of the bank, traders and asset managers) from which we collected the 445 subjects observed during the analysis. The condition of involving in the analysis people taking real financial decisions (either for familial or for professional duties) influences the socio-demographic features of our sample. For example, only 11.2 per cent of the sample is under 30 years of age because, especially in Italy, young people tend to delay acquiring economic and financial independence. At the same time, the need to analyse financial professions (traders and asset managers), typically between 30 and 60 years old, reduced the 10.3 per cent over-60s subgroup component. Nevertheless, our numbers are wide enough, in absolute value, to allow reliable deductions for all the age clustering showed in Figure 8.2 (50 individuals are under 30 years old, and 46 are over 60 years old).

The title given to Figure 8.2 is honestly quite provocative because it is reminiscent of the lifecycle hypothesis formulated originally in the early 1950s by Franco Modigliani and his student Richard Brumberg (Modigliani and Brumberg, 1954). At this time they developed a theory of spending, which later became a theory of saving (Modigliani, 1975, 1976, 1998), based on the idea that people tailor their consumption and saving patterns at different ages. The variable which conceptually is closer to the Modigliani idea of saving is the RLC indicator, which behaves across the ages coherently with the lifecycle hypothesis. Savings and overall risk capacity are low when people are young, then gradually increase reaching the highest level for the last age cluster in working activity (between 45 and 60), then decrease during the retirement stage. The risky choices assumed in real life (RLA) replicate consistently the trend of the capacity (RLC): the risk attitude is low for young people, then increases to the top for the first cluster of ages in working activity (between 30 and 45), then gradually decreases for the older age groups.

Figure 8.2 contributes to the existing literature on the long-life trend of the biased and unbiased risk tolerance. It is interesting to notice that

	Freq.	Percent
under_30	50	11.2
between_30_45	237	53.3
between_45_60	112	25.2
over_60	46	10.3
Total	**445**	**100.0**

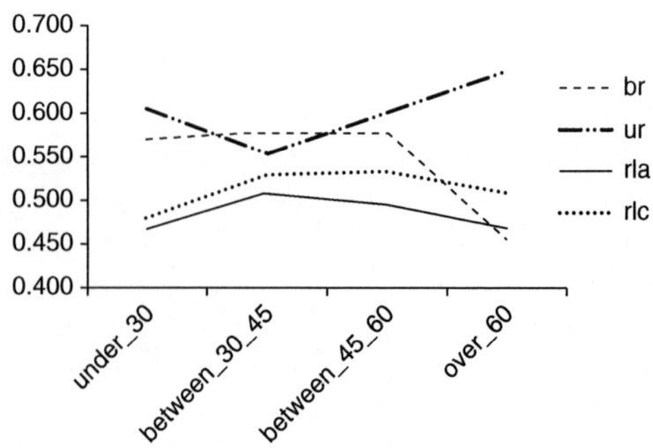

Figure 8.2 The long lifecycle of risk tolerance

the levels of the risk self-evaluation (BR) are mainly the same for the first three clusters of ages (with a small increase visible in the 30–45 cluster). Then, for those people over 60 years of age, BR sharply decreases. Self-confidence, which is perhaps one of the most relevant components of biased risk, typically decreases at the end of the normal working activity lifecycle and the onset of retirement tends to induce older individuals to often assume the risk averter role. This is certainly true both in relation to BR, and, albeit to a lesser degree, to RLA; however getting old cannot take away the fantasy of profits, of the lucky investment, or of the dreamed hope. In psychological terms, the true sign of ageing is in the reduction or loss of daydreaming.

Surprisingly, the UR indicator reveals a trend which is completely different: it shows high levels in the under-30 cluster (it is not strange to think that young people may emotionally love risk); it reaches the lowest level when the real life risk attitude is highest (the the 30–45 cluster); then, unpredictably it increases regularly and sharply, arriving at the top level for people over 60 years old. It seems to be that people within the most economically active working age groups appear more secure and less emotionally attracted towards risk, while people in retirement especially appear more risk seeking in their behaviour. Indeed, their physiologically recorded love for risk appears primarily in the autonomic nervous system activation caused by the parallel process of the fantasy of winning. In real life, retired people are able to wisely recognise the interests of a prudent behaviour. So the low level of BR for over-60s allows us to deduce that their unbiased risk attraction is strongly unconscious. This class of age seemed to be most exposed to the unconscious sleeping factor.

The residence of individuals involved in our sample is influenced by the location of the financial intermediaries involved in the analysis. For example, in Italy asset managers are mainly located in Milan, as well as the Borsa Italiana spa (the Italian Stock Exchange) where many traders have been observed. So, almost 50 per cent of the sample declared that they have a residence in the northern part of Italy, more than 45 per cent declared to be in the centre and only a small percentage was observed in the south. We created a dummy variable *metropol*, which is set at 1 if the individual lives in a city belonging to a province which is known as a metropolitan area (for example Milan or Rome) and 0 in the opposite case. According to this new variable, almost 32 per cent of the sample lives in a metropolitan area, while the residual 68 per cent do not. Some correlation tests[1] induced us to use the *metropol* variable in the multivariate analysis, instead of the precise location of the individuals.

Examining the gender variable provides further interesting evidence. Again, the sampling criteria, which involved obtaining people who are in charge of financial decisions, is the main reason why we have only 21.8 per cent of females under analysis (in any case there are 97 females in the sample, which is enough to deduce the gender effect). In fact, the bank that provided the sub-sample of its customers indicated that the sample was made up of people who generally have the final responsibility of financial choices. An important Italian sociological condition is that generally males are in charge of these financial choices, within the family unit. Moreover, some financial jobs, such as that of trader, are typically occupied more by males than females. To evidence this statement, we can see that in our sample only two of the 49 traders are indeed females.

The histograms of Figure 8.3 reveal an interesting gender effect for risk tolerance. Ordinarily within the existing literature (for example, Hallahan et al., 2003), it has been observed that the BR level is higher for males than for females: males tend to be much more self-confident than females. In some cases, male over-confidence is also proven to exist (Barber and Odean, 2001). The female risk aversion is confirmed most strongly in regard to RLA: females tend to assume real life decisions at a level of risk much lower than males. The 0.426 score is the lowest RLA value ever obtained for any of our sub-samples. This is true even if we have to consider that the female capacity is clearly lower than that of the males in our sample.

	Freq.	Percent
Male	348	78.2
Female	97	21.8
Total	**445**	**100.0**

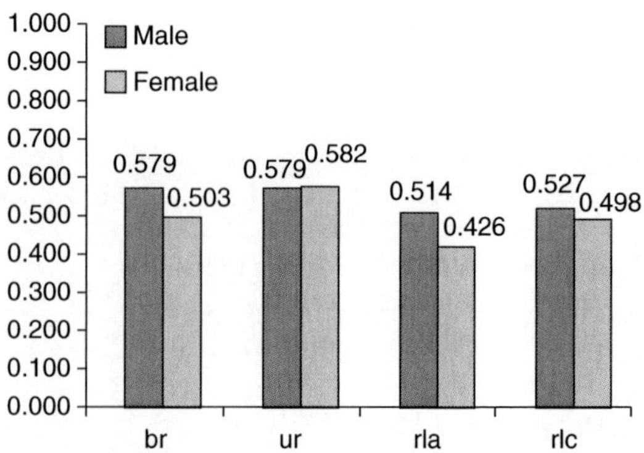

Figure 8.3 The gender features

Surprisingly, if females evaluate themselves as being risk averse and taking very cautious financial decisions, their emotional risk attraction is slightly higher than that of males (the female UR is 0.582 while the male UR is 0.579). Tables 8.1 and 8.2 provide evidence that while the BR levels are significantly different between male and females, the UR ones are not.

This would appear to be in contrast with the previous findings of Bolla et al. (2004), who proved that men show better task performance at the IGT, and that the brain mechanisms engaged by men and women when solving the same decision making task are different.

Marital status is considered to give evidence of any change in risk tolerance due to the presence/absence of familial linkages. Precisely, 30.9

Table 8.1 Significance of gender differences (BR)

Two-sample t test with equal variances

Group	Obs	Mean	Std. Err.	Std. Dev.	[95% Conf. Interval]	
0	345	0.5787664	0.0071781	0.133327	0.564648	0.5928849
1	96	0.502907	0.014288	0.1399931	0.4745417	0.5312722
combined	441	0.5622528	0.006583	0.1382437	0.5493147	0.5751909
diff		0.0758595	0.0155545		0.0452889	0.10643

diff = mean(0) – mean(1) t = 4.8770
Ho: diff = 0 degrees of freedom = 439
Ha: diff < 0 Ha: diff != 0 Ha: diff > 0
Pr(T < t) = 1.0000 Pr(|T| > |t|) = 0.0000 Pr(T > t) = 0.0000

Table 8.2 Significance of gender differences (UR)

Two-sample t test with equal variances

Group	Obs	Mean	Std. Err.	Std. Dev.	[95% Conf. Interval]	
0	345	0.578903	0.0246428	0.4577203	0.5304334	0.6273726
1	96	0.5821159	0.0470373	0.4608691	0.4887352	0.6754967
combined	441	0.5796024	0.021804	0.4578843	0.5367495	0.6224554
diff		−0.0032129	0.0528959		−0.1071736	0.1007478

diff = mean(0) – mean(1) t = −0.0607
Ho: diff = 0 degrees of freedom = 439
Ha: diff < 0 Ha: diff != 0 Ha: diff > 0
Pr(T < t) = 0.4758 Pr(|T| > |t|) = 0.9516 Pr(T > t) = 0.5242

Table 8.3 Marital status

	Freq.	%
Single	139	30.9
w_Family*	275	61.1
nw_Family**	36	8.0
Total	**450*** **	**100.0**

* Married and common law wife/husband.
** Divorced or widowed.
*** Multiple choices.

	br	ur	rla	rlc
Single	0.591	0.564	0.516	0.513
w_Family	0.546	0.572	0.483	0.520
nw_Family	0.583	0.698	0.495	0.552

per cent of our sample is made up of *singles*, 61.1 per cent of people have a family (*w_family*, either married or common law) and the residual 8 per cent represents people without family (*nw_family*), because they are either divorced or widowed. Note that multiple choices were allowed here because one could be, for example, both divorced and living with another new family (see Table 8.3).

It is relevant to note that singles show the highest level of BR, while the lowest BR is seen for people with family; the same ranking is revealed as far as RLA is concerned. The light grey shading is to evidence the lowest recorded value; the dark grey for the highest value. We might think that singles, even though they possess the lowest capability (lowest RLC), may develop a high self-evaluation of risk tolerance (BR) with corresponding high financial risk choices in real life (RLA), even if their emotional risk attraction is not noticeably relevant (lowest UR). On the contrary, divorced or widowed people, even if they show a good capacity, reveal the highest level of UR ever obtained in any of the sub-samples. We might say that this personal condition, combined with ageing, gives rise to a considerable increase in the emotional risk attraction (UR), which is frequently inconsistent with self-evaluation and the financial choices taken in real life (what we called the unconscious sleeping risk factor).

If this last point is particularly crucial in this univariate framework, the three variables of marital status (*single*, *w_family* and *nw_family*) should be strongly correlated with the age variable (negatively regarding the single variable, and positively with the other two); so we use only the latter in the multivariate analysis.

8.3 Knowledge

The second set of variables which could explain the different levels of risk tolerance shown in our sample relates to the varying degree of knowledge each subject possesses. Knowledge is obviously a significant internal feature which influences the behaviour of individuals. In particular, considering our focus on financial risk, we are interested in understanding the role of financial knowledge specifically, both in terms of knowledge of financial instruments *strictu sensu*, and in terms of financial competences. The latter will be linked to the professions declared by the individuals.

The first basic question we addressed to subjects under analysis was the highest educational qualification they hold: only 5.2 per cent have a secondary school qualification, 39.5 per cent possess the high school qualification, 42.2 per cent have achieved a university degree and 13 per cent hold a Master's degree or a PhD. Given our interest in financial risk, we then asked the subjects in regard to their knowledge of a set of financial instruments, items generally used in the MiFID questionnaires. More precisely, we asked them to mark, within a multiple choice scheme, which of the following financial products the subject was confident with: bank account, bank deposit, certificate of deposit, repo contract, postal deposit, treasury bills, stocks, bonds, mutual funds, financial management, Exchange Traded Fund (ETF), hedge funds, structured products, derivatives, index and unit linked insurance policies. After having evaluated different alternatives, we built up a dummy variable, namely *high_fk*, which is 1 if the individual declared themselves to be confident with at least four of the last five financial instruments (ETF, hedge funds, structured products, derivatives, index and unit linked insurance policies), 0 in the opposite case. We are aware that these criteria may be too sharp because we assign a low financial knowledge to those who are, for example, confident with three, and not four, of those financial products. Nevertheless, understanding of the real financial knowledge of individuals is very difficult and our sample is made up of people who are, on average, very qualified in finance, given the fact that they take financial decisions on a regular basis. So we decided that this incisive condition was the best solution as it could separate those with a noticeably high financial knowledge from the others. In doing so, the results which materialised were acceptable because the *high_fk* variable is equally balanced in our sample. Moreover, *high_fk* is significantly and positively correlated with the higher levels of educational qualification (university degree and Master's or PhD). So, we

	Freq.	Percent
Secondary School	23	5.2
High School	176	39.6
University Degree	188	42.3
Master or Ph. D.	58	13.0
Total	**445**	**100.0**

	Freq.	Percent
Low_fk	235	52.8
High_fk	210	47.2
Total	**445**	**100.0**

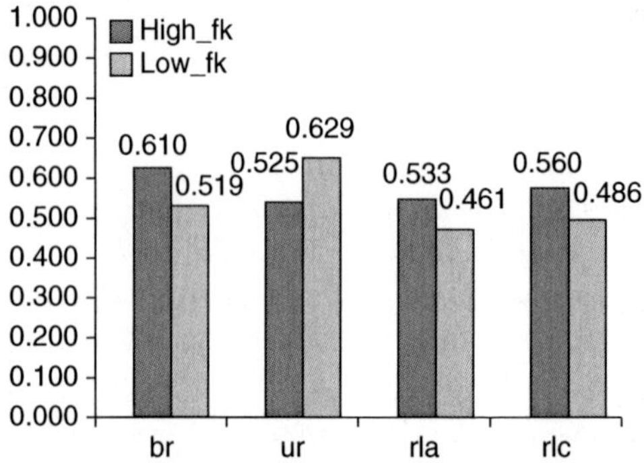

Figure 8.4 Educational qualifications and financial knowledge

simplify the variables used in the multivariate framework, using only *high_fk* for both education and financial knowledge.

The histograms of Figure 8.4 show one of the most pertinent pieces of evidence of our research. Let us keep in mind that for the overall sample (see Figure 8.1), people generally assume a real life risk that is much lower than the one indicated by the psycho-physiological test. It is surprising that when we select people with high financial knowledge, the discrepancy between RLA and UR is minimum and, in any case, positive. If we keep in mind that our sample is almost divided in two very similar sub-samples (47.2 per cent with high financial knowledge and 52.0 per cent without), we can deduce that the difference between UR and RLA is at the minimum for those people (210 units) with high financial knowledge, and it is at the maximum for the others (235 units). This evidence allows us to make two separate deductions. First, no moral hazard behaviour may explain the high levels of UR referring to the overall sample, if a relevant sub-sample reveals a different situation (the real life risk is almost at the same level, or even higher, than the unbiased risk). Secondly, the variable which helps to separate people with more coherent behaviours, on the one hand, and non-consistent behaviours, on the other hand, is particularly crucial and reasonable: the way people feel confident with uncommon or risky financial products (ETFs, hedge funds, derivatives, and so on).

The last component of knowledge that we considered in the analysis relates to the profession declared. We offered several alternatives, as shown in Table 8.4, and allowed multiple choices because we are aware that some people can manage two or three jobs at the same time (sometimes, it is also considered a hobby). For example, the profession of trader is frequently a secondary job, which integrates further personal/family incomes.

It is important to note that results for the biased risk are in line with expectations, where pensioners (coherently with the age effect) are those with the lowest self-evaluated risk tolerance, while asset managers possess the highest BR. Nevertheless, the comparisons of the extreme scores for UR and RLA (highest marked with dark grey; lowest with light grey) show two paradoxes. On the one hand, those showing the highest emotionally driven risk attraction (highest UR: that is for salaried employees, pensioners and freelancers) tend to take the lowest risky decisions in real life (lowest RLA). On the other hand, those with lower emotionally driven risk attraction (lowest UR: that is for traders and asset managers), take the riskiest decisions in real life (highest RLC). Levels of familial, economic and financial restrictions (RLC) are the highest and at the lowest levels for managers and freelancers, respectively, and seem not to be particularly related to RLA.[2]

A further point of interest pertains to the levels of UR within the financial professions. Let us keep in mind (see Chapter 7) that this indicator was carefully obtained observing the behaviour of each

Table 8.4 Professions

	Freq.	%
Salaried employee	139	27.7
Pensioner	49	9.8
Manager	34	6.8
Freelancer	80	15.9
Entrepreneur	41	8.2
Trader	50	10.0
Asset manager	84	16.7
Others	25	5.0
Total	502*	100.0

	br	ur	rla	rlc
Salaried employee	0.533	0.658	0.466	0.513
Pensioner	0.469	0.646	0.466	0.520
Manager	0.588	0.474	0.524	0.673
Freelancer	0.546	0.669	0.472	0.469
Entrepreneur	0.596	0.591	0.490	0.546
Trader	0.596	0.457	0.553	0.507
Asset manager	0.613	0.456	0.547	0.578

* Multiple choices.

individual during a complex experiment allowing us to observe both preferences for risky solutions and the emotional physiological reaction to these choices. Each individual received a score which could move within the 0 to 1 scale. It is quite fascinating to see that for the 50 traders and 84 asset managers, the average score of UR recorded was 0.457, and 0.456 respectively. They are almost at the same levels, while other professional conditions obtained very different average scores (for example salaried and employees hold an average score of 0.658). The two financial professions, as already underlined, showed a homogenous behaviour in assuming the real life risk (high RLA), while they possess different levels of BR and noticeably dissimilar restrictions (RLC). All these considerations encourage us to reason that their specific profession, based on assuming day-by-day financial risk, could represent a training experience that is of help to them in controlling their emotional attraction towards risk (thus reducing their unconscious sleeping factor). These findings are indirectly linked with those of Lo and Repin (2002) who observed significant differences in mean physiological responses among the traders; differences systematically related to the amount of trading experience. Specifically, less experienced traders showed a much higher number of significant mean responses in the number of SCRs. Coherently, Lo et al. (2005) show that one component of successful trading may be a reduced level of emotional reactivity.

This last consideration induces us to simplify the list of professions of Table 8.4, grouping financial professions (*financial_professions*), against

	Freq.	Percent
Not financial prof.	310	70.3
Financial prof.	131	29.7
Total	**445**	**100.0**

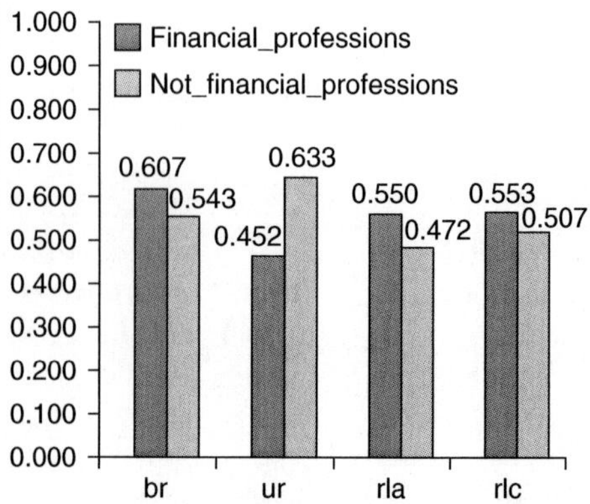

Figure 8.5 Financial professions

the others. Figure 8.5 offers a summary for the levels of risk tolerance indicators comparing these two main groups. The histograms of 8.5 clearly confirm and reinforce the asymmetries of the error (RLA-UR). If this error is negative (UR is higher than RLA), comparing average values for the overall sample, it is widely negative for people without a high financial knowledge and for those not working within financial professions; on the contrary, the error is positive (UR is lower than RLA) for those who have good financial knowledge and who are within financial professions. Obviously, the need of synthetic variables for the multivariate analysis causes us to use only the *financial_professions* dummy which testifies to whether the individual is a trader or an asset manager or not.

8.4 Information used

The following two sections (namely, 'Information used' and 'Decision process') are developed to take into consideration those external strengths which could influence the risks assumed in real life, reducing the role of the personal inside perspective of the biased and unbiased risk tolerance. One can assume more or less financial risk, controlling emotion or personal behaviours, in relation to the information held while taking financial decisions, or also if strongly influenced by others (for example friends or financial advisers).

As far as the information used in the financial decision process is concerned, we asked the frequency of the access to economic and financial newspapers and magazines, the time devoted to collecting information used to take decisions and the frequency of any updating decision. Keeping in mind that our sample is made up of qualified people taking financial decisions, it is not surprising that more than the 60 per cent of the interviewed regularly access economic and financial specialised information (see Figure 8.6). Nevertheless, this percentage corresponds to more than 180 individuals. Considering that those in a financial profession number 131, we have to admit that the people who frequently utilise technical information are mainly, but not only, professionals. To simplify computations, we grouped answers in terms of those people who frequently use financial information (*high_freq_news*, for those reading information several times per day, on the Internet or every day), and the people who are comparatively speaking less informed (*low_freq_news*, if reading information once a week, once a month or never).

	Freq.	Percent
Several times per day	156	35.1
Every day	137	30.8
Once a week	68	15.3
Once a month	36	8.1
Never	48	10.8
Total	**445**	**100.0**

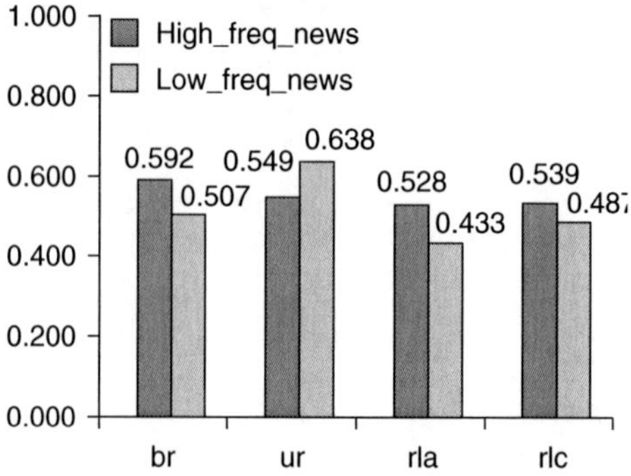

Figure 8.6 Use of financial information

Confirming the previous evidence in regard to financial knowledge and financial professions, less informed people tend to show a UR which is noticeably higher than both the RLA and the BR, revealing the presence of a strong sleeping factor component. Nevertheless, well-informed people, not strictly coinciding with financial professionals or people with high financial knowledge, have an RLA which is lower than UR; however, it is crucial to point out that this difference is quite minuscule (0.528 against 0.549). This may allow us to affirm that people with good financial information, together with holding good financial knowledge, tend to behave in real life very coherently and as they emotionally are (RLA is seen to be almost at the same level as UR).

Then, we asked how much time the interviewed usually spend in obtaining information that is useful to take decisions about investments, debts and mortgages.

Surprisingly, the time dedicated to making a financial decision reveals that individuals in our sample are not very impulsive, even if we include a considerable share of investors specialised in short-term financial operations, as traders are (look at Figure 8.7 for an overall view and at Table 8.5 for precise percentages). In fact, almost 40 per cent of our sample claims to need at least several hours before taking an investment decision, which is almost the same percentage (43.4 per cent) of those admitting requiring several hours to take a decision for a mortgage.

On the contrary, an impulsive behaviour is seen in taking decisions as far as consumer debt is concerned (16.2 per cent of our sample declares to make a debt decision in less than 5 minutes). This point is crucial and will be focused on in Chapter 9.

Table 8.5 Time to take financial decisions

	Investments		**Debts**		**Mortgage**	
	Freq.	**%**	**Freq.**	**%**	**Freq.**	**%**
Less than 5 minutes	32	7.2	72	16.2	20	4.5
About 15 minutes	40	9.0	34	7.6	11	2.5
About 30 minutes	53	11.9	31	7.0	33	7.4
About 1 hour	59	13.3	29	6.5	30	6.7
A few hours	71	16.0	35	7.9	50	11.2
Several hours	175	39.3	77	17.3	193	43.4
I do not take any decision	15	3.4	167	37.5	108	24.3
Total	**445**	**100.0**	**445**	**100.0**	**445**	**100.0**

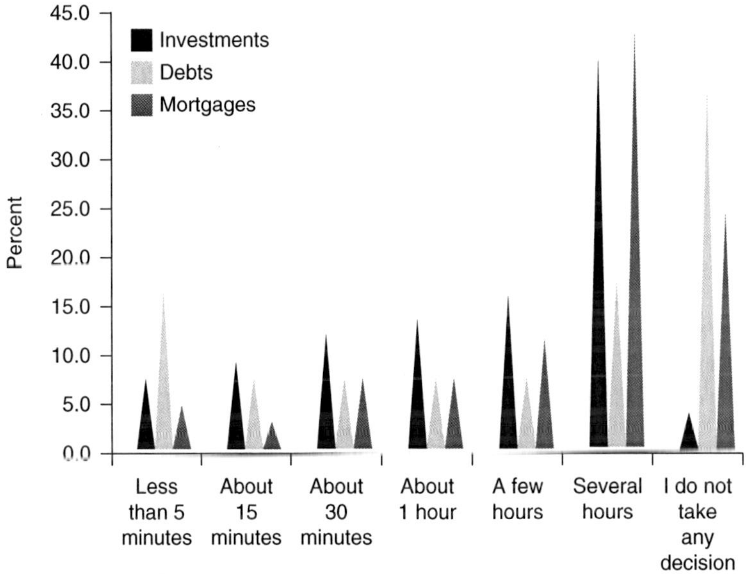

Figure 8.7 Time to take financial decisions (at a glance)

In order to reach a synthetic view of the risk tolerance behaviour in relation to the time addressed to take financial decisions, we created the following synthetic variables: *i_quick*, *d_quick* and *m_quick*. These are dummies which assume a value of 1 if the decision is taken in less than

30 minutes, for investments, debts and mortgages, respectively. The short time taken for a consumer debt decision is significantly and positively correlated with the Barrat Impulsivity Scale (BIS) variable (we use the latter in the multivariate framework), while this correlation is not proven for investment and mortgage decisions. Also the organisation of the decision process (alone or with an external advice), which will be described in the following section, does not correlate significantly with these items. Therefore they are used separately in the multivariate framework.

The analysis of the risk tolerance indicators, offered by Table 8.6 in regard to those people who take decisions quickly, shows that individuals belonging to this category, particularly for the investment decision process (*i_quick*), hold an above average UR, a RLA which is below average, and a BR under the average – even if RLC is not always under the average. This means that those who tend to make investment decisions specifically, dedicating little time in the process, are also those exposed to the sleeping risk factor.

Finally, we asked the frequency of financial decision updating, and found that a significant and positive correlation of those updating

Table 8.6 Time to take financial decisions and risk tolerance indicators

	br	**Ur**	**rla**	**rlc**
i_quick	0.526	0.643	0.468	0.516
d_quick	0.573	0.630	0.480	0.510
m_quick	0.557	0.581	0.469	0.538
Overall sample	***0.562***	***0.580***	***0.495***	***0.521***

Table 8.7 Frequency of updating decisions (traders and asset managers excluded)

	Freq.	**%**
Daily	44	14.1
Weekly	50	16.0
Intra-year	133	42.6
Yearly	42	13.5
Every two or three years	16	5.1
I do not take any financial decision	27	8.7
Total	**312**	**100.00**

frequently with the *financial_profession* variable exists. Accordingly, we omit to consider this information in the multivariate framework, but we offer the updating behaviours of non-professionals interviewed in Table 8.7.

Most of the individuals tend to update their decision very frequently; more than the 30 per cent of the sample updates its financial choices on the daily or weekly basis and only 5.1 per cent is coherent with a long-run portfolio strategy.

8.5 The decision process

A further set of information in the questionnaire has the main objective of understanding the investment decision process. We are aware that the level of risk assumed in real life may diverge from the personal inside risk tolerance (either biased or unbiased) for the presence of third parties conditioning the financial choices. We asked primarily with whom these financial choices are generally shared. Then, we built up three variables, which the multiple choice questions allowed. As far as Table 8.8 is concerned, the *inv_alone* stands if the subject declares that they make decisions by him/herself; the *inv_clan* if the decision is taken together with the family, friends and colleagues; the *inv_ext*, if an external adviser provides advice or completely takes care of the investment. The same meaning, for the debt side, applies to the variables *debt_alone*, *debt_clan* and *debt_ext*.

Almost half of the sample takes decisions by him/herself, both at the investment and at the debt side. On the contrary, while the investment decision is shared with family, friends and colleagues in the same percentage of that relying on external advisers, it is relevant that only 8 per cent of the sample make use of the help of external professionals to take

Table 8.8 The organisation of the decision process

	Freq.	%		Freq.	%
inv_alone	272	53.4	debt_alone	178	52.8
inv_clan	121	23.8	debt_clan	132	39.2
inv_ext	116	22.8	debt_ext	27	8.0
Total	**509***	**100.0**	**Total**	**337****	**100.0**

*Multiple choices.
**Multiple choices and only for those assuming debt.

Table 8.9 Correlations among financial knowledge, profession and decision process

	high_fk	**financial_profession**	**d_inv_ext**	**d_inv_ alone**
high_fk	1			
financial_profession	0.4097*	1		
inv_ext	−0.3272*	−0.2757*	1	
inv_alone	0.3804*	0.3389*	−0.4083*	1

*Significance at 1%

debt decisions. In any case, both the alone decisions and the advised decisions are mainly driven by a condition of trust: self-trust in the case of alone decisions and trust of external experts in the case of advised decisions. Nevertheless, in this latter case, among those using external advice of some sort, 132 individuals declared a medium level of trust, 40 a high level of trust and 77 a low level of trust.

One might think that financial knowledge, the financial profession and the decision process (either alone or with some external adviser) may be strongly related. Table 8.9 shows evidence of this. All the same, for financial knowledge and the financial profession, even if the correlation is high (0.4097 with a significance at the 1 per cent confidence level), the different levels of UR between the sub-samples of *high_fk* (0.525) and of *financial_profession* (0.452) demonstrate that the two groups of subjects do not overlap. In any case, taking decisions alone or with the help of an adviser is significantly related with financial knowledge and financial profession (positively and negatively, respectively). Obviously, also *inv_ext* and *inv_alone* are significantly and negatively related.

All these considerations allow us to conclude that in the multivariate analysis we will use each of the four variables of Table 8.9 alternatively.

8.6 Vulnerability, odds and trust

Further conclusive questions were asked in order to contextualise the financial risk tolerance behaviour in relation to some personal conditions of those interviewed. First, we asked their income expectations (in particular, if they are stable or growing); then we asked if the individual suffered from any negative events recently (job loss, job reduction, disease, death, disability, divorce, in the last 12 months); finally, we asked the level of self-trust felt at the moment of the experiment and the degree of trust in the future.

The category of people who forecast a stable income by definition excludes the condition of having a growing income (that is why the correlation is significant and strongly negative). Moreover, the occurrence of negative events did not in any way affect any condition of trust (both self-trust and trust in the future). More interesting and informative is the variable self-trust which may be the synthesis of the other three associated variables. In fact, the correlations shown in Table 8.10 (the star stands for significance at the 1 per cent level) show that people's self-trust is higher if they have expectations of growing income, and is lower if their income is expected to stand stable. This explains why the self-trust variable is taken as representative of all the others and used for the following comparisons of risk tolerance indicators.

Figure 8.8 shows another germane piece of information: people with a good level of self-trust seem to make their real life financial decisions

Table 8.10 Correlations among drivers of trust

	stable_ income	*growing_ income*	*odds*	*self-trust*	*trust_future*
stable_income	1				
growing_income	−0.8411*	1			
odds	−0.0538	−0.0205	1		
self-trust	−0.1524*	0.2206*	0.0635	1	
trust_future	−0.1006	0.2084*	−0.0403	0.2361*	1

	Freq.	Percent
Low_self_trust	240	54.4
High_self_trust	201	45.6
Total	**441**	**100.0**

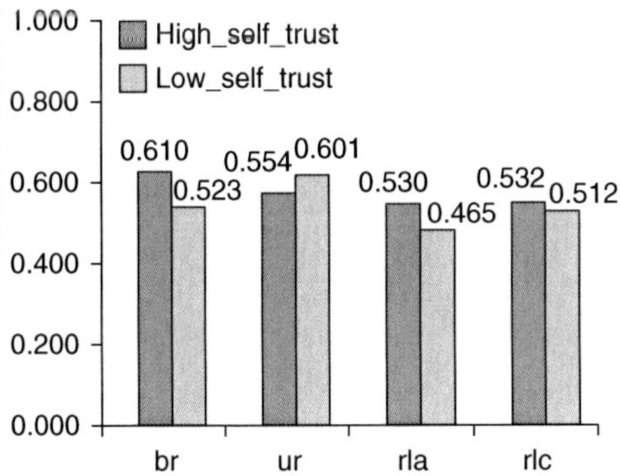

Figure 8.8 Self-trust and risk tolerance

Table 8.11 Profiles of people's exposure to the unconscious sleeping factor

	Higher risk	Lower risk
Age	People in retirement (over-60s)	People in working activity (30–60 years old)
Gender	Females	Males
Marital status	Divorced or widowed	People with family
Financial knowledge	Low financial knowledge	High financial knowledge
Professions	Salaried employees; pensioners	Financial professions (for example, traders and asset managers)
Information used	Low use of economical and financial news	Heavy users of economic and financial news
Time to take decisions	Impulsive investment decisions	Reasoned decisions
Self-trust	Low self-trust	High self-trust

coherently with their emotional risk tolerance. Levels of RLA are almost in line with those of UR. On the contrary, people with low self-trust may be considered to be susceptible to the sleeping factor condition as they have UR levels that are higher than RLA and also BR.

All these descriptive statistics persuade us to develop two separate profiles for those who are more and less exposed to the sleeping factor risk, as shown in Table 8.11.

Being aware that Table 8.11 offers an overall view of descriptive results and that some features may be overlapping (for example financial knowledge and profession), the profile of those most affected by the sleeping factor is quite clear. This finding could be somewhat helpful because we may reasonably argue that those holding a strong emotional attraction towards risk, without being necessarily aware of it, may behave unpredictably. For example, they may be particularly sensitive to mass media news on financial market trends, intensifying emotional reactions of fear and greed and finally overall systemic risk, as will be explained in our conclusions.

8.7 The multivariate analysis: what determines RLA?

The final step of the empirical research carried out on the investment side is aimed at understanding the variables which may explain the financial risk assumed in real life (RLA). All the considerations of previous sections represent the rationale for the setting of the cross-section models (8.1) and (8.2). RLA should be related, as theory suggests, to the real life capacity (RLC): we expect that the familial, financial and economic conditions of each individual should influence the level of risk assumed in real life. Furthermore, we consider the effect on the RLA played by our personal inside risk tolerance indicators (BR and UR). The BIS (from the Barratt Impulsivity Scale, see Chapter 6) is to control any influence due to impulsive behaviour. The age and the gender (with the dummy variable female) are the two drivers included to consider the most relevant demographical variable. Then, as stated in Section 8.6., the high correlation between financial knowledge, financial profession and the organisation of the decision process (either alone or with the help of an external financial adviser) induces us to consider each of the four variables, alternatively (*high-fk, financial_profession, inv_alone* and *inv_ext*). Given that the latter two show a significant and negative correlation with each other, we present two distinct models (8.1 with the first, and 8.2 with the second). Finally, we include a variable to acknowledge when the experiments took place. In fact, the nature of our analysis did not allow us to carry out all the interviews over a short interval. It took us more than nine months to conduct the empirical work, from October 2008 to June 2009. We have to keep in mind that this period was particularly crucial as the interviews started right after the Lehman Brothers crash and the first semester of 2009 was influenced by strong financial instability and recessionary worries worldwide. So we build up a dummy variable named crisis which is 1 is for those interviews carried out just at the beginning of the crisis (October 2008), and 0 in the other cases. Thus, the models we estimated are:

$$\begin{aligned} rla_i = {} & cons_i + \beta_1 rlc_i + \beta_2 br_i + \beta_3 ur_i + \beta_4 bis_i + \beta_5 age_i + \beta_6 female_i \\ & + \beta_7 metropol_i + \beta_8 inv\_alone_i + \beta_9 crisis_i + \varepsilon_i \end{aligned} \tag{8.1}$$

where:
rla_i is the real life risk attitude indicator, for subject i;
rlc_i is the real life capacity indicator;
br_i is the biased risk tolerance indicator;
ur_i is the unbiased risk tolerance indicator;
bis_i is the total score obtained by the subject at the Barratt Impulsivity test;
age_i is the age of the interviewed;

metropol$_i$ is the dummy variable indicating the residence of the individual;
female$_i$ is the dummy variable to indicate the gender of the subject;
inv_alone$_i$ is the variable to testify if the subject takes decision by him/herself;
crisis$_i$ is the dummy variable to testify the period of the interviews;
ε_i~i.i.d.$(0,\sigma_\varepsilon^2)$ is the model disturbance.

$$rla_i = cons_i + \beta_1 rlc_i + \beta_2 br_i + \beta_3 ur_i + \beta_4 bis_i + \beta_5 age_i + \beta_6 female_i + \beta_7 metropol_i + \beta_8 inv\_ext_i + \beta_9 crisis_i + \varepsilon_i \quad (8.2)$$

where:
inv_ext$_i$ is the variable to testify whether the subject takes decisions with the help of an external adviser.

Estimations of models 8.1 and 8.2 are shown in Tables 8.12 and 8.13.

First we point out that we discarded two further variables *inv_quick* and *t_self* because they appear to be non-significant. The overall view of the estimations persuade us to deduce that the risk assumed in real life is not related with the risk capacity, an opposite finding compared to the theoretical view which was discussed at the beginning of Chapter 7. Moreover, not surprisingly considering the results of the previous descriptive statistics, we can see that RLA is positively related with the biased risk

Table 8.12 Cross-section estimation for drivers of RLA model 8.1

Source	**SS**	**df**	**MS**			
				Number of obs = 441		
				F(9, 431)	=	22.48
Model	3.20781175	9	.356423528	Prob > F	=	0.0000
Residual	6.83472213	431	0.015857824	R-squared	=	0.3194
Total	10.0425339	440	0.022823941	Adj R-squared	=	0.3052
				Root MSE	=	.12593

rla	**Coef.**	**Std. Err.**	**t**	**P>|t|**	**[95% Conf.**	**Interval]**
rlc	–.0298782	.0463924	–0.64	0.520	–.1210616	.0613053
br	.4026934	.0481568	8.36	0.000	.3080421	.4973447
ur	–.0416164	.0134241	–3.10	0.002	–.0680012	–.0152315
bis	.0019839	.0007946	2.50	0.013	.0004221	.0035458
age	.0011049	.0005513	2.00	0.046	.0000214	.0021885
female	–.0382679	.015406	–2.48	0.013	–.0685481	–.0079877
metropol	.0239025	.0142601	1.68	0.094	–.0041255	.0519304
inv_alone	.058532	.0136228	4.30	0.000	.0317567	.0853074
crisis	.0537513	.020407	2.63	0.009	.0136418	.0938609
_cons	.1036668	.0625037	1.66	0.098	–.0191833	.2265168

Table 8.13 Cross-section estimation for drivers of RLA model 8.2

Source	SS	df	MS		
				Number of obs	= 441
				F(9, 431)	= 19.93
Model	2.95101852	9	.327890947	Prob > F	= 0.0000
Residual	7.09151536	431	0.016453632	R-squared	= 0.2939
Total	10.0425339	440	0.022823941	Adj R-squared	= 0.2791
				Root MSE	= .12827

rla	Coef.	Std. Err.	t	P>|t|	[95% Conf.	Interval]
rlc	−.0278191	.047253	−0.59	0.556	−.1206941	.0650559
br	.4418677	.0481481	9.18	0.000	.3472334	.5365021
ur	−.0431059	.0136745	−3.15	0.002	−.069983	−.0162289
bis	.001982	.0008097	2.45	0.015	.0003905	.0035735
age	.0011617	.0005667	2.05	0.041	.0000478	.0022756
female	−.0466464	.0155489	−3.00	0.003	−.0772076	−.0160852
metropol	.0333592	.0144988	2.30	0.022	.0048621	.0618563
inv_ext	−.0217491	.0147119	−1.48	0.140	−.0506652	.007167
crisis	.0609419	.0207169	2.94	0.003	.0202232	.1016607
_cons	.1189338	.0636796	1.87	0.062	−.0062273	.244095

BR and negatively with the unbiased risk UR. This confirms that people tend to behave coherently to their self-representation and almost in stark contrast to what they feel. The univariate analysis conducted in previous sections already anticipated this important evidence: people who generally self-represent themselves as risk averse tend to assume low risk in real life, even if they possess a relevant emotional attraction toward risk (the sleeping factor). This is particularly true for people with low financial knowledge and non-financial professions (see Section 8.3).

The UR has a significant and negative relationship with BR even if the absolute value of the β_3 parameter is much lower than β_2 (β_2 for BR is 0.4027, in model 8.1, and 0.4419, in model 8.2, while β_3 for UR is −0.0416 in model 8.1, and −0.0431 in model 8.2). This sounds strange but also worrying. Our study would mean, surprisingly, that the higher the risk assumed in real life, the lower the emotional risk attraction; in contrast, the lower the real life risk, the higher the emotional risk attraction. This would mean that people taking non-risky financial decisions in real life may hold an unaware emotional risk attraction. At the same time, their self valuation is not informative of this love for risk. These relationships stand still even after considering the role of the impulsivity (the *bis* variable), which is significant but only with a small positive impact on RLA (β_4 for *bis* is roughly 0.002 for both models).

One might think that moral hazard behaviour, potentially assumed during the IGT/SCR experiment, could be the reason for the widespread risky choices revealed by our subjects. Nevertheless the moral hazard hypothesis is groundless because a considerable number of individuals in our sample have the same level of UR and RLA (those with a higher level of financial education) while another sub-sample shows levels of UR much lower than RLA (traders and asset managers). If the restless mind is the psychological explanation of the presence of the risk sleeping factor, we might suggest that those occupying financial professions tend to practise in the domain of gains and losses. This practice allows them to be able to break the influence of the restless mind evident in financial choice behaviours, inducing the control/reduction of the sleeping factor.

The variables showing a significant relationship with RLA are age, gender and residence. The role of *age* on RLA is significant and positive. The absolute value of the β_4 coefficient is small. This is mainly due to the different metrics for RLA, which goes from 0 to 1, on the one hand, and for *age*, which goes from 18 to 80, on the other. Nevertheless, the relationship is positive, meaning that ageing people tend to take riskier choices in real life. Gender plays its role as expected from previous findings in the literature, and shows the condition of being female as a significant driver for risk reduction.[3] The residence appears to drive significantly the risk assumed in real life. The variable *metropol*, which testifies as to whether the subject lives in a metropolitan area or not, seems to say that those living in these areas tend to assume riskier financial choices. Nevertheless, we are aware that some socio-demographical features overlap. In fact, the variable *metropol* shows a correlation of 45.61 per cent (p-value at 1 per cent) with the variable *high_fk*. This suggests that the most appropriate interpretation for *metropol* is as indirectly testifying to the degree of financial knowledge of the individual. More directly, people living in metropolitan areas are more likely to have higher financial education.[4] This component finally causes RLA to be higher.

The last two variables indicate the effect on RLA of two further components: the period in which the analysis took place and the way the financial decision process is organised. The dummy variable *crisis* shows a significant and positive relationship with RLA. This indicates that when crisis moves from 1 (October 2008, the beginning of the financial instability) to 0, individuals observed in our analysis, ceteris paribus, tend to decrease their exposition towards financial risks. This is coherent with a more prudent behaviour induced by highly volatile financial markets and the beginning of the economic recession.

Finally, the variable *inv_alone* and *inv_ext*, separately considered in models 8.1 and 8.2, suggests that when taking decisions without any external counselling people tend to assume higher risks (β_8 for *inv_alone* is 0.0585), while the presence of professional advisers acts to reduce RLA ($\beta_{8'}$ for *inv_ext* is –0.0217). We cannot state, by definition, if increasing or reducing RLA is an adequate decision for any individuals, given their overall familiar, financial and economical condition. Nevertheless, if we keep in mind that the sleeping factor is relevant for peculiar subjects (those with lower levels of financial knowledge, who read less economic and financial news, and are more inclined to take quick investment decisions) we might affirm that the latter should be more interested in being supported by third parties. External advisers, especially if they are not affected by the sleeping factor, could be of help to them in controlling their unconscious risk attraction.

Notes

1. We built up three dummy variables: the dummy north which is 1 if people live in the north of Italy, 0 in the other case; the same for the variable centre and south. We compute the correlation among these dummies and *north* is significantly and positively related to *metropol*, while the *centre* is significantly and negatively related to this variable. South is indifferent to *metropol*, because it is made up of only a few individuals (17).
2. Even if theory suggests considering restrictions (RLC) in explaining the real life risk tolerance, and specifically the RLA, this result anticipates what the multivariate framework will confirm: the real life risk attitude (RLA) is not conditioned by the risk capacity (RLC).
3. Remember that the descriptive statistics show that females tend to assume the lowest level of risk in real life, they tend to evaluate themselves as risk averse even if they feel the same emotional attraction towards risk as males.
4. We have to admit that if we run the estimations of models 8.1 and 8.2 using *high_fk* instead of *metropol*, *high_fk*, ceteris paribus, is not significant, because its role is totally absorbed by BR (high correlation between people showing high financial knowledge and self-evaluated risk tolerance).

9

The Determinants of Household Debt Holding: An Empirical Analysis

Daniela Vandone and Cristina Ottaviani

9.1 Socio-demographic, economic and psychological variables

As already pointed out in Chapter 2, the theoretical economic framework for indebtedness decisions is developed within inter-temporal consumption choice models which are based on the economic rationality of individuals, who seek to increase their living standards and maximise their expected utility by smoothing consumption over different periods of their lives through saving and borrowing decisions.

Within this framework, the determinants of household demand for debt have been investigated with a considerable amount of theoretical and empirical studies, among others Crook (2006), Del Rio and Young (2006), Duygan and Grant (2008), Fabbri and Padula (2004), Fay et al. (2002), Grant and Padula (2006), Gropp et al. (1997), Jappelli and Pagano (2006) and Magri (2007).

All these empirical studies commonly include a set of socio-demographic and economic explanatory variables to analyse the determinants of household debt, such as age, level of education, income, wealth and work status. Results have generally led to the conclusion that the Permanent Income Theory is not completely verified, and this may be determined by the myopia of the individuals, who would not have rational expectations (Magri, 2007).

With this last point in mind, we use the data collected on our sample of 445 subjects randomly selected among traders, asset managers and bank customers in order to shed some light on the effect of emotional traits on the demand for debt and to contribute to new discussion issues in the still growing literature on behavioural economics.

The aim of this chapter is to analyse the determinants of the individuals' probability of holding debt including, together with the explanatory variables commonly used in applied economic literature, the role of psychological factors.

We also empirically investigate whether the effect of such explanatory variables is different for secured debt (mortgages) and unsecured debt (consumer credit). In fact, it is likely that secured debt demand well follows the lifecycle since such decisions last for a long time, while unsecured debt demand is more subject to variables like impulsivity, materialism and satisfaction, since consumer credit is frequently used to finance daily shopping (for example, credit cards).

The dependent variable is a dummy which is equal to 1 if the household is indebted and 0 otherwise. We draw this information from question n. 26 of the survey, which also allows us to distinguish between the holding of consumer credit and mortgages.

In our sample, the percentage of households holding debt totalled 61 per cent; regarding participation in the secured and unsecured credit market, the percentages are 47 per cent and 27 per cent respectively.

The explanatory variables can be grouped into two classes:

- socio-demographic and economic variables commonly used in applied economic literature to investigate the determinants of households participation in the credit market
- psychological variables, aimed at collecting information on the emotional side of debt decisions and analysing the possible limitation of the traditional theoretical framework in predicting real life choices.

Among the first group of explanatory variables we include age (*age*), level of education (*education*), size of family (*dependent children*), work status (*work*), real financial wealth (*wealth*), and income (*income*). We also include a dummy (*divorced*) aimed at taking into account shocks; that is, unexpected adverse events which negatively impact an individual's financial situation, and the variable *fragility* aimed at describing the household's financial situation.[1] Among the second group of variables we include the household's impulsivity, measured by the Barratt Impulsiveness Scale, and the household risk propensity, measured by the psycho-physiological test (unbiased risk – UR) already described in Chapter 7.

The role of socio-demographic and economic variables in determining household debt demand has already been reviewed in Chapter 2.

In particular, the age of the head of household is generally included in the analysis to take account of the lifecycle model of consumption. The theoretical model predicts that demand for debt should be higher for young households expecting their income to grow with demand dropping over time both because income becomes sufficient to cover expenditures and because households adopt a more conservative attitude as regards borrowing.

With regard to education, higher education reflects a quicker increase in future income, greater employment stability and reduced entry costs in the market due to the ability to better understand financial information.

As for the size of the family, indebtedness is higher or the capacity to save is lower also in the case of large families with children at preschool or school age when in this lifecycle phase spending is typically high.

Net wealth generally has an ambiguous effect on the demand for debt. One would expect the increase in wealth to be accompanied by a reduction in households' debt demand due to their improved ability to finance consumption. However, empirical evidence and theoretical reasons suggest a possible opposing relationship: as wealth increases, the demand for debt increases as well, in particular for medium-low levels of wealth where the marginal utility of consumption is higher than that of wealth.

Current income is expected to have a negative effect on household debt demand: if the current income increases, demand for debt drops because, as for wealth, individuals are able to meet their needs with greater autonomy.

For the variable work status, participation in the consumer credit market is higher for employees compared to the self-employed whose income is subject to greater variability.

As for the variable divorced, indebtedness is higher or the capacity to save is lower in case of events like separation or divorce, which can determine a shock in individual's income source or unexpected liabilities.

Finally, the variable fragility is included in order to investigate whether debt, in particular unsecured debt, is used not only for optimising inter-temporal consumption but also as a way of managing financial distress.

Regarding psychological variables, as we already pointed out in Chapter 2, one of the main aspects that may influence household decision making, and thus debt demand, is that individuals tend to systematically overvalue immediate costs and benefits and undervalue those in the future (that is, hyperbolic discount). In other words, their preferences are not time-consistent and they give greater importance to present events in comparison to those in the future. As regards the decision to apply for debt, and in particular unsecured debt, that is consumer credit, the hyperbolic discount factor pushes individuals in the moment they have to decide whether to purchase on credit terms or not to opt for immediate purchase. This decision is made despite the fact that the individual is rationally able to judge that the level of debt taken on is unsustainable in comparison to future income receipts. This behavioural factor explains why individuals choose 'buy now, pay later' solutions that bring immediate gratification at a future cost; in fact, it means that individuals adopt impatient, short-sighted behaviour patterns which make it difficult for them to be fully aware of the consequences of their spending decisions on the sustainability of personal debt (Meier and Sprenger, 2007).

As already highlighted in Chapter 6, the economic concept of hyperbolic discounting has been associated with the psychological notion of impulsivity showing that impulsive individuals are biased towards immediate rewards and are less sensitive to the long-term consequences of their choices (Bickel and Marsch, 2001; Martin and Potts, 2009; Potts et al., 2006; Takahashi, 2007). Thus, we might expect that impulsivity positively influences debt demand, particularly in the case of unsecured debt.

With regard to household risk preferences, the nature of an individual's risk preferences arguably plays an important role in the decision to use debt to finance current consumption. In particular, according to traditional economic theory the more risk averse a household is, the lower the debt they incur will be if there is a non-zero probability that the debt cannot be repaid in the future. In fact, in the presence of uncertain future income streams risk preferences may negatively influence the demand for debt: the higher the level of risk aversion, the lower the level of debt accumulation by households. In order to measure individual risk propensity, we use the psycho-physiological test (Unbiased Risk – UR) already described in Chapter 7. This indicator of risk propensity should provide a more objective evaluation of the risk tolerance, given the fact that it relies on risky choices influenced by spontaneous somatic responses. To our purposes it should be a better indicator compared to the traditional financial risk tolerance test (Biased Risk – BR) which relies on the self-evaluation of the individual about their own risk tolerance. We might expect a positive link between debt demand and risk: the lower the risk propensity, the lower the debt demand because the higher is the fear to default.

Table A.1 in Appendix 2 synthesises individual characteristics of the sample concerning the variables used. All socio-economic variables considered are categorical, either because of their nature (educational qualifications, professional status, dependent children, divorced) or because they are transformed so as to identify any non-linearities in relation to the probability of having debt (age, income, wealth). Psychological variables (Impulsiveness and Unbiased Risk) are scale variables.

9.2 Descriptive analysis

We first reprocess the data in order to determine the percentage of households with debt in relation to the categorical explanatory variables mentioned previously. The percentage of households holding debt was calculated with reference to each chosen variable (Table 9.1).

In line both with theory and previous research (Crook, 2006; Fabbri and Padula, 2004), household liabilities are concentrated principally among younger households, in particular those with an age between 30 and 40, who borrow in order to smooth consumption over their lifetime and consequently to improve lifestyle.

Having children is associated with a higher concentration of households having debt; the same holds for individuals who are divorced.

The percentage of households with debt is higher among the second quartile of wealth, consistent with the evidence in the literature (Del Rio and Young, 2006; Magri, 2007), showing that households with higher wealth are able to cover consumption needs autonomously without recourse to debt. The analysis furthermore shows that the percentage of individuals holding debt rises with higher income; this may also be due to the reduced probability of supply-side restrictions. Probably for the same reason, the percentage of households with debt is higher for employees; this could stem from the fact that employees' pay represents an *ex ante* guarantee for financial intermediaries.

Table 9.1 Percentage of households holding debt in relation to their socio-economic characteristics

	Households without debt (%)	**Households with debt (%)**	**Total**
Number of households	**172**	**269**	**441**
Age			
Up to 30 years	13.95%	6.69%	9.52%
31 to 40 years	30.81%	43.49%	38.55%
41 to 50 years	25.58%	26.77%	26.30%
50 to 61 years	11.63%	16.36%	14.51%
Older than 61 years	18.02%	6.69%	11.11%
Education			
Elementary school	5.81%	4.83%	5.22%
Middle school	38.37%	40.52%	39.68%
High school	43.02%	42.01%	42.40%
University degree	12.79%	12.64%	12.70%
Work status			
Employee (ref.)	51.16%	67.66%	61.22%
Self-employed	25.58%	25.28%	25.40%
Not employed	23.26%	7.06%	13.38%
Wealth (quartile)			
Up to €350,000	31.40%	22.68%	26.08%
€350,001 to €425,000	17.44%	31.23%	25.85%
€425,001 to €1,100,000	31.98%	28.25%	29.71%
More than €1,100,001	19.19%	17.84%	18.37%
Monthly income (quartile)			
Up to €2,500	41.28%	33.46%	36.51%
€2,501 to €3,500	17.44%	19.70%	18.82%
€3,501 to €5,500	16.28%	24.16%	21.09%
More than €5,501	25.00%	22.68%	23.58%
Dependent children			
No (ref.)	56.98%	42.75%	48.30%
Yes	43.02%	57.25%	51.70%
Divorced			
No (ref.)	94.77%	92.19%	93.20%
Yes	5.23%	7.81%	6.80%
Fragility			
No (ref.)	81.40%	79.93%	80.50%
Yes	18.60%	20.07%	19.50%

Education does not appear to be a particularly significant variable in contrast to both what is normally expected and the findings presented in the literature, which typically report higher levels of education as an effective proxy of rising future income and consequently positively correlated to the amount of debt outstanding (Del Rio and Young, 2006; Grant, 2003).

Interestingly, having financial difficulties is associated with a higher concentration of households holding debt. This evidence may indicate that a selection of population may have to borrow not only to smooth consumption over time, but also to face conditions of financial stress.

9.3 Multivariate analysis

In order to take into account the relations between variables, we then performed a probit analysis to study how the probability of holding debt varies according to individual characteristics and socio-economic context. We also single out the determinants of the two main categories of debt: secured and unsecured (Table 9.2).

The variable age is significant and the sign is positive: for individuals aged between 30 and 40 years the probability of having debt increases approximately 45 percentage points compared to individuals younger than 30 years. The result is similar when we analyse for secured and unsecured debt. The relationship between age and household indebtedness is coherent with previous findings and the lifecycle model of consumption which predicts that demand for debt should be higher for young households expecting their income to grow with demand dropping over time both because income becomes sufficient to cover expenditures and because households adopt a more conservative attitude as regards borrowing (Crook, 2006; Del Rio and Young, 2006; Magri 2007).

The probability of participation in the household debt market is lower for not-employees – almost 97 percent compared to the reference category – and the reason is likely due to problems in accessing credit. With reference to consumer credit, like Magri (2007) we found that the probability of holding consumer credit is higher for the self-employees than for employed (+35 percent), suggesting that individuals in this category use unsecured debt also as a mean of funding their work activities.

Among socio-economic variables, the level of education is not significant. Although one can argue that education reflects a quicker increase

Table 9.2 Participation in the debt market: Probit estimation

	1 Marginal effects (total debt)	2 Marginal effects (mortgages)	3 Marginal effects (consumer credit)
Age (Ref. = younger than 30 years)			
31 to 40 years	.4519 (.2378) *	.3991 (.2386)*	.5003 (.2613)*
41 to 50 years	.0446 (.2629)	.1957 (.2625)	–.0165 (.2952)
50 to 61 years	.2960 (.2966)	–.0100 (.2892)	.5724 (.3155)*
Older than 61	.1757 (.3613)	–.1453 (.3646)	.6944 (.3913)*
Work status (Ref. = employee)			
Self-employed	–.2104 (.1609)	–.3381 (.1555)**	.3560 (.1625)**
Not employed	–.9737 (.2879)***	–.6314 (.2826)**	–.8535 (.3436)**
Education (Ref. = elementary school)			
Middle school	–.0780 (.3241)	–.0772 (.3380)	–.2447 (.3258)
High school	–.2224 (.3360)	–.1350 (.3501)	–.2707 (.3414)
University degree	–.2685 (.3672)	–.2251 (.3822)	–.0412 (.3802)
Wealth (Ref. = up to first quartile)			
First to second quartile	.5661 (.1860) ***	.3995 (.1760)**	.1433 (.1814)
Second to third quartile	.1455 (.1955)	.1122 (.1978)	.0787 (.2064)
More than third quartile	.1148 (.2381)	.3126 (.2201)	–.6160 (.2584)**
Monthly income (Ref. = up to first quartile)			
First to second quartile	.1510 (.1945)	.2022 (.1806)	.0310 (.1977)
Second to third quartile	.3071 (.1961)	.3769 (.1922)*	–.2028 (.2136)
More than third quartile	.1463 (.2093)	.1833 (.2063)	–.0976 (.2361)
Fragility (Ref. = no)	.2254 (.1793)	–.0683 (.1709)	.5564 (.1714)***
Dependent children (Ref. = no)	.3637 (.1442)**	.3731 (.1427)***	.2356 (.1564)
Divorced (Ref. = no)	.3412 (.2457)	.1935 (.2329)	–.0375 (.2861)
UR	.0550 (.1427)	–.1471 (.1411)	–.0343 (.1528)
Bis	.0248 (.0087)***	.0118 (.0084)	.0275 (.0089)***
Cons	–1.6744 (.6376)***	–1.587 (.6502)***	–2.4983 (.6703)***
Number of obs	441	441	441
Wald chi2(20)	69.08	54.63	55.45
Prob > chi2=0.0000	–260.08354	–275.17324	–222.22528
Pseudo R2	0.1181	0.0974	0.1324

in future income, greater employment stability and reduced entry costs in the market due to a better ability to understand financial information, in previous studies education was a significant factor only for King and Leape (1998), while it did not play an important role for Cox and Jappelli (1993). Moreover, in our case almost two-thirds of the sample have a high level of education and this may further render the link unclear.

The probability of having debt increases 56 per cent moving from the first quartile to the second quartile of net wealth. Similar results hold for the probability of holding mortgages, while for unsecured debt the variable is significant and the sign is negative moving from the first to the last quartile of net wealth (−61 per cent). As far as income is concerned, the variable is significant only for mortgages, moving from the first to the third quartile.

In line with King and Leape (1998), the relationship between the probability of debt and net wealth is positive, while, in agreement with Magri (2007), net wealth has a negative effect on the holding of consumer credit; the same different relationship remains for the effect of current income. The relationship between net wealth and current income with household indebtedness is coherent with previous findings, which generally outline an ambiguous effect of those variables on the determinant for debt. In particular, a negative sign is consistent with determinants on the demand side; that is, higher levels of wealth allow individuals to cope more independently with consumption needs. Conversely, a positive sign is coherent with the determinants supply side of the market, which likely act in an opposite direction as wealth or income represents a guarantee for the bank and which are likely stronger for mortgages whose value is normally far higher than that of consumer credit.

Having children increases the probability of debt by 36 per cent. The same result holds for the probability of holding mortgages, while for consumer credit the variable is not significant.

With regard to financial fragility, results show that the variable is significant and positive only on the consumer credit market where it increases the probability of being indebted: the probability of having unsecured debt increases for financially fragile borrowers with a marginal effect of 55 per cent. Although we are not able to ascertain whether the financial position is a determinant of consumer credit demand or whether it is a consequence of accumulated debt, the result in itself highlights that a relatively consistent part of unsecured debt is concentrated in the hands of financially fragile households, in line with

Cavalletti et al. (2008), who use debt not only to smooth consumption over time but also to make ends meet.

Overall, as far as traditional socio-demographic and economic variables are concerned, the decision making process for mortgages has different determinants than that for consumer credit; the last appearing to be less related to the lifecycle, and more influenced by the willingness to apply for credit in order to finance consumption.

As for psychological variables, results show that real life indebtedness decisions, in particular those related to unsecured risk, are largely influenced by individuals' impulsivity, even after controlling for the traditional predictors. In fact, impulsivity is significant and the sign is positive: an increase in the inability to act without thinking increases the probability of holding unsecured debt by 2.4 per cent. A similar result is found for the probability of holding unsecured debt, while the variable is not significant for secured debt (Ottaviani and Vandone, 2010). Conversely, the Unbiased Risk is not a determinant of participation in the debt market.

To conclude, up to now the role played by psychological factors as determinants of debt demand has been erroneously ignored. Although common sense might suggest that these two elements are connected, our results seem to show that impulsivity, much more than the willing ness to take risks, plays a role in determining debt holding. If present results will be further confirmed, concerns should be raised especially for consumer credit granted through revolving credit cards, which are payment instruments that make impulsive shopping easier to realise. These methods of payment may in fact induce impulsive subjects at risk of over-indebtedness. The importance of the phenomenon lies in the fact that over-indebtedness mainly affects the economically and socially weakest members of society, with potentially high costs not only at individual level but for the financial system and society as a whole.

Note

1. This variable is identified from question 13): *'What is the monthly income–daily expenses ratio within your family? Income is not enough to cover daily expenses and we are forced to borrow money; We are forced to use our savings; Income is enough to cover daily expenses; We are able to save some money; We are able to save a considerable amount of money'*. For our purposes, individuals are fragile if they need to borrow, to use savings or if income is just enough to make ends meet.

10

The Implications for Market Participants and Regulators

Gianni Brighetti, Caterina Lucarelli and Daniela Vandone

10.1 The overall empirical results

The overall empirical findings of our study on risk tolerance are two-fold: on the one hand, we revealed relevant incoherencies among alternative measures of risk tolerance, on the investment side of decision processes. On the other hand, we found that unknown psychological drivers affect the choice to assume debts, especially with regard to unsecured debts. The commonly shared trait of these results is that a large number of dysfunctional behaviours take place when financial decisions are considered. It is thus evidently true that correct knowledge of human mental processing is essential to control conscious/responsible investing and lending.

As far as the first set of evidence is concerned, we wanted to understand the degree of coherence among how we *are* (or, more technically, at which level of phase synchrony the neural populations that guide our choices oscillate); how we *consider ourselves to be* (or better, which representation we have of ourselves); and how we *act*, given our constraints. Specifically, we studied whether our biased self-representation, on the one hand, or our unbiased emotional risk attraction (sympathetic effect), on the other hand, *differently* affect our real life attitude in relation to a set of socio-demographical and cultural variables. Our findings reveal that a strong component of unconscious/unaware risk attraction is proven to exist. We observed many subjects who seem to exhibit a strong risk attraction without any further signal of being gamblers, neither considering how they evaluate themselves, nor how they practically act. In other words, we discovered many individuals who consider themselves, and act, as risk averters but they simultaneously and unconsciously appear to be risk lovers. When this condition occurs, the unbiased risk (UR) is much higher than the risk assumed in real life (RLA) but, at the same time, it is higher than the self-evaluation (BR). We state, in this case, the presence of an 'unconscious sleeping factor'. The psychological explanation of these incoherencies among different risk tolerance indicators is the presence of the 'wandering mind', the daydreaming, the fantasy of profits, of the lucky investment, or of the dreamed hope. Even if the 'wandering mind' is inherent in human psychology, it tends to work in 'domains' (the 'domain of gains and losses', the 'domain of sexuality', the 'domain of driving cars'). One can have an active 'wandering mind' in one domain, and not in others. This explains why the 'sleeping factor' varies for different individual sub-samples. We discover groups of people whose sleeping factor is completely absent, at least in the 'financial domain': this was confirmed for people who have a financial profession, like traders and asset managers. On the contrary, some other groups seem to be strongly affected by the sleeping factor. This feature is strong for old people (a long lifecycle of risk tolerance is uncovered), for those who are widowed or divorced, for people who seldom acquire financial information, with low financial knowledge, for those who do not read the news regularly, and also for those who take quick investment decisions. It is also strong for those with low self-trust.

The multivariate analysis, which aimed to study those variables affecting actual financial choices, proved that the real life risk attitude (RLA) is positively related with the biased risk (the self-evaluated one) and negatively with the unbiased risk (the emotionally driven one). This finding affirms that people tend to behave coherently according to their self-representation and almost in stark contrast to what they feel. Moreover, the real life risk seems to be uninfluenced by any familial, economic or financial constraints, while it increases with the impulsivity and the age of individuals. Being female or living far from big cities reduces the risk assumed in real life, and so does the sharing of the decision process with external advisers.

Regarding the debt side, we analysed the determinants of the individuals' probability of holding debt, including the role of psychological factors. We also empirically investigated whether the effect of such explanatory variables is different for secured debt (mortgages) and unsecured debt (consumer credit). In fact, it is likely that secured debt demand follows the lifecycle well since such decisions have a long lifespan, whereas unsecured debt demand is more subject to variables (like impulsivity, materialism, satisfaction) since consumer credit is frequently used to finance daily shopping (for example, credit cards). Overall, as far as traditional socio-demographic and economic variables are concerned, the decision making process for mortgages has different determinants than that for consumer credit; the latter appearing to be less related to the lifecycle, and more influenced by the willingness to demand credit to finance further consumption. Pertaining to psychological variables, results show that real life indebtedness decisions, in particular those related to unsecured risk, are largely influenced by individuals' impulsivity, even after controlling for the traditional predictors. In fact, impulsivity is significant and the sign is positive: an increase in the inability to act without thinking increases the probability of holding unsecured debt by 2.4 per cent. A similar result is found to exist for the probability of holding unsecured debt, while the variable is not significant for secured debt. Conversely, the unbiased risk (UR) did not appear to be a determinant of participation in the debt market.

10.2 Implications on the investment side

The presence of information about the emotional (psychophysiological) behaviour of a wide range of individuals induces us to foresee at least two future research developments, concerning the investment side of the decision process. First we hope to adapt the theoretical utility function, a mathematical expression that models the decision process of the individual, by making use of our alternative measures of risk tolerance. Specifically, we intend to simulate the different portfolio choices which arise when using biased and unbiased risk measures, respectively. Furthermore, we aim to employ these subjective measures of risk in the empirical validation of recent theoretical studies on spectral risk measures, especially from the portfolio optimisation perspective.

Many further operational implications of our findings appear relevant. The presence of the sleeping factor in specific sub-groups of people (especially: older people, people with low financial education and/or less used to reading economic news) give rise to the idea that this condition may represent a source of risk. The discrepancy between what appears outside (from actual choices and from self-representation) and what is hidden inside represents a disequilibrium which may induce unconscious or apparently irrational behaviours. We may wonder why, unpredictably, strong stock exchange price volatility may exist, together with some other occurrences, such as bank runs. We think that the 'fear and greed' emotional sentiment of the financial marketplace may be reasonably reinforced by the presence of the individual sleeping factor component.

What may induce the sleeping factor to surface and cause unforeseeable emotional behaviours? We might suggest that the relevant presence of this feature in those less financially educated or also less used to reading economic news regularly may give some hint as to what can act as a 'catalyst' for the 'explosion' of emotionally driven behaviours. In fact, some economic and financial events, like stock market bubbles or even worldwide crises (such as the sub-prime crisis or the sovereign credit risk issue), may suddenly become news spread by even non-specialised media. In this case, people who are not ardent followers of technical financial information developments may become particularly impressed, which stimulates their sleeping agent to awake.

These considerations appear particularly worrying for those who are responsible for the care of global financial stability and the management of systemic risk. At this point, we suggest three separate streams of implications for market participants and for regulators.

The first implication that we propose is caution, *warning* relevant parties about the role that potentially should be assigned to the *'questionnaire' tool* which aims to detect the individual financial risk tolerance. The documented fallacies are twofold: first, in the case where the questionnaire's content was coherent with what the literature states as being a good financial risk tolerance test (as the one we used in our analysis), the questionnaire would be 'biased' by the individual self-evaluation. This instrument may act as a good reference point of the individual risk tolerance in 'normal' market conditions, because people tend to act as they self-represent. Nevertheless, it loses any relevance in periods of market turmoil, because those affected by the sleeping factor may radically and unforeseeably change their risk tolerance, and thus their financial behaviour. Secondly, the suitability questionnaires enforced by the Markets in Financial Instruments Directive (MiFID, henceforth) requirements appear to be far from being a risk tolerance detection instrument. Rather, from our analysis of the suitability questionnaires provided by a significant sample of Italian financial intermediaries, we discovered that the implementation of the suitability assessment and, within it, the valuation of risk tolerance, is achieved in a highly variable manner. The majority of intermediaries seem to derive the risk tolerance assessment by asking the risk–return expectations for future investments, while the subjective risk profile of the client is less frequently requested. In particular, the individual's past financial investments (risk attitude in the real life), along with current financial constraints (risk capacity), are often neglected. Moreover, we uncovered many inconsistencies in the profiles produced from different questionnaires submitted to the same person. We ran an experiment by submitting three anonymous questionnaires to a sample of 100 potential investors in order to verify the steadiness of their profiles. Depending on the bank questionnaire that is used, at least for some subjects, the risk profiles obtained varied. In 77 per cent of the cases, the same subject obtains profiles that are different across the three banks. In 14 per cent of the cases, the profiles are totally different: they range from the highest to the lowest profile across the three banks for the same subject. In this sense, we should recognise that the questionnaires are strongly different as far as their structures and scoring methods are concerned. In terms of structure, they mainly neglect risk attitude and risk capacity information. On the subject of scoring, we might think that 'different business models' may justify scoring discrepancies. Nevertheless, no real effort to profile the *true* risk tolerance of the individual seems to have been undertaken.

All these findings should be taken into consideration by market authorities and regulators, because they should be aware of the pros, but also of the limits, of a technical tool (the questionnaire) which may not always be completely informative of the financial risk tolerance of individuals. Paradoxically, in peculiar market conditions it may even supply misleading information about this risk tolerance, leading to a situation whereby there is a lack of protection provided to both customers and to intermediaries.

The fallacies (or in any case the limitations) of the 'questionnaire' tool lead us to the second stream of implications of our findings. If the standardised format of the questionnaire may play the role, in optimal conditions, of a 'biased' detection instrument of the individual risk tolerance, we believe that a more customised and careful approach should be followed to understand and monitor the risk profile of investors. Further findings of our research demonstrate that when people choose by themselves, they take higher risks. In general, the sharing of the financial decision process with others, and even better, with external financial advisers, is proven to mediate subjectivity and to reduce the riskiness of choices. Hence, we think that a spread of the advisory support and mediation involving professional third parties may help to contain the emotional reactions of individuals, especially those with less experience or financially educated. In aggregate these conciliations of thoughts and of personalities may be of help, finally, for the slowdown of systemic crises.

The last suggestion for market participants is addressed again to authorities and regulators. Our findings provide evidence that people with low financial knowledge tend to suffer from the presence of the sleeping factor the most. The mediation of professional third parties (such as financial advisers) may be an immediate solution to break the dangerous implications of an uncontrolled sleeping factor blow-up. Nevertheless, a long-term solution should be conceived in order to progressively moderate the sleeping factors at its root. That is why, coherently with the following remarks referred to the debt side of the marketplace, we add to the widespread stream of studies and institutional initiatives which suggest investment and participation in financial literacy programmes, because people with higher levels of financial knowledge tend to be less affected by the sleeping factor.

10.3 Implication on the debt side

On the debt side of the decision process, our empirical analyses show that household debt demand, especially consumer credit demand, seems less rational but more driven by emotional factors, such as overconfidence, impulsivity in consumption attitudes and myopia: that is, the inability to perceive the long-term consequences of today's debt decisions. In fact individuals tend, on the one hand, to overestimate their capacity to manage domestic financial resources and, on the other, to underestimate the possibility of being affected by negative events, such as illness or job loss. Furthermore, they overestimate immediate benefits and undervalue future costs; such behaviour leads to the decision to purchase, using debt if necessary, regardless of the effect this choice may have on the sustainability of future debt levels.

The fact that over-indebtedness may be caused by individual irrational behaviours is relevant and has to be taken into account by policy makers in order to appoint appropriate measures designed to prevent or manage situations of financial difficulties and to evaluate their effectiveness.

Developed countries are becoming increasingly concerned about the phenomenon of over-indebtedness, not only for its size but also for its nature and its impact on the welfare of society. In fact, it disproportionately affects persons who are weak from a social and economic point of view.

Among preventive measures that seek to achieve more responsible borrowing by individuals, financial education plays an important role in the prevention of over-indebtedness both by increasing an individual's ability to understand financial information relating to the state of his or her financial assets and liabilities and by helping raise awareness about the effects consumption and lifestyle behaviour have on a household's finances. Indeed, financial education targets behaviour patterns due to inability, irresponsibility or short-sightedness that lead individuals into excess debt. By helping individuals understand the difference between what they want and what they need and can afford, and between essential items and those that can be purchased at a later date, significant inroads into the behavioural causes of over-indebtedness can be made.

However, although financial education initiatives certainly help to improve individuals' abilities to borrow responsibly, these measures on their own cannot be realistically expected to prevent over-indebtedness. Individuals, in fact, may continue to have difficulties understanding correctly the financial information made available to them or may not be able to alter significantly behaviour patterns that lead them to over-borrow, as suggested by the literature on psychological factors.

Moreover, many studies on biases in judgement and decision making have shown that individuals not only tend to display overconfidence about their ability to manage resources, but they are also overconfident with regard to their own knowledge. Due to overconfidence, people often believe that they know more than they actually do, and this can in turn have negative consequences since it affects decision making; individuals can overweight their own judgements relative to other inputs (for example, all the technical information provided by banks on credit). Thus, financial education is not a panacea and behavioural experiments have highlighted that the results of financial advice have not led to, as expected, better financial decisions when behavioural factors prevail. Furthermore, individuals often have little awareness of the existence and consequences these psychological mechanisms have. Indeed, individuals in job and family difficulties tend to lay the blame on exogenous factors, which reduce incomes levels below those expected. Rarely do individuals recognise that the causes for their difficulties lie principally or at least also with their inability to manage money and the decisions made regarding spending and indebtedness. In this perspective, policy makers involved in financial education should investigate what kind of financial knowledge has the most impact on financial behaviours, taking into account also individual biases and heuristics.

More generally, we think that further work is needed to analyse the link between psychological factors and debt demand. Additionally, we believe that the definition of policies designed to prevent and manage the risk of over-indebtedness cannot ignore the evaluation of the role of behavioural variables in determining non-rational debt behaviours. Indeed, individuals' incapacity to take corrective steps, despite knowing of the dangers of over-indebtedness, may have significant repercussions in designing effective policies for the management of situations of indebtedness that are already (or are at risk of becoming) pathological. In this direction an important contribution, at least for unsecured debt, may come from the New Consumer Credit Directive, which among its goals seeks to increase consumer protection not only by improving levels of disclosure regarding credit products and thereby helping consumers make informed decisions, but also by raising awareness of consumer risks, by explaining at the pre-contractual and agreement stages the costs incurred in case of insolvency.

The overall findings on the debt side suggest that the so-called sleeping factor, hypothesised for the investment side, is (in the case of indebtedness decisions) specifically linked to impulsivity. Interestingly, Ottaviani and Vandone (2010) showed in the same sample that the motor component of impulsivity specifically predicted consumer credit, while the non-planning component was significantly related to mortgages. Again, our participants may not seem impulsive when they programme future expenditure but then, in daily life, they might obey the part of themselves that pushes them into a choice dictated by a particular spur of the moment. Of specific interest is the fact that the same person can effectively reflect on whether to spend money wisely, and also schedule these decisions over time; however, at the same time, they are often unable to resist the urge to implement irreversible actions, such as handing over the credit card in a store, or typing a PIN code at the ATM. These mental operations, that seem to be closely related to the internal consistency, may be split into partially autonomous processes, leaving intact the identity of the subject. An illuminating example is that we can be totally aware of the level of probability associated with the lottery game but this knowledge is not enough to prevent us ending up at the bookmaker on a Saturday and we often cannot resist the temptation to play again. These considerations confirm the overall final interpretation of our findings, that our rational mind can coexist with such a pervasive process as the wandering mind that temporarily transports us in to life of fantasy and which inevitably influences our actions.

10.4 *'Nosce te ipsum'*: know who you are

Our daily life decision making is not based uniquely on rationality or on our ability to calculate: we are not computers. Evolution has provided us with both a nervous system and also emotional capacity, which have been used successfully for hundreds of centuries in dealing with environment and with our fellows. If we choose to listen to the system of our emotions, we would have a guide for our actions, anticipated by the signals coming from the body, in order to cope with opportunities or dangers coming from the living system we have built.

The findings described in this book induce us to propose a model of mental functioning that places rationality and emotion side by side with a third factor: the counterfactual thinking and the wandering mind. These processes rely on ample scientific references but will need much more empirical research. So our decision process results in a mix of rational forces, emotional responses and also the continuous activity of counterfactual thoughts together with the parallel process of mind wandering. It is a normal mechanism, which guides our daily lives and makes us not only purely rational beings or emotionally sensitive, but also capable of dreams and hopes, even while we are wide awake. Hopes and dreams may become true or not, but this does not stop us from thinking about them.

These processes are often unconscious and could be considered to be parasitic, because they act to divert us from our daily activities as efficient reasoning. Nevertheless, various authors (Byrne, 2002; Mason et al., 2007) suggest that the wandering mind enables individuals to maintain an optimal level of arousal, thereby facilitating performances on mundane tasks, or stimulating independent thought. Thus the wandering mind should be essential to assure a sense of coherence to one's past, present and future experiences. In fact, in counterfactual thinking, the contemplation 'What if...?' may also apply to our personal past and, in some cases, to history.

And yet, may we think of the process related to 'hope' or 'regret' as a strict calculation of probability? Why should we have regrets about something that has already happened? Perhaps the old adage 'Do not cry over spilt milk' is of relevance here; however, researchers, such as Coricelli et al. (2005), have more formally suggested that the orbitofrontal cortex (OFC) is a candidate neural substrate for the generation of such emotions. The OFC modulates the gain of emotion using a top-down method in which a paradigmatic cognitive process, specifically counterfactual thinking, contributes to an emotional response and ensuing choice behaviour. Evidence that high-level emotions such as regret depend upon a specific neuroanatomical substrate comes from studies which show that the normal expression of this cognitively based emotion depends on the integrity of the OFC. Patients with selective lesions to the anterior medial OFC do not experience regret and, unlike healthy controls, are unable to adjust their behaviour to avoid regret-inducing situations.

Remember that our subjects had no disease, and the avoidance of regret (negative emotions) is valid also as a possibility to have hope. Of course you could object that hope is nothing but the trust on those behaviours that are on the side of highest probability. Nevertheless, in this case, the act of buying lottery tickets which have millionaire premiums should be considered to be the behaviour of people ignorant of statistics and also of the calculation of probabilities.

It is necessary to remember that the initial instructions of the IGT test underline that the purpose of the experiment was to win as much as possible. This sentence, which is very easy to understand in cognitive terms, triggers many parallel thoughts made available by the neural network, that immediately activate the choice mechanism for the cards. Imagine dividing the time in seconds, or even tenths of a second, to show what happens to the subject who is preparing to do the test, starting from his or her previous decision to adhere to the test. Was he or she intrigued? Did he or she believe to be compelled to do so? What did he or she expect? All these are functions of prospective memory, cognitive processes of memory, projected towards the future and strongly influenced by expectations and scenario construction. Then, the individual faces the computer, to the machine that measures levels of skin conductance and also to the researchers who explain the task; the subject wonders whether there is a trap, whether it is a test of intelligence. In the meantime, the neural network called 'default mode' (Raichle and Snyder, 2007) begins simultaneously to work on the experimental task which requires him or her to earn as much as possible. At this point, our subjects begin the test and when they choose the disadvantageous cards, as predicted by the model of the somatic marker, they begin to be conditioned, activating themselves emotionally. At the same time, their mind wandering system leads them to try again, and again, to repair themselves, to earn choosing decks that give not only heavy losses, but also big wins. They dare more. In addition, for reasons related to the functioning of our autonomous nervous system, after any choice each subject has to wait about 10 seconds before proceeding to the next selection (the time physiologically required for the system to return back to the baseline condition). This is an infinite time for the processing speed of our brain. During this period, the attention should not focus on any particular task, and the processes of rational thought, of listening to emotional states of body and mind wandering, are free to fluctuate and interact with each other. There is a very 'quiet' and 'unconscious' mind working while our gaze is directed at the reassuring blue uniform of the computer screen. We can be tempted not to listen to the somatic marker, and to leave the default network prevailing, the one that relates to fantasies and hopes, which are domain specifically activated.

Since the test was designed to be cognitively impenetrable, there is no rule that allows consistent winning: those who have invested with some regularity on a rational search of algorithms have always lost. The 'dreamers' guided by hope that a favourable cycle of choice would last for ever also lost.

Again, we remember that our subjects were not suffering from any neurological disorder or addiction, and the results we obtained on a large scale (441 individuals), have some similarities with that reported by Bechara and Damasio (2002) who found that in a small sample of 31 non-clinical subjects, 20 per cent have behaviours similar to those of addicted persons. Based on their observations, the authors point out that normal subjects, who perform poorly on the IGT but generate anticipatory SCR, describe themselves to be high risk takers, thrill seekers or gamblers in real life. In our large sample, subjects are very reluctant to take risks in real life, and a plausible explanation is that the wandering and the counterfactual thought are a good interpretation of the results. The test retains its full value and is particularly effective when a cerebral area is damaged, due to trauma or from drug use (Bechara and Damasio, 2002). However, when applied to a non-clinical population, its interpretation must take account of the functioning of the 'default mode network'.

Experience and knowledge, accompanied by a good ability to listen to the emotional messages coming from the body, seem to be the best conditions for accepting the (inevitable) losses from our test, while taking prudent decisions is the more rewarding strategy at the end of the experiment. The role of emotion, and its impact on trading performance, has been extensively analysed and reported by Fenton-O'Creevy et al. (2008). They found that successful expert traders are more likely to engage in self-monitoring and emotional regulation, and it is true to say that ultimately this carries important benefits in terms of trading performance. Although Lo and Repin (2002) documented significant emotional responses among the most experienced traders, the same authors subsequently showed that being emotionally affected by one's own daily profits and losses is counterproductive from the perspective of trading performance. Specifically, subjects whose emotional reactions to monetary gains and losses were more intense, on both the positive and negative sides, exhibited significantly worse trading performance, therefore supporting the common wisdom (Lo et al., 2005). It has to be noted that the latter study consisted of survey data, such as daily emotional state questionnaires and trading reports, whereas the Lo and Repin (2002) study included perhaps more revealing psycho-physiological measures.

Our sample includes a considerable number of people who specialise in the financial profession (more than 130 individuals). A relevant finding of our research is that they behave regularly during the IGT/SCR test, and their UR levels, compared to BR and real life risk do not reveal any 'sleeping factor'. We might easily suggest that their accumulated expertise is capable of inhibiting the activation of the 'default network' that would inevitably lead them to an enhancement of easy money. It seems that financial experts have developed a kind of cynicism towards the piece of good fortune, a serene pessimism about market stability and continued growth in prices; their imagination can therefore roam into other domains, but it does not venture into the 'lucky gain domain', and it shows more concreteness. This principle does not apply to those inexperienced in financial markets who cannot erase from their memory, even after the pain of a bearish market, some fantastically extraordinary price hikes that make financial market participation like playing the lottery and which might never ever happen again. (Who knows, after all?)

The result of these simultaneous processes (rationality, emotions and the wandering mind) is a kind of personality that is split without being pathological, most likely developed with that level of inconsistency that everyone finds within with a minimum of honest introspection. This interpretation basically originates from the pioneering work of Kahneman, who, in the essay that he wrote with Tversky (1982), posed a key question for cognitive scientists: 'How do people mentally "undo" reality?' Do not forget also Pirandello's masterpiece 'One, no one and one hundred thousand' which ironically depicts how we are, under the surface of the skin.

Appendix 1

Part 1 – Survey on the Financial Risk Tolerance

(Grable and Lytton, 1999)
N.B.: The situations you are provided with in this section are absolutely ***hypothetical*** *and are not connected with the current financial situation; moreover some questions ask you to take decisions based on a* ***limited set of information****.*

1. In general, how would your best friend describe you as a risk taker?
   - ❑ A real gambler
   - ❑ Willing to take risks after completing adequate research
   - ❑ Cautious
   - ❑ A real risk avoider

2. You are on a TV game show and can choose one of the following. Which would you take?
   - ❑ €1,000 in cash
   - ❑ A 50% chance at winning €5,000
   - ❑ A 25% chance at winning €10,000
   - ❑ A 5% chance at winning €100,000

3. You have just finished saving for a 'once-in-a-lifetime' vacation. Three weeks before you plan to leave, you lose your job. You would:
   - ❑ Cancel the vacation
   - ❑ Take a much more modest vacation
   - ❑ Go as scheduled, reasoning that you need the time to prepare for a job search
   - ❑ Extend your vacation, because this might be your last chance to go first class

4. How would you respond to the following statement? 'It's hard for me to pass up a bargain.'
   - ❑ Very true
   - ❑ Sometimes true
   - ❑ Not at all true

5. If you unexpectedly received €20,000 to invest, what would you do?
   - ❑ Deposit it in a bank account, money market account, or an insured CD
   - ❑ Invest it in safe high-quality bonds or bond mutual funds
   - ❑ Invest it in stocks or stock mutual funds

6. In terms of experience, how comfortable are you investing in stocks or stock mutual funds?
   - ❑ Not at all comfortable
   - ❑ Somewhat comfortable
   - ❑ Very comfortable

7. Which situation would make you the happiest?
   - ❑ You win €50,000 in a publisher's contest
   - ❑ You inherit €50,000 from a rich relative
   - ❑ You earn €50,000 by risking €1,000 in the options market
   - ❑ Any of the above – after all, you're happy with the €50,000

8. When you think of the word 'risk', which of the following words comes to mind first?
   - ❑ Loss
   - ❑ Uncertainty
   - ❑ Opportunity
   - ❑ Thrill

9. You inherit a mortgage-free house worth €80,000. The house is in a nice neighbourhood, and you believe that it should increase in value faster than inflation. Unfortunately, the house needs repairs. If rented today, the house would bring in €600 monthly, but if updates and repairs were made, the house would rent for €800 per month. To finance the repairs you'll need to take out a mortgage on the property. You would:
   - ❑ Sell the house
   - ❑ Rent the house as is
   - ❑ Remodel and update the house, and then rent it

10. In your opinion, is it more important to be protected from rising consumer prices (inflation) or to maintain the safety of your money from loss or theft?
    - ❑ Much more important to secure the safety of my money
    - ❑ Much more important to be protected from rising prices (inflation)

11. You've just taken a job at a small fast-growing company. After your first year you are offered the following bonus choices. Which one would you choose?
    - ❑ A five-year employment contract
    - ❑ A €25,000 bonus
    - ❑ Stock in the company currently worth €25,000 with the hope of selling out later at a large profit

12. Some experts are predicting prices of assets such as gold, jewels, collectibles and real estate (hard assets) to increase in value. Bond prices may fall; however, experts tend to agree that government bonds are relatively safe.

Most of your investment assets are now in high-interest government bonds. What would you do?

- ❑ Hold the bonds
- ❑ Sell the bonds, put half the proceeds into money market accounts, and the other half into hard assets
- ❑ Sell the bonds and put the total proceeds into hard assets
- ❑ Sell the bonds, put all the money into hard assets, and borrow additional money to buy more

13. Assume you are going to buy a home in the next few weeks. Your strategy would probably be:

- ❑ To buy an affordable house where you can make monthly payments comfortably
- ❑ To stretch a bit financially to buy the house you really want
- ❑ To buy the most expensive house you can qualify for
- ❑ To borrow money from friends and relatives so you can qualify for a bigger mortgage

14. Given the best and worst case returns of the four investment choices below, which would you prefer?

- ❑ €200 gain best case; €0 gain/loss worst case
- ❑ €800 gain best case; €200 loss worst case
- ❑ €2,600 gain best case; €800 loss worst case
- ❑ €4,800 gain best case; €2,400 loss worst case

15. Assume that you are applying for a mortgage. Interest rates have been coming down over the past few months. There's the possibility that this trend will continue. But some economists are predicting rates to increase. You have the option of locking in your mortgage interest rate or letting it float. If you lock in, you will get the current rate, even if interest rates go up. If the rates go down, you'll have to settle for the higher locked in rate. You plan to live in the house for at least three years. What would you do?

- ❑ Definitely lock in the interest rate
- ❑ Probably lock in the interest rate
- ❑ Probably let the interest rate float
- ❑ Definitely let the interest rate float

16. In addition to whatever you own, you have been given €1,000. You are now asked to choose between:

- ❑ A sure gain of €500
- ❑ A 50% chance to gain €1,000 and a 50% chance to gain nothing

17. In addition to whatever you own, you have been given €2,000. You are now asked to choose between:

- ❑ A sure loss of €500
- ❑ A 50% chance to lose €1,000 and a 50% chance to lose nothing

18. Suppose a relative left you an inheritance of €100,000, stipulating in the will that you invest ALL the money in ONE of the following choices. Which one would you select?

   - ❑ A savings account or money market mutual fund
   - ❑ A mutual fund that owns stocks and bonds
   - ❑ A portfolio of 15 common stocks
   - ❑ Commodities like gold, silver and oil

19. If you had to invest €20,000, which of the following investment choices would you find most appealing?

   - ❑ €12,000 in low-risk investments, €6,000 in medium-risk investments, €2,000 in high-risk investments
   - ❑ €6,000 in low-risk investments, €8,000 in medium-risk investments, €6,000 in high-risk investments
   - ❑ €2,000 in low-risk investments, €8,000 in medium-risk investments, €10,000 in high-risk investments

20. Your trusted friend and neighbour, an experienced geologist, is putting together a group of investors to fund an exploratory gold mining venture. The venture could pay back 50 to 100 times the investment if successful. If the mine is a bust, the entire investment is worthless. Your friend estimates the chance of success is only 20%. If you had the money, how much would you invest?

   - ❑ Nothing
   - ❑ One month's salary
   - ❑ Three month's salary
   - ❑ Six month's salary

Part 2 – Impulsivity Test

N.B.: In this section you will find a list of situations that people usually face during their life. For each situation you should choose the answer that fits you best. You are kindly requested to answer all of the questions ***based on your opinion*** *and* ***without the help of others****. There is no right or wrong answer; just fill in the answers to the questions using your* ***personal feelings****.*

	Rarely/ Never	Occasionally	Often	Almost always/Always
I plan tasks carefully.	❑	❑	❑	❑
I do things without thinking.	❑	❑	❑	❑
I make up my mind quickly.	❑	❑	❑	❑
I am happy-go-lucky.	❑	❑	❑	❑
I don't 'pay attention'.	❑	❑	❑	❑
I have 'racing' thoughts.	❑	❑	❑	❑
I plan trips well ahead of time.	❑	❑	❑	❑
I am self-controlled.	❑	❑	❑	❑
I concentrate easily.	❑	❑	❑	❑
I save regularly.	❑	❑	❑	❑
I 'squirm' at plays or lectures.	❑	❑	❑	❑
I am a careful thinker.	❑	❑	❑	❑
I plan for job security.	❑	❑	❑	❑
I say things without thinking.	❑	❑	❑	❑
I like to think about complex problems.	❑	❑	❑	❑
I change jobs.	❑	❑	❑	❑
I act 'on impulse'.	❑	❑	❑	❑
I get easily bored when solving thought problems.	❑	❑	❑	❑
I act on the spur of the moment.	❑	❑	❑	❑
I am a steady thinker.	❑	❑	❑	❑

I change residences.	❑	❑	❑	❑
I buy things on impulse.	❑	❑	❑	❑
I can only think about one thing at a time.	❑	❑	❑	❑
I change hobbies.	❑	❑	❑	❑
I spend or charge more than I earn.	❑	❑	❑	❑
I often have extraneous thoughts when thinking.	❑	❑	❑	❑
I am more interested in the present than the future.	❑	❑	❑	❑
I am restless at the theatre or lectures.	❑	❑	❑	❑
I like puzzles.	❑	❑	❑	❑
I am future oriented.	❑	❑	❑	❑

Part 3 – Socio-economic section

N.B.: In this section some questions refer to your ***family****. This category includes all of the people you share incomes, expenses, investments and debts with. In the case where you do not share economics and financial situations with others, you are your 'family'.*

1. **Age** ....

2. **City of official address and ZIP code, postcode, CAP** ....

3. Gender:
   - ❒ M
   - ❒ F

4. Marital status:
   - ❒ Single
   - ❒ Married
   - ❒ Common-law wife/husband
   - ❒ Divorced
   - ❒ Widowed

5. People belonging to your family who are dependent on you (multiple choice):
   - ❒ Nobody
   - ❒ Wife/Husband
   - ❒ Children
   - ❒ Elderly

6. Educational qualification (refer to the highest qualification you hold):
   - ❒ Secondary school
   - ❒ High school
   - ❒ University
   - ❒ Master's or PhD

7. Working condition (multiple choice):
   - ❒ Salaried employee (workman, office worker, teacher)
   - ❒ Pensioner
   - ❒ Company director
   - ❒ Freelancer
   - ❒ Businessman
   - ❒ Financial adviser
   - ❒ Trader
   - ❒ Asset manager
   - ❒ Not working
   - ❒ Other

8. Type of working contract:
   - ❒ Fixed-term
   - ❒ Open-ended
   - ❒ Other

9. Composition of family income (multiple choice):
   - ❒ Work income
   - ❒ Retirement income
   - ❒ Real estate income
   - ❒ Financial income
   - ❒ Other

10. Total amount of family income (monthly net income):
    - ❒ < 500 euros
    - ❒ between 500 and 1,000 euros
    - ❒ between 1,000 and 2,000 euros
    - ❒ between 2,000 and 3,000 euros
    - ❒ between 3,000 and 4,000 euros
    - ❒ between 4,000 and 5,000 euros
    - ❒ between 5,000 and 6,000 euros
    - ❒ more than 6,000 euros

11. Expectations about future income:
    - ❒ lower
    - ❒ stable
    - ❒ higher

12. Did any unexpected or bad event impact upon your family in the past 12 months thus causing an income decrease? (e.g. job loss, job reduction, disease, death, disability, divorce)
    - ❒ Yes
    - ❒ No

13. What is the monthly income–daily expenses ratio within your family?
    - ❒ Income is not enough to cover daily expenses; we are forced to borrow money
    - ❒ We are forced to use our savings
    - ❒ Income is enough to cover daily expenses
    - ❒ We are able to save some money
    - ❒ We are able to save a considerable amount of money

14. Number of real estate properties:
    - ❒ 0
    - ❒ 1
    - ❒ 2
    - ❒ 3
    - ❒ more than 3

15. What is the global estimated value of your real estate properties?
    - ❒ I do not have any real estate property
    - ❒ below 200,000 euros
    - ❒ between 200,000 and 500,000 euros
    - ❒ between 500,000 and 1,000,000 euros
    - ❒ above 1,000,000 euros

16. What is the global estimated value of your financial properties?
    - ❒ I do not have any financial property
    - ❒ below 50,000 euros
    - ❒ between 50,000 and 100,000 euros
    - ❒ between 100,000 and 200,000 euros
    - ❒ between 200,000 and 500,000 euros
    - ❒ above 500,000 euros

17. Which of the following financial products are you confident with? (Multiple choice)
    - ❒ Bank account
    - ❒ Bank deposit
    - ❒ Certificate of deposit
    - ❒ Repo contract
    - ❒ Postal deposit
    - ❒ Treasury bills
    - ❒ Stocks
    - ❒ Bonds
    - ❒ Mutual funds
    - ❒ Exchange traded fund (ETF)
    - ❒ Financial management
    - ❒ Hedge funds
    - ❒ Structured products
    - ❒ Derivatives
    - ❒ Index and unit linked insurance policies

18. If 100 is the total amount of your financial properties, how are they approximately divided into:

	Percentage
Bank account	________
Bank deposit, Certificate of deposit, Repo contract	________
Postal deposit	________
Treasury bills and bonds	________
Financial management, Mutual funds and ETF shares	________
Stocks	________
Foreign financial products	________
Structured products and derivatives	________
Hedge funds	________
Financial insurance policies	________
Total	**100%**

19. What is the frequency of your financial decision updating?

    - ❒ Daily
    - ❒ Weekly
    - ❒ Intra-year
    - ❒ Yearly
    - ❒ Every two or three years
    - ❒ I do not take any financial decisions

20. Have you ever invested a huge amount of money in a risky asset just to feel the thrilling sensation of knowing its return?

    - ❒ No
    - ❒ Rarely
    - ❒ Yes

21. What level of risk did you bear <u>in the past</u> when taking financial decisions?

    - ❒ I never took financial decisions
    - ❒ Very low
    - ❒ Low
    - ❒ Medium
    - ❒ High
    - ❒ Very high

22. What level of risk are you <u>now</u> willing to bear when taking financial decisions?

    - ❒ I never take financial decisions
    - ❒ Very low
    - ❒ Low
    - ❒ Medium
    - ❒ High
    - ❒ Very high

23. What is the maximum financial loss you bore in the past before deciding to withdraw your investments?

    - ❒ I never bore financial losses
    - ❒ Very little
    - ❒ Up to 1/4
    - ❒ Half
    - ❒ More than half
    - ❒ I kept the investment even if it was in a loss

24. What insurance coverage do you have at the moment (apart from car accident policies)? (Multiple choice)

    - ❒ No insurance coverage
    - ❒ Life insurance (death, index/unit linked)
    - ❒ Disease or disability insurance

- ❒ Burglary and burning insurance
- ❒ Civil liability insurance
- ❒ Pension fund

25. How did you financially react to the recent financial crisis? (Multiple choice)
    - ❒ I bought undervalued stocks
    - ❒ I sold part of my financial assets
    - ❒ I sold the majority of my financial assets
    - ❒ I did nothing

26. Your family borrowed money to (multiple choice):

		Amount of debt now
Buy family house	❒	....
Make other real estate investments	❒	....
Make financial investments	❒	....
Buy a car	❒	....
Buy other useful devices (TV, PC, etc.)	❒	....
Buy holidays and beauty farm treatments	❒	....
Cover daily expenses	❒	....
Pay gambling debts	❒	....
Other (specify)...	❒	....
No debts	❒	

27. Amount of the global monthly instalment required to finance the debts you are paying at the moment:
    - ❒ no debt
    - ❒ < 200 euros
    - ❒ between 200 and 400 euros
    - ❒ between 400 and 600 euros
    - ❒ between 600 and 800 euros
    - ❒ between 800 and 1.000 euros
    - ❒ between 1,000 and 2,000 euros
    - ❒ more than 2,000 euros

28. Have you ever borrowed money from relatives, friends, colleagues or neighbours?
    - ❒ Yes
    - ❒ No

29. How do you usually take investment decisions? (Multiple choice)
    - ❒ I do not have investments
    - ❒ I take decisions about investments by myself
    - ❒ I take decisions about investments with my family
    - ❒ I listen to the advice I am given by friends and colleagues

- ❒ I take decisions with the advice of an analyst or, in general, of an expert
- ❒ An expert takes care of my investments

30. If you make use of an adviser or expert, what is your level of trustworthiness in him/her?
    - ❒ I do not make use of any adviser
    - ❒ Low
    - ❒ Medium
    - ❒ High

31. How has your trust in an adviser evolved over the past few years?
    - ❒ I do not make use of any adviser
    - ❒ It has gotten worse
    - ❒ It is the same
    - ❒ It has gotten better

32. How do you usually take <u>debt</u> decisions? (Multiple choice)
    - ❒ I do not have any debt
    - ❒ I take decisions about debts by myself
    - ❒ I listen to the advice I am given by friends and colleagues
    - ❒ I take decisions about debts with my family
    - ❒ I take decisions with the advice of the salesperson or of the bank employee

33. How much time do you usually spend in getting information that is useful to take decisions about:

	Investments	**Debts**	**Mortgage**
Less than 5 minutes	❒	❒	❒
About 15 minutes	❒	❒	❒
About 30 minutes	❒	❒	❒
About 1 hour	❒	❒	❒
A few hours	❒	❒	❒
Several hours	❒	❒	❒
I dot take any decisions	❒	❒	❒

34. How frequently do you read economic and financial newspapers and magazines?
    - ❒ several times per day, on the Internet
    - ❒ every day
    - ❒ once a week
    - ❒ once a month
    - ❒ never

35. Are you aware of the return that your <u>investments</u> produced in the last year?
    - ❐ No
    - ❐ Yes
    - ❐ Yes but not exactly
    - ❐ I do not hold any investment

36. Are you aware of how the cost of your debt has evolved over time?
    - ❐ No
    - ❐ Yes
    - ❐ Yes but not exactly
    - ❐ I do not have any debt

37. Do you trust in your capacity to take good financial decisions?
    - ❐ Not at all
    - ❐ Quite enough
    - ❐ A lot
    - ❐ Very much
    - ❐ Absolutely

38. Do you trust in the future?
    - ❐ No
    - ❐ Yes
    - ❐ I do not know

Appendix 2

Table A.1 Households socio-demographic, economic and psychological characteristics: descriptive statistics

Variables	*Freq.*	%
Dependent variable		
Participation in the debt market		
No	172	39.00
Yes	269	61.00
Participation in the consumer credit market		
No	323	73.24
Yes	118	26.76
Participation in the mortgage market		
No	234	53.06
Yes	207	46.94
Explanatory variables		
Age		
Up to 30 years (ref.)	42	9.52
31 to 40 years	170	38.55
41 to 50 years	116	26.30
50 to 61 years	64	14.51
Older than 61 years	49	11.11
Education		
Elementary school (ref.)	23	5.22
Middle school	175	39.68
High school	187	42.40
University degree	56	12.70
Work status		
Employee (ref.)	270	61.22
Self-employed	112	25.40
Not employed	59	13.38
Net wealth (quartile)		
Up to €350,000 (ref.)	115	26.8
€350,001 to €425,000	114	25.85
€425,001 to €1,100,000	132	29.71
More than €1,100,001	81	18.37

Monthly income (quartile)		
Up to €2,500 (ref.)	161	36.51
€2,501 to €3,500	83	18.82
€3,501 to €5,500	93	21.09
More than €5,501	104	23.58
Dependent children		
No (ref.)	213	48.30
Yes	228	51.70
Divorced		
No (ref.)	411	93.20
Yes	30	6.80
Fragility		
No (ref.)	355	80.50
Yes	86	19.50
	Mean	**Std dev.**
UR	0.5722	.4576
Bis	58.6576	7.8880

References

C. Acerbi (2002) 'Spectral measures of risk: a coherent representation of subjective risk aversion', *Journal of Banking and Finance*, 26, 7, 1505–1518.

C. Acerbi (2004) 'Coherent representation of subjective risk aversion', in G. Szegö (ed.) *Risk Measures for the 21st Century* (New York: Wiley).

D. R. Addis, A. T. Wong and D. L. Schacter (2007) 'Remembering the past and imagining the future: Common and distinct neural substrates during event construction and elaboration', *Neuropsychologia*, 45, 1363–1377.

Y. Aït-Sahalia and A. Lo (2000) 'Nonparametric risk management and implied risk aversion', *Journal of Econometrics*, 94, 9–51.

L. Allen, J. Boudoukh and A. Saunders (2004) *Understanding Market, Credit and Operational Risk* (Oxford: Blackwell Publishing).

M. Alpert and H. Raiffa (1982) 'A progress report on the training of probability assessors', in D. Kahneman, P. Slovich and A. Tversky (eds) *Judgment Under Uncertainty: Heuristics and biases* (Cambridge and New York: Cambridge University Press).

L. Anderloni (1997) 'Il sovraindebitamento in Italia e in Europa', in R. Ruozi (ed.) *L'usura in Italia* (Milano: Egea).

L. Anderloni, D. Braga and E. Carluccio (2007) *New Frontiers in Banking Services. Emerging needs and taylored products for untapped market* (Berlin: Springer-Verlag).

P. B. Andreassen and S. J. Kraus (1990) 'Judgmental extrapolation and the salience of change', *Journal of Forecasting*, 9, 347–372.

M. Arellano and S. Bond (1991) 'Some tests of specification for panel data: Monte Carlo evidence and an application to employment equations', *Review of Economic Studies*, 58, 277–297.

L. Argote, M. Turner and M. Fichman (1988) 'To centralize or not to centralize: the effects of uncertainty and threat on group structure and performance', *Organizational Behavior*, 42, 1–17.

H. R. Arkes, L. T. Herren and A. M. Isen (1988) 'The role of potential loss in the influence of affect on risk-taking behavior', *Organizational Behavior and Human Decision Processes*, 42, 181–193.

W. B. Arthur (1994) 'Inductive reasoning and bounded rationality', *American Economic Review*, 84, 2, 406–411.

P. Artzner, F. Delbaen, J. M. Eber and D. Heath (1997) 'Thinking coherently', *Risk*, 10, 11, 68–71.

E. Arzac and V. Bawa (1977) 'Portfolio choice and equilibrium in capital markets with safety-first investors', *Journal of Financial Economics*, 4, 3, 277–288.

Assogestioni (2009) 'Mappa del risparmio gestito (third quarter 2009)', 1–59.

T. K. Au (1983) 'Chinese and English counterfactuals: The Sapir–Whorf hypothesis revisited', *Cognition*, 15, 155–187.

L. M. Ausubel (1999) 'Adverse selection in the credit card market', *University of Maryland, Working Paper.*

B. J. Baars (2010) 'Spontaneous repetitive thoughts can be adaptive: Postscript on mind wandering', *Psychological Bulletin*, 136, 2, 208–210.

J. B. Baesel (1974) 'On the assessment of risk: Some further consideration', *Journal of Finance*, 29, 5, 1491–1494.

F. C. Bagliano and G. Bertola (2004) *Models for Dynamic Macroeconomics* (Oxford: Oxford University Press).

R. Bagozzi, H. Baumgartner, R. Pieters and M. Zeelenberg (2000) 'The role of emotions in goal-directed behavior', in S. Ratneshwar, D. G. Mick and C. Huffman (eds) *The Why of Consumption* (London: Routledge), pp. 36–58.

H. K. Baker and J. R. Nofsinger (2002) 'Psychological biases of investors', *Financial Services Review*, 11, 2, 97–116.

M. Baker and J. Wurgler (2007) 'Investor sentiment in the stock market', *Journal of Economics Perspectives*, 21, 2, 129–151.

A. L. Balzer (1994) 'Measuring investment risk: A review', *Journal of Investing*, 3, 3, 47–58.

Bank for International Settlement (BIS) (2008) 'Customer suitability in the retail sale of financial products and services', Basel Committee on Banking Supervision.

Banque de France (1996) 'Traitement du surendettement: nouvelles perspectives', Bulletin 2 trimestre (Supplement Etudes).

R. W. Banz (1981) 'The relationship between return and market value of common stocks', *Journal of Financial Economics*, 9, 3–18.

B. Barber and T. Odean (2000) 'Trading is hazardous to your wealth: the common stock investment performance of individual investors', *Journal of Finance*, 55, 2, 773–806.

B. Barber and T. Odean (2001) 'Boys will be boys: Gender, overconfidence and common stock investment', *The Quarterly Journal of Economics*, 116, 1, 261–292.

N. Barberis and R. Thaler (1993) 'A survey of behavioural finance', in G. M. Costantinides, M. Harris and R. M. Stultz (eds) *Handbook of the Economics of Finance* (New York: Elsevier), pp. 1052–1121.

N. Barberis and M. Huang (2001) 'Mental accounting, loss aversion, and individual stock returns', *Journal of Finance*, 56, 4, 1247–1292.

N. Barberis and M. Huang, (2008) 'Stocks as lotteries: the implications of probability weighting for security prices', *American Economic Review*, 98, 5, 2066–2100.

N. Barberis, M. Huang and T. Santos (2001) 'Prospect theory and asset prices', *Quarterly Journal of Economics*, 116, 1, 1–53.

N. Barberis, A. Shleifer and R. Vishny (1998) 'A model of investor sentiment', *Journal of Financial Economics*, 49, 3, 307–343.

N. Barberis and R. Thaler (2002) 'A survey of behavioral finance', *NBER Working Paper No. W9222*, 1–67.

N. Barberis and R. H. Thaler (2003) 'A survey of behavioural finance', in G. M. Costantinides, M. Harris and R. Stultz (eds) *Handbook of the Economics of Finance* (New York: Elsevier Science).

N. Barberis and W. Xiong (2009) 'What drives the disposition effect? An analysis of a long standing preference based explanation', *Journal of Finance*, 64, 2, 751–784.

M. Bar-Hillel and E. Neter (1996) 'Why are people reluctant to exchange lottery tickets?', *Journal of Personality and Social Psychology*, 70, 1, 17–27.

G. Barone-Adesi (1985) 'Arbitrage equilibrium with skewed asset returns', *Journal of Financial and Quantitative Analysis*, 20, 3, 299–313.

G. Barone-Adesi, P. Gagliardini and G. Urga (2004) 'Testing asset pricing models with coskewness', *Journal of Business and Economic Statistics*, 22, 1, 474–485.

S. Basu (1983) 'The relationship between earnings yield, market value and return for NYSE common stocks: Further evidence', *Journal of Financial Economics*, 12, 129–156.

M. D. Bauman, P. Lavenex, W. A. Mason, J. P. Capitanio and D. G. Amaral (2004) 'The development of mother–infant interactions following neonatal amygdala lesions in rhesus monkeys', *Journal of Neuroscience*, 24, 711–721.

V. Bawa (1975) 'Optimal rules for ordering uncertain prospects', *Journal of Financial Economics*, 2, 95–121.

S. E. Beatty and M. E. Ferrel (1998) Impulsive buying: modeling its precursors, *Journal of Retailing*, 74, 2, 169–191.

A. Bechara (2004) 'The role of emotion in decision-making: Evidence from neurological patients with orbitofrontal damage', *Brain and Cognition*, 55, 30–40.

A. Bechara and H. Damasio (2002) 'Decision-making and addiction (part I): Impaired activation of somatic states in substance dependent individuals when pondering decisions with negative future consequences', *Neuropsychologia*, 40, 1675–1689.

A. Bechara, A. R. Damasio, H. Damasio and S. W. Anderson (1994) 'Insensitivity to future consequences following damage to human prefrontal cortex', *Cognition*, 7–15.

A. Bechara, D. Tranel, H. Damasio and A. R. Damasio (1996) 'Failure to respond autonomically to anticipated future outcomes following damage to prefrontal cortex', *Cerebral Cortex*, 6, 215–225.

A. Bechara, H. Damasio, D. Tranel and A. R. Damasio (1997) 'Deciding advantageously before knowing the advantageous strategy', Science, 275, 1293–1295.

D. Bell (1982) 'Regret in decision making under uncertainty', *Operations Research*, 30, 5, 961–981.

S. Benartzi (2001) 'Excessive extrapolation and the allocation of 401 (k) accounts to company stock', *Journal of Finance*, 56, 5, 1747–1764.

S. Benartzi and R. H. Thaler (1995) 'Myopic loss aversion and the equity premium puzzle', *Quarterly Journal of Economics*, 110, 73–92.

S. Benartzi and R. H. Thaler (2001) 'Naïve diversification strategies in defined contribution savings plan', *American Economic Review*, 91, 1, 79–98.

S. Benartzi and R. H. Thaler (2002) 'How much is investor autonomy worth?', *Journal of Finance*, 57, 4, 1593–1616.

D. Bernoulli (1738) 'Specimen Theoriae Novae de Mensura Sortis' in *Commentarii Academiae Scientiarum Imperialis Petropolitannae* (1738); translated from Latin into English by L. Sommer (1954) 'Exposition of a New Theory on the Measurement of Risk' *Econometrica*, 22, 1, 23–36.

G. S. Berns, J. Chappelow, M. Cekic, C. F. Zink, G. Pagnoni and M. E. Martin-Skurski (2006) 'Neurobiological Substrates of Dread', *Science*, 312, 754–758.

P. L. Bernstein and A. Damodaran (1998) *Investment Management* (New York: John Wiley & Sons).

C. C. Bertaut, M. Haliassos and M. Reiter (2008) 'Credit card debt puzzles and debt revolvers for self control', *Working Paper.*

R. K. Bhardwaj and L. D. Brooks (1993) 'Dual betas from bull and bear markets: reversal of the size effect', *The Journal of Financial Research*, 16, 4, 269–283.

W. K. Bickel and L. A. Marsch (2001) 'Toward a behavioral economic understanding of drug dependence: Delay discounting processes', *Addiction*, 96, 73–86.

J. Bischof and M. Ebert (2009) 'Bank disclosures under IFRS and biases in the risk perception of financial instruments', *Working Paper*, 1–35.

F. Black (1993) 'Beta and return', *Journal of Portfolio Management*, 20, 8–18.

F. Black, M. C. Jensen and M. Scholes (1972) 'The capital asset pricing model: Some empirical tests' in M. Jensen (ed.) *Studies in the Theory of Capital Market* (New York: Praeger Publishers), pp. 79–121.

M. E. Blume (1971) 'On the assessment of risk', *The Journal of Finance*, 26, 1, 1–10.

K. I. Bolla, D. A. Eldreth, J. A. Matochik and J. L. Cadet (2004) 'Sex-related differences in a gambling task and its neurological correlates', *Cerebral Cortex*, 14, 11, 1226–1232.

P. Boyle, G. Garlappi, R. Uppal and T. Wang (2009) 'Keynes meets Markowitz: The tradeoff between familiarity and diversification', *Working Paper*, 1–41.

M. Brand, E. C. Recknor, F. Grabenhorst and A. Bechara (2007) 'Decisions under ambiguity and decisions under risk: correlations with executive functions and comparisons of two different gambling tasks with implicit and explicit rules', *Journal of Clinical and Experimental Neuropsychology*, 29, 86–99.

B. Brehmer (1987) 'The psychology of risk', in W. T. Singleton and J. Howden (eds) *Risk and Decisions* (New York: John Wiley and Sons), pp. 25–40.

G. Brighetti and C. Lucarelli (2010) 'Biased or unbiased risk tolerance in the financial decision making' in F. Fiordelisi, P. Molyneux and D. Previati (ed.) *New issues* in Financial Institutions and Markets I. (Bangstoke: Palgrave McMillan).

P. L. Brockett and L. L. Golden (2007) 'Biological and psychobehavioural correlates of credit scores and automobile insurance' losses: toward an explication of why credit scoring works, *Journal of Risk and Insurance*, <http://onlinelibrary.Wiley.com/doi/10.1111/jori.2007.74.issue-1/issueetoc> 74, 1, 23–63.

S. Brown, G. Garino, P. Simmons and K. Taylor (2008) 'Debt and risk preferences: A household level analysis', *Working Paper*.

R. L. Buckner and J. L. Vincent (2007) 'Unrest at rest: Default activity and spontaneous network correlations', *Neuroimage*, 37, 4, 1091–1096.

E. A. Butler and J. J. Gross (2004) 'Hiding feelings in social contexts: out of sight is not out of mind', in P. Philippot and R. S. Feldman (eds) *The Regulation of Emotion* (Mahwah, NJ: Erlbaum), pp. 101–126.

R. M. J. Byrne (1997) 'Cognitive processes in counterfactual thinking about what might have been', *The Psychology of Learning and Motivation, 37,* pp. 105–154.

R. M. Byrne (2002) 'Mental models and counterfactual thoughts about what might have been', *Trends in Cognitive Science*, 6, 10, 426–431.

R. M. Byrne (2007) 'Précis of the rational imagination: how people create alternatives to reality', *Behavioral and Brain Sciences*, 5–6, 439–453.

R. M. Byrne and P. N. Johnson-Laird (2009) '"If" and the problems of conditional reasoning', *Trends in Cognitive Science*, 13, 7, 282–287.

V. J. Callan and M. Johnson (2002) 'Some guidelines for financial planners in measuring and advising clients about their levels of risk tolerance', *Journal of Personal Finance*, 1, 1, 31–44.

J. Y. Campbell, J. Hilscher and J. Szilagyi (2008) 'In search of distress risk', *Journal of Finance*, 63, 6, 2899–2939.

A. Capli and J. Leahy (2004) 'The social discout rate', *Journal of Political Economy*, 112, 6, 1257–1268.

Z. Carmon, K. Wertenbroch and M. Zeelenberg (2003) 'Option attachment: when deliberating makes choosing feel like losing', *Journal of Consumer Research*, 30, 15–29.

K. E. Case and R. Shiller (1990) 'The behavior of home buyers in boom and post-boom markets', *New England Economic Review*, 80, 29–46.

F. X. Castellanos, E. J. S. Sonuga-Barke, A. Scheres, A. Di Martino, C. Hyde and J. R. Walters (2005) 'Varieties of attention-deficit/hyperactivity disorder-related intra-individual variability', *Biological Psychiatry*, 57, 11, 1416–1423.

B. Cavalletti, C. Lagazio and D. Vandone (2008) 'Il credito al consumo in Italia: benessere economico o fragilità finanziaria?', *Università di Milano, DEAS Working Paper.*

K. C. L. Chan, H. Yasushi and J. Lakonishok (1991) 'Fundamentals and Stock Returns in Japan', *Journal of Finance*, 46, 5, 1739–1764.

S. N. Chen (1982) 'An examination of risk-return relationship in bull and bear markets: using time varying betas', *Journal of Financial and Quantitative Analysis*, 17, 2, 265–286.

S. Chew (1983) 'A generalization of the quasilinear mean with applications to the measurement of income inequality and decision theory resolving the Allais Paradox', *Econometrica*, 51, 4, 1065–1092.

S. Chew (1989) 'Axiomatic utility theories with the betweenness property', *Annals of Operations Research*, 19, 273–298.

S. Chew and K. MacCrimmon (1979) 'Alpha-nu Choice Theory: an axiomatization of Expected Utility', *University of British Columbia Working Paper.*

J. J. Choi, D. Laibson, B. C. Madrian and A. Metrick (2009) 'Reinforcement learning and savings behavior', *Journal of Finance*, 64, 6, 2515–2534.

C. T. Clotfelter and P. J. Cook (1993) 'The "gambler's fallacy" in lottery play', *Management Science*, 39, 93–95.

J. Cochrane (2005) *Asset Pricing*, 2nd edn (Princeton, NJ: Princeton University Press).

J. Conlisk (1996) 'Why bounded rationality?', *Journal of Economic Literature*, 34, 2, 669–700.

Consumer and Financial Literacy Task Force (2004) 'Australian consumer and money', Discussion Paper.

D. M. Cordell (2002) 'Risk tolerance in two dimensions', *Journal of Financial Planning*, May, 30–36.

G. Coricelli, H. D. Critchley, M. Joffily, J. P. O'Doherty, A. Sirigu and R. J. Dolan (2005) 'Regret and its avoidance: a neuroimaging study of choice behavior', *Nature Neuroscience*, 8, 9, 1255–1262.

J. Cotter and K. Dowd (2007) 'Exponential spectral risk measures', *Working Paper*, 1–16.

D. Cox and T. Jappelli (1993) 'The effect of borrowing constraints on consumer liabilities', *Journal of Money, Credit and Banking*, 25, 197–213.

J. N. Crook (2006) 'Household debt demand and supply' in G. Bertola, R. Disney and C. Grant (eds) *The Economics of Consumer Credit* (Cambridge, MA: MIT Press), pp. 63–92.

J. Crook and S. Hochguertel (2007) 'US and European household debt and credit constraints: comparative micro evidence from the last 15 years', Tinbergen Institute, Discussion Paper, 087/3.

E. Cuvelier and M. Noirhomme-Fraiture (2005) 'Clayton copula and mixture decomposition', ASMDA 2005, 699–708.

A. R. Damasio (1994) *Descartes Error: Emotion, Reason and the Human Brain* (New York: Avon Books).

A. R. Damasio (1996) 'The somatic marker hypothesis and the possible functions of the prefrontal cortex', *Philosofical Transactions of the Royal Society of London. Series B, Biological Sciences,* 351, 1413–1420.

A. R. Damasio (1998) 'Emotion in the perspective of an integrated nervous system', *Brain Research Review,* 26, 83–86.

K. D. Daniel, D. Hirshleifer and A. Subrahmanyam (1998) 'Investor psychology and security market under- and overreaction', *The Journal of Finance,* 53, 6, 1839–1885.

K. D. Daniel, D. Hirshleifer and A. Subrahmanyam (2001) 'Mispricing, covariance risk, and the cross section of security returns', *The Journal of Finance,* 56, 921–965.

K. Daniel and S. Titman (1999) 'Market efficiency in an irrational world', *Financial Analysts Journal,* 55, 6, 28–40.

S. Das, H. Markowitz, J. Scheid and M. Statman (2010) 'Portoflio optimization with mental account', *Journal of Financial and Quantitative Analysis,* 45, 2, 311–334.

R. J. Davidson, D. C. Jackson and N. H. Kalin (2000) 'Emotion, plasticity, context and regulation: Perspectives from affective neuroscience', *Psychological Bulletin,* 126, 890–906.

W. F. M. DeBondt (1998) 'A portrait of the individual investor', *European Economic Review,* 42, 3–5, 831–844.

E. G. De Giorgi (2009) 'Goal-based with cumulative prospect theory and satisficing behavior', *Working Paper,* 1–53.

S. Dehaene and J. P. Changeux (2005) 'Ongoing spontaneous activity controls access to consciousness: A neuronal model for inattentional blindness', *PLOS: Biology,* 3, 910–927.

E. Dekel (1986) 'An axiomatic characterization of preferences under uncertainty: weakening the independent axiom', *Journal of Economic Theory,* 40, 2, 304–318.

A. Del Rio and G. Young (2006) 'The determinants of unsecured borrowing: Evidence from the British Household Panel Survey', *Applied Financial Economics,* 15, 1119–1144.

P. Delamillieure, G. Doucet, B. Mazoyer, M. R. Turbelin, N. Delcroix, E. Mellet, L. Zago, F. Crivello, L. Petit, N. Tzourio-Mazoyer and M. Joliot (2009) 'The resting state questionnaire: an introspective questionnaire for evaluation of inner experience during the conscious resting state', *Brain Research Bulletin,* 81, 6, 565–573.

R. J. Dolan (2002) 'Emotion, cognition, and behavior', *Science,* 298, 1191–1194.

B. Donkers and A. Van Soest (1999) 'Subjective measures of household preferences and financial decisions', *Journal of Economic Psychology,* 20, 6, 613–642.

D. Dorn and G. Huberman (2009) 'Preferred risk habitat of individual investors', *Working Paper,* 1–58.

K. Dowd (1998) *An Introduction to Market Risk Measurement* (Chichester: John Wiley and Sons).

K. Dowd, J. Cotter and G. Sorwar (2008) 'Spectral risk measures: properties and limitations', *Journal of Financial Services Research,* 34, 71–75.

M. Dowling and B. M. Lucey (2004) 'The role of feelings in investor decision-making', *Working Paper*, 1–36.
D. Dremen and E. Lufkin (2000) 'Investor overreaction: evidence that its basis is psychological', *Journal of Psychology and Financial Markets*, 1, 61–75.
DTI-MORI (2004) Over-indebtedness in Britain: A DTI report on the MORI Financial Services survey 2004', DTI Report.
B. D. Dunn, T. Dalgleish and A. D. Lawrence (2006) 'The somatic marker hypothesis: A critical evaluation', *Neuroscience & Biobehavioral Reviews*, 30, 239–271.
T. Durking (2002) 'Consumer and credit disclosures: credit cards and credit insurance' *Federal Reserve Bulletin*, 201–213.
B. Duygan and C. Grant (2008) 'Household debt repayment behaviour: what role do institutions play?', *FRB of Boston Quantitative Analysis Unit, Working Paper n.3*.
A. Edmans, D. Garcia and O. Norli (2008) 'Sports sentiment and stock returns', *Journal of Finance*, 62, 4, 1967–1998.
S. M. Egan, J. A. García-Madruga and R. M. Byrne (2009) 'Indicative and counterfactual "only if" conditionals', *Acta Psychologica*, 132, 3, 240–249.
A. Elliott (2005) *Not Waving but Drowning: Over-indebtedness by misjudgement* (London: CSFI).
E. J. Elton and M. J. Gruber (1995) *Modern Portfolio Theory and Investment Analysis* (New York: Wiley).
E. J. Elton, M. J. Gruber, S. J. Brown and W. N. Goetzman (2007) *Modern Portfolio Theory and Investment Analysis*, 7th edn (Hoboken: John Wiley and Sons, Inc.).
R. F. Engle (1982) 'Autoregressive conditional heteroscedasticity with estimates of variance of United Kingdom inflation', *Econometrica*, 50, 987–1008.
A. Etzioni (2010) 'Behavioural economics: A methodological note', *Journal of Economic Psychology*, 31, 51–54.
D. Fabbri and M. Padula (2004) 'Do poor legal enforcement make households credit constrained?', *Journal of Banking and Finance*, 28, 10, 2369–2397.
F. J. Fabozzi and J. C. Francis (1977) 'Stability tests for alphas and betas over bull and bear market conditions', *The Journal of Finance*, 32, 4, 1093–1099.
F. Fabozzi and J. Francis (1978) 'Beta as a random coefficient', *Journal of Financial and Quantitative Analysis*, 101–116.
R. W. Faff and R. D. Brooks (1998) 'Time-varying beta risk for Australian industry portfolios: An exploratory analysis', *Journal of Business Finance & Accounting*, 25, 5–6, 721–745.
E. Fama (1970) 'Efficient capital markets: a review of theory and empirical work', *Journal of Finance*, 25, 383–417.
E. F. Fama and K. R. French (1992) 'The cross-section of expected stock returns', *Journal of Finance*, 47, 2, 427–465.
E. F. Fama and K. R. French (1995) 'Size and book-to-market factors in earnings and returns', *Journal of Finance*, 50, 131–155.
E. F. Fama and K. R. French (1996) 'Multifactor explanations of asset pricing anomalies', *Journal of Finance*, 51, 55–84.
E. F. Fama and J. MacBeth (1973) 'Risk, return and equilibrium: Empirical tests', *Journal of Political Economy*, 81, 607–636.
L. Farinha (2004) 'Households' debt burden: An analysis based on microeconomic data, Banco de Portugal', Economic Bulletin (September).

S. Fay, E. Hurst and M. White (2002) 'The household bankruptcy decision', *The American Economic Review*, 92, 3, 706–718.
M. P. Fenton-O'Creevy, P. Gooderham and O. Nordhaug (2008) 'HRM in US subsidiaries in Europe and Australia: centralisation or autonomy?' *Journal of International Business Studies*, 39, 151–166.
M. S. Finke and S. J. Huston (2003), 'Factors affecting the probability of choosing a risky diet', *Journal of Family and Economic Issues*, 24, 291–303.
B. Fischhoff, P. Slovich and S. Lichtenstein (1977) 'Knowing with certainty: the appropriateness of extreme confidence', *Journal of Experimental Psychology: Human Perception and Performance*, 3, 4, 552–564.
P. C. Fishburn (1977) 'Mean–risk analysis with risk associated with below-target returns', *American Economic Review*, 67, 2, 116–126.
I. Fisher (1928) *The Money Illusion* (New York: Adelphi Company).
I. Fisher (1930) *The Theory of Interest* (New York: The Macmillan Company).
D. Forlani (2002) 'Risk and rationality: the influence of decision domain and perceived outcome control on managers' high-risk decisions', *Journal of Behavioral Decision Making*, 15, 2, 125–140.
A. Fossati, A. Di Ceglie, E. Acquarini and E. S. Barratt (2001) 'Psychometric properties of an Italian version of the Barratt Impulsiveness Scale-11 (BIS-11) in nonclinical subjects', *Journal of Clinical Psychology*, 57, 815–828.
D. C. Fowles, M. J. Christie, R. Edelberg, W. W. Grings, D. T. Lykken and P. H. Venables (1981) 'Committee report. publication recommendations for electrodermal measurements', *Psychophysiology*, 18, 3, 232–239.
M. D. Fox, A. Z. Snyder, J. L. Vincent, M. Corbetta, D. C. Van Essen and M. E. Raichle (2005) 'The human brain is intrinsically organized into dynamic, anticorrelated functional networks' *Proceedings of the National Academy of Sciences of the U S A*, 102, 27, 9673–9678.
C. Fox and A. Tversky (1995) 'Ambiguity aversion and comparative ignorance', *Quarterly Journal of Economics*, 110, 3, 585–603.
K. Frade (2004) *The Fable of the Grasshopper and the Ant: A Research Project on Overindebtedness and Unemployment in Portugal* (Coimbra: University of Coimbra).
I. H. Franken, J. W. Van Strien, I. Nijs and P. Muris (2008) 'Impulsivity is associated with behavioral decision-making deficits', *Psychiatry Research*, 158, 155–163.
P. Fransson (2005) 'Spontaneous low-frequency BOLD signal fluctuations: an fMRI investigation of the resting-state default mode of brain function hypothesis', *Human Brain Mapping*, 26, 1, 15–29.
P. Fraser, F. Hamelink, M. Hoesli and B. MacGregor (2004) 'Time-varying betas and cross-sectional return-risk relation: evidence from the UK', *The European Journal of Finance*, 10, 4, 255–276.
X. Freixas and J. C. Rochet (1996) *Microeconomics of Banking* (London: MIT Press).
R. Frey, A. J. McNeil and M. Nyfeler (2001) 'Copulas and credit models', *Risk*, 14, 10, 111–114.
M. Friedman (1957) 'The permanent income hypothesis: comment', *American Economic Review*, 48, 990–991.
M. Friedman and L. J. Savage (1948) 'The Utility Analysis of choices involving risk', *The Journal of Political Economy*, 56, 4, 279–304.
I. Friend and R. Westerfield (1981) 'Risk and capital asset prices', *Journal of Banking and Finance*, 5, 291–315.

N. H. Frijda (1986) *The Emotions* (Cambridge: Cambridge University Press).
N. H. Frijda (2006) *The Laws of Emotion* (Mahwah, NJ: Erlbaum).
FSA (2005) 'Measuring financial capability: an explanatory study' FSA Report n.37 (June).
FSA (2006) 'Levels of financial capability in the UK: Results of a baseline survey' FSA Report n.47 (March).
R. J. Fuller and J. L. Farrel (2003) *Modern Investment and Security Analysis* (New York: McGraw-Hill).
R. Gallou and P. Le Queau (1999) 'Les Personnes Interdite de Chequiers', *Bank de France Report* (Paris).
GAO (2006) 'Financial literacy and education commission', US Government Accountability Office, Report to congressional committees, (December).
D. Genesove and C. Mayer (2001) 'Loss aversion and selling behavior: evidence from the housing market', *Quarterly Journal of Economics*, 116, 4, 1233–1260.
D. T. Gilbert, C. K. Morewedge, J. L. Risen and T. D. Wilson (2004) 'Looking forward to looking backward: the misprediction of regret', *Psychological Science*, 15, 346–350.
I. Gilboa and D. Schmeidler (1995) 'Maxmin expected utility with non-unique prior', *Journal of Mathematical Economics*, 18, 2, 141–153.
T. Gilovich, D. Griffin and D. Kahneman (2002) *Heuristics and Biases: The Psychology of Intuitive Judgment* (Cambridge: Cambridge University Press).
T. Gilovich, R. Vallone and A. Tversky (1985) 'The hot hand in basketball: on the misperception of random sequence', *Cognitive Psychology*, 17, 3, 295–314.
G. Gloukoviezoff (2006) 'Surendettement des particuliers en France', *International Labour Office Geneva, Working Paper n. 43.*
U. Gneezy (1997) 'An experiment on risk taking and evaluation periods', *Quarterly Journal of Economics*, 112, 631–645.
W. N. Goetzmann and A. Kumar (2008) 'Equity portfolio diversification', *Review of Finance*, 12, 3, 433–463.
J. Grable and S. Joo (2000) 'A cross-disciplinary examination of financial risk tolerance', *Consumer Interests Annual*, 46, 151–157.
J. E. Grable and R. H. Lytton (1999) 'Financial risk tolerance revisited: the development of a risk assessment instrument', *Financial Services Review*, 8, 163–181.
C. Grant (2003) 'Estimating credit constraints among US households', *European University Institute, Working Paper.*
C. Grant and M. Padula (2006) 'Informal credit markets, judicial costs and consumer credit: Evidence from firm level data', *CSEF – Centre for Studies in Economics and Finance, Working Paper n.155.*
D. Griffin and A. Tversky (1992) 'The weighing of evidence and the determinants of overconfidence', *Cognitive Psychology*, 24, 3, 411–435.
M. Grinblatt and M. Keloharju (2000) 'The investment behavior and performance of various investor types: a study of Finland's unique data set', *Journal of Financial Economics*, 55, 1, 43–67.
M. Grinblatt, S. Titman and R. Wermers (1995) 'Momentum investment strategies, portfolio performance, and herding: a study of mutual fund behavior', *American Economic Review*, 85, 5, 1088–1105.
R. Gropp, J. K. Scholz and M. J. White (1997) 'Personal bankruptcy and credit supply and demand', *Quarterly Journal of Economics*, 112, 217–252.

F. Gul (1991) 'A theory of disappointment in decision making under uncertainty', *Econometrica,* 59, 3, 667–686.
O. Haas (2006) 'Overindebtedness in Germany', *Employment Sector International Labour Office Geneva, Working Paper n. 44.*
T. Hallahan, R. Faff and M. McKenzie (2003) 'An exploratory investigation of the relation between risk tolerance scores and demographic characteristics', *Journal of Multinational Financial Management,* 13, 483–502.
J. Hammond, R. Keeney and H. Raiffa (1998) 'The hidden traps in decision making', *Harvard Business Review,* 76, 5, 47–58.
S. D. Hanna and S. Lindamood (2004) 'An improved measure of risk aversion', *Financial Counseling and Planning,* 15, 2, 27–38.
Y. Hanoch, J. G. Johnson and A. Wilke (2006) 'Domain specificity in experimental measures and participant recruitment: an application to risk-taking behavior', *Psychological Science,* 17, 4, 300–304.
C. R. Harvey and A. Siddique (2000) 'Conditional skewness in asset pricing tests', *Journal of Finance,* 55, 1263–1295.
M. G. Hasselton and T. Ketelaar (2006) 'Irrational emotions or emotional wisdom? The evolutionary psychology of emotions and behavior' in J. P. Forgas (ed.) *Affect in Social Thinking and Behavior* (New York: Psychology Press), pp. 21–39.
I. Hathaway and S. Khatiwada (2008) 'Do financial education programs work?', *FRB of Cleveland, Working Paper n. 3.*
J. M. Heath and A. Tversky (1991) 'Preference and belief: ambiguity and competence in choice under uncertainty', *Journal of Risk and Uncertainty,* 92, 323–336.
D. Hirshleifer (2001) 'Investor psychology and asset pricing', *The Journal of Finance,* 56, 4, 1533–1597.
R. Hockey, J. Maule, P. Clough and L. Bdzola (2000) 'Effects of negative mood states on risk in everyday decision making', *Cognition and Emotion,* 14, 823–855.
D. R. Hofstadter (1985) *Metamagical Themas: Questing for the Essence of Mind and Pattern* (New York: Basic Books).
A. Hung and J. Yoong (2010) 'Asking for help: Survey and experimental evidence on financial advice and behavior change', *RAND Working Paper Series* WR-714-1, 1–47.
M. Isen and N. Geva (1987) 'The influence of positive affect on acceptable level of risk: the person with a large canoe has a large worry', *Organizational Behavior and Human Decision Processes,* 39, 145–154.
A. M. Isen, T. E. Nygren and F. G. Ashby (1988) 'Influence of positive affect on the subjective utility of gains and losses: it is just not worth the risk', *Journal of Personality and Social Psychology,* 55, 710–717.
M. Isen and R. Patrick (1983) 'The effect of positive feelings on risk taking: when the chips are down', *Organizational Behavior and Human Decision Processes,* 31, 194–202.
T. Jappelli and M. Pagano (2006) 'The role and effects of credit information sharing', in G. Bertola, R. Disney and C. Grant (eds) *The Economics of Consumer Credit* (Cambridge, MA: MIT Press).
N. Jegadeesh (1992) 'Does market risk really explain the size effect?', *Journal of Financial and Quantitative Analysis,* 27, 337–351.

M. W. Johansson and M. Persson (2006) 'Swedish households' indebtedness and ability to pay – a household level study', *Penning Och Valutapolitik*, vol. 3/2006.

E. Johnson and A. Tversky (1983) 'Affect, generalization, and the perception of risk', *Journal of Personality and Social Psychology*, 45, 20–31.

P. Jorion (1994) 'Mean–variance analysis of currency overlays', *Financial Analysts Journal*, 50, 3, 48–56.

P. Jorion (1997) *Value at Risk: The New Benchmark for Controlling Financial Risk*. (Chicago: Irwin Professional).

P. Jorion (2000) *Value at Risk: The New Benchmark for Managing Financial Risk*, 2nd edn (New York: McGraw-Hill).

D. Kahneman (2003) 'Maps of bounded rationality: psychology for behavioral economics', *American Economic Review*, 93, 5, 1449–1475.

D. Kahneman, J. L. Knetsch and R. H. Thaler (1990) 'Anomalies: the endowment effect, loss aversion, and status quo bias', *Journal of Economic Perspective*, 5, 193–206.

D. Kahneman, J. L. Knetsch and R. H. Thaler (1991) 'The endowment effect, loss aversion, and status quo bias: anomalies', *Journal of Economic Perspectives*, 5, 1, 193–206.

D. Kahneman, P. Slovic and A. Tversky (1982) *Judgment under Uncertainty: Heuristic and Biases* (New York: Cambridge University Press).

D. Kahneman and A. Tversky (1974) 'Judgment under uncertainty: heuristics and biases', *Science*, 185, 4157, 1124–1131.

D. Kahneman and A. Tversky (1979) 'Prospect Theory: an analysis of decision under risk', *Econometrica*, 47, 2, 263–291.

D. Kahneman and A. Tversky (1982) 'The simulation heuristic', in D. Kahneman, P. Slovic and A. Tversky (eds), *Judgment under Uncertainty: Heuristics and biases* (New York: Cambridge University Press), pp. 201–208.

D. Kahneman and D. T. Miller (1986) 'Norm theory: comparing reality to its alternatives', *Psychological Review*, 93, 136–153.

V. G. Kahneman and A. Tversky (1996) 'On the reality of cognitive illusion', *Psychological Review*, 103, 3, 582–591.

N. H. Kalin, S. E. Shelton and R. J. Davidson (2004) 'The role of the central nucleus of the amygdala in mediating fear and anxiety in the primate', *The Journal of Neurosicence*, 24, 5506–5515.

M. J. Kamstra, L. A. Kramer and M. D. Levi (2003) 'Winter blues: A SAD stock market cycle', *American Economic Review, American Economic Association*, 93, 324–343.

S. Kandel and R. F. Stambaugh (1996) 'On the predictability of stock returns: An asset-allocation perspective', *Journal of Finance*, 51, 2, 385–424.

N. Karlsson, P. Dellgran, B. Klingander and T. Garlin (2004) 'Household consumption: influences of aspiration level, social comparison and money management', *Journal of Economic Psychology*, 25, 753–769.

P. Kenning and H. Plassmann (2005) 'Neuroeconomics: an overview from an economic perspective', *Brain Research Bulletin*, 67, 343–354.

T. Ketelaar (2004) 'Ancestral emotions, current decisions: using evolutionary game theory to explore the role of emotions in decision-making', in C. Crawford and C. Salmon (eds) *Darwinism, Public Policy and Private Decisions* (Mahwah, NJ: Erlbaum), pp. 145–168.

J. M. Keynes (1936) *The General Theory of Employment, Interest and Money* (London: Macmillan).

J. Kilborn (2002) 'Behavioural economics, overindebtedness and comparative consumer bankruptcy: searching for causes and evaluating solutions', *Bankruptcy Developments Journal*, 22, 13–46.

M. K. Kim and J. K. Zumwalt (1979) 'An analysis of risk in bull and bear markets', *Journal of Financial and Quantitative Analysis*, 14, 5, 1015–1025.

M. A. King and J. I. Leape (1998) 'Wealth and portfolio composition: theory and evidence', *Journal of Public Economics*, 69, 155–193.

A. Kish (2006) 'Perspectives on recent trends in consumer debt', *Federal Reserve Bank of Philadelphia, Discussion Paper (June).*

R. C. Klemkosky (1973) 'The bias in composite performance measures', *Journal of Financial and Quantitative Analysis*, 8, 3, 505–514.

F. H. Knight (1921) *Risk, Uncertainty, and Profit*, 1st edn (Boston and New York: Houghton Mifflin Company).

R. T. Knight and M. Grabowecky (1995) 'Escape from linear time: prefrontal cortex and conscious experience', in M. S. Gazzaniga (ed.) *The Cognitive Neurosciences* (Cambridge, MA: MIT Press), pp. 1357–1371.

V. Koljonen and T. Romer-Paakkanen (2000) 'Overindebtedness from the viewpoint of young debtor', County Administrative Board of Southern Finland Publications.

A. Kraus and R. H. Litzenberger (1976) 'Skewness preference and the valuation of risk assets', *Journal of Finance*, 31, 1085–1100.

A. Kraus and R. Litzenberger (1983) 'On the distributional conditions for a consumption-oriented three moment CAPM', *The Journal of Finance*, 38, 5, 1381–1391.

Y. Kroll, H. Levy and A. Rapoport (1988) 'Experimental tests of the mean-variance model for portfolio selection', *Organizational Behavior and Human Decision Processes*, 42, 388–410.

S. Lea, P. Webley and C. Walker (1995) 'Psychological factors in consumer debt: money management, economic socialization and credit use', *Journal of Economic Psychology*, 16, 681–701.

D. Laibson, A. Repetto and J. Tobacman (2003) 'A debt puzzle', in P. Aghion, R. Frydman, J. Stiglitz and M. Woodford (eds) *Knowledge, Information and Expectations in Modern Economics: in Honor of Edmund S. Phelps* (Princeton: Princeton University Press), pp. 228–266.

D. J. Laughhunn, J. W. Payne and R. Crum (1980) 'Managerial risk preferences for below-target returns', *Management Science*, 26, 1238–1249.

J. LeDoux (1996) *The Emotional Brain: the Mysterious Underpinnings of Emotional Life* (New York: Simon and Schuster).

K. P. Leith and R. F. Baumeister (1996) 'Why do bad moods increase self-defeating behavior? emotion, risk taking, and self-regulation', *Journal of Personality and Social Psychology*, 71, 1250–1267.

J. S. Lerner, R. M. Gonzales, D. A. Small and B. Fischhoff (2003) 'Effects of fear and anger on perceived risks of terrorism: a national field experiment', *Psychological Science*, 14, 2, 144–150.

R. A. Levy (1974) 'Beta coefficients as predictors of returns', *Financial Analysts Journal*, 30, 61–69.

H. Levy and M. Sarnat (1995) *Capital Investment and Financial Decisions*, 5th edn (London: Prentice Hall College).
N. Linciano (2010) 'Errori cognitivi e instabilità delle preferenze nelle scelte di investimento dei risparmiatori retail: le indicazioni di policy della finanza comportamentale', *Quaderno di Finanza CONSOB*, 66, 1–46.
J. Lintner (1965) 'The valuation of risk assets and the selection of risky investments in stock portfolios and capital budgets', *Review of Economic Statistics*, 47, 13–37.
W. Lo and D. V. Repin (2002) 'The psychophysiology of real-time financial risk processing', *Journal of Cognitive Neuroscience*, 14, 323–339.
W. A. Lo, D. V Repin and B. N. Steenbarger (2005) 'Fear and greed in financial markets: a clinical study of day-traders', *American Economic Review*, 95, 2, 352–359.
G. Loewenstein (1996) 'Out of control: visceral influences on behavior', *Organizational Behavior and Human Decision Processes*, 65, 272–292.
G. Loewenstein and J. Lerner (2003) 'The role of emotion in decision making' in R. J. Davidson, H. H. Goldsmith and K. R. Scherer (eds) *Handbook of Affective Science* (Oxford: Oxford University Press), pp. 619–642.
G. Loewenstein, E. U. Weber, C. K. Hsee and N. Welch (2001) 'Risk as feelings', *Psychological Bulletin*, 127, 267–286.
G. Loomes and R. Sugden (1982) 'Regret theory: an alternative theory of rational choice under uncertainty', *The Economic Journal*, 92, 368, 805–824.
L. Lopes (1987) 'Between hope and fear: the psychology of risk', *Advances in Experimental Social Psychology*, 20, 255–295.
D. G. MacGregor, P. Slovic, D. Dreman and M. Berry (2000) 'Imagery, affect, and financial judgment', *Journal of Psychology and Financial Markets*, 1, 2, 104–110.
P. D. MacLean (1949) 'Psychosomatic disease and the visceral brain; recent developments bearing on the Papez theory of emotion', *Psychosomatic Medicine*, 11, 338–353.
S. Magri (2002) 'Italian households' debt: determinant of demand and supply', Banca d'Italia, Temi di discussione, 454.
S. Magri (2007) 'Italian households' debt: determinant of demand and supply', *Empirical Economics*, 33, 401–426.
S. Maital, R. Filer and J. Simon (1986) 'What do people bring to the stock market (besides money)? The economic psychology of stock market behavior' in B. Gilad and S. Kaish (eds) *Handbook of Behavioral Economics* (Greenwich: JAI press Inc.), pp. 273–307.
J. K. Maner, J. A. Richey, K. Cromer, M. Mallott, C. W. Lejuez, T. E. Joiner and N. B. Schmidt (2007) 'Dispositional anxiety and risk-avoidant decision-making', *Personality and Individual Differences*, 42, 665–675.
J. K. Maner and N. B. Schmidt (2006) 'The role of risk-avoidance in anxiety', *Behavior Therapy*, 37, 181–189.
H. Mano (1994) 'Risk-taking, framing effects, and affect', *Organizational Behavior and Human Decision Processes*, 57, 35–58.
J. C. T. Mao (1970) 'Models of capital budgeting, E-V vs. E-S', *Journal of Financial and Quantitative Analysis*, 5, 5, 657–676.
H. M. Markowitz (1952a) 'The utility of wealth', *Journal of Political Economy*, 60, 2, 151–158.
H. Markowitz (1952b) 'Portfolio selection', *The Journal of Finance*, 7, 1, 77–91.
M. Markowitz (1959) *Portfolio Selection* (New York: John Wiley & Sons, Inc.).

H. Markowitz (1999) 'The early history of portfolio theory: 1600–1960', *Financial Analysts Journal*, 55, 4, 5–16.

L. E. Martin and G. F. Potts (2009) 'Impulsivity in decision-making: an event-related potential investigation', *Personality and Individual Differences*, 46, 303–308.

M. F. Mason, M. I. Norton, J. D. Van Horn, D. M. Wegner, S. T. Grafton and C. N. Macrae (2007) 'Wandering minds: the default network and stimulus-independent thought', *Science*, 315, 5810, 393–395.

T. H. McInish (1982) 'Individual investors and risk taking', *Journal of Economic Psychology*, 2, 2, 125–136.

M. N. McMullen and K. D. Markman, (2002) 'Affective impact of close counterfactuals: implications of possible futures for possible pasts', *Journal of Experimental Social Psychology*, 38, 64–70.

S. Meier and C. Sprenger (2007) 'Impatience and credit behaviour: evidence from a field experiment', *Centre for Behavioral Economics and Decision Making, Federal Reserve Bank of Boston, Working Paper n. 07–3.*

H. E. Merriken (1994) 'Analytical approaches to limit downside risk: Semi variance and the need for liquidity', *Journal of Investing*, 3, 3, 65–72.

R. C. Merton (1987) 'A simple model of capital market equilibrium with incomplete information', *The Journal of Finance*, 42, 3, 483–510.

N. Mirza (2005) 'The death of CAPM: A critical review', *The Lahore Journal of Economics*, 10, 2, 35–54.

S. Mitra (2009) 'Risk measures in quantitative finance', *Quantitative Finance Papers*, Cornell University, New York.

K. Mitte (2007) 'Anxiety and risky decision-making: the role of subjective probability and subjective costs of negative events', *Personality and Individual Differences*, 43, 243–253.

A. C. Miu, R. M. Heilman and D. Houser (2008) 'Anxiety impairs decision-making: psychophysiological evidence from an Iowa gambling task', *Biological Psychology*, 77, 353–358.

F. Modigliani (1975) 'The life-cycle hypothesis of saving twenty years later', in M. Parkin (ed.) *Contemporary Issues in Economics* (Manchester: Manchester University Press), pp. 2–35.

F. Modigliani (1976) 'Life-cycle, individual thrift, and the wealth of nations', *American Economic Review*, 76, 3, 297–313.

F. Modigliani (1998) 'The role of intergenerational transfers and life-cycle saving in the accumulation of wealth', *Journal of Economic Perspectives*, 2, 2, 15–20.

F. Modigliani and R. H. Brumberg (1954) 'Utility analysis and the consumption function: an interpretation of cross-section data' in K. K. Kenneth (ed.) *Post- Keynesian Economics* (New Brunswick, NJ: Rutgers University Press), pp. 388–436.

P. Molyneux (2006) 'What are the specific economic gains from improved financial inclusion? a tentative for estimating these gains', in L. Anderloni, D. Braga, E. Carluccio (eds) *New Frontiers in Banking Services. Emerging Needs and Tailored Products for Untapped Market* (Berlin: Springer-Verlag).

T. J. Moskowitz and A. Vissing Jorgensen (2002) 'The returns to entrepreneurial investment: a private equity premium puzzle?', *American Economic Review*, 92, 4, 745–778.

J. Mossin (1966) 'Equilibrium in a capital asset market', *Econometrica*, 34, 768–783.

A. H. Mowbray and R. H. Blanchard (1961) *Insurance* (New York: McGraw-Hill Book Company).

D. N. Nawrocki (1999) 'A brief history of downside risk measures' *The Journal of Investing*, 8, 3, 9–25.

R. M. A. Nelissen and M. Zeelenberg (2007) 'The motivational function of emotions: a "feeling is for doing" perspective', in L. V. Brown (ed.) *Psychology of Motivation* (New York: NOVA Science Publishers), pp. 47–63.

R. B. Nelsen (2006) *An Introduction to Copulas* (New York: Springer Science and Business Media, Inc.).

N. Nicholson, M. Fenton-O'Creevy, E. Soane and P. Willman (2002) *Risk Propensity and Personality* (London: London Business School).

R. E. Nisbett and T. D. Wilson (1977) 'The halo effect: evidence from unconscious alteration of judgments', *Journal of Personality and Social Psychology*, 35, 4, 250–256.

J. R. Nofsinger and R. W. Sias (1999) 'Herding and feedback trading by institutional and individual investors', *Journal of Finance*, 54, 6, 2263–2295.

P. S. Norum (2008) 'The role of time preference and credit card usage in compulsive buying behaviour', *International Journal of Consumer Studies*, 32, 3, 269–275.

Observatoire du Crédit et de l'Endettement (2005) 'Rapport général sur la consommation et le crédit aux particulier'. Report (Paris).

T. Odean, (1998) 'Volume, volatility, price, and profit when all traders are above average', *The Journal of Finance*, 53, 6, 1887–1934.

T. Odean (1999) 'Do investors trade too much?', *American Economic Review*, 89, 5, 1279–1298.

OECD (2005) *Improving Financial Literacy. Analysis of issues and policies* (Paris OECD Publishing).

R. A. Olsen (2000) 'The instinctive mind on Wall Street: evolution and investment decision-making', *The Journal of Investing*, 9, 4, 47–54.

C. Ottaviani and D. Vandone (2010) 'Impulsivity and household indebtedness', Department of Economics, Business and Statistics, University of Milan, Working Paper, 28, 1–30.

J. Panksepp (1998) *Affective Neuroscience* (New York: Oxford University Press).

J. M. Patton, M. S. Stanford and E. S. Barratt (1995) 'Factor structure of the Barratt Impulsiveness Scale', *Journal of Clinical Psychology*, 51, 768–774.

V. G. Perry: (2008) 'Is ignorance bliss? Consumer accuracy in judgements about credit ratings'. *Journal of Consumer Affairs*, 42, 189–205.

K. Pilbeam (1998) *International Finance* (Basingstoke: Palgrave Macmillan) (see http://www.amazon.co.uk/International-Finance-Keith-Pilbeam/dp/1403948372/ref=ntt_at_ep_dpt_1).

F. Piron (1991) 'Defining impulse purchasing', *Advances in Consumer Research*, 18, 509–514.

V. Polkovnichenko (2005) 'Household portfolio diversification: a case for rank dependent preferences', *Review of Financial Studies*, 18, 4, 1467–1502.

C. Poppe (2008) 'Into the debt quagmire. How defaulters cope with severe debt problems', University of Oslo, Department of Sociology and Human Geography, Series of Dissertation n.124.

G. F. Potts, M. R. George, L. E. Martin and E. S. Barratt (2006) 'Reduced punishment sensitivity in neural systems of behavior monitoring in impulsive individuals', *Neuroscience Letters*, 397, 130–134.

J. Quiggin (1982) 'A theory of anticipated utility', *Journal of Economic Behavior and Organization*, 3, 4, 323–343.

J. P. Quirk and R. Saposnik (1962) 'Admissability and measurable utility functions', *Review of Economic Studies*, 29, 140–146.

M. Rabin (1998) 'Psychology and economics', *Journal of Economic Literature*, 36, 1, 11–46.

M. Rabin (2002) 'Inference by believers in the law of small numbers', *Quarterly Journal of Economics*, 117, 3, 775–816.

S. Rahman, B. J. Sahakian, N. C. Rudolph, R. D. Rogers and T. W. Robbins (2001) 'Decision making and neuropsychiatry', *Trends in Cognitive Sciences*, 6, 271–277.

M. E. Raichle and A. Z. Snyder (2007) 'A default mode of brain function: a brief history of an evolving idea', *Neuroimage*, 37, 4, 1083–1090.

D. Read, G. Loewenstein and M. Rabin (1999) 'Choice bracketing', *Journal of Risk and Uncertainty*, 19, 1–3, 171–197.

D. Redelmeier and A. Tversky (1992) 'On the framing of multiple prospects', *Psychological Science*, 3, 3, 191–193.

A. Resti and A. Sironi (2007) *Risk Management and Shareholders Value in Banking* (New York: John Wiley).

V. Ricciardi (2004) 'A risk perception primer: A narrative research review of the risk perception literature in behavioral accounting and behavioral finance' (20 July 2004). Available at SSRN: http://ssrn.com/abstract=566802.

V. Ricciardi (2008) 'The psychology of risk: the behavioral finance perspective' in F. J. Fabozzi (ed.) *Handbook of Finance: Investment Management and Financial Management*, vol. 2 (New York: John Wiley & Sons).

V. Ricciardi and H. Simon (2001) Behavioral finance: a new perspective for investors and financial professionals, *Working Paper.*

J. M. Richards, E. A. Butler and J. J. Gross (2003) 'Emotion regulation in romantic couples: the cognitive consequences of concealing feelings', *Journal of Social and Personal Relationships*, 20, 599–620.

I. Ritov and J. Baron (1990) 'Reluctance to vaccinate: omission bias and ambiguity', *Journal of Behavioral Decision Making*, 3, 4, 263–277.

J. R. Ritter (1991) 'The long-run performance of initial public offerings', *Journal of Finance*, 46, 1, 3–27.

R. Roenfeldt (1978) 'Further evidence on the stationarity of beta coefficients', *Journal of Financial and Quantitative Analysis*, 13, 117–121.

R. D. Rogers, B. J. Everitt, A. Baldacchino, A. J. Blackshaw, R. Swainson, K. Wynne, N. B. Baker, J. Hunter, T. Carthy, E. Booker, M. London, J. F. Deakin, B. J. Sahakian and T. W. Robbins (1999) 'Dissociable deficits in the decision-making cognition of chronic amphetamine abusers, opiate abusers, patients with focal damage to prefrontal cortex, and tryptophan-depleted normal volunteers: evidence for monoaminergic mechanisms', *Neuropsychopharmacology*, 20, 322–339.

K. I. M. Rohde (2009) 'Decreasing relative impatience', *Journal of Economic Psychology*, 30, 831–839.

B. Rohrmann and O. Renn (2000) 'Risk perception research: An introduction', in B. Rohrmann and O. Renn (eds) *Cross-cultural Risk Perception: A Survey of Empirical Studies* (Boston, MA: Kluwer Academic Publishers), pp. 13–53.

R. Roll (1977) 'A critique of the asset pricing theory's tests Part I: On past and potential testability of the theory', *Journal of Financial Economics*, 4, 2, 129–176.

R. Roll and S. A. Ross (1980) 'An empirical investigation of the Arbitrage pricing theory', *The Journal of Finance*, 35, 5, 1073–1103.

R. Roll and S. A. Ross (1994) 'On the cross-sectional relation between expected returns and betas', *The Journal of Finance*, 49, 1, 101–122.

B. M. Rom and K. W. Ferguson (1993) 'Post-modern portfolio theory comes of age', *Journal of Investing*, reprinted Fall 1994a, 3, 3, 11–17.

B. M. Rom and K. W. Ferguson (1997/1998) 'Using post-modern portfolio theory to improve investment performance measurement', *Journal of Performance Measurement*, 2, 2, 5–13.

D. W. Rook (1987) 'The buying impulse', *Journal of Consumer Research*, 14, 189–199.

J. Rosenberg and R. Engle (2002) 'Empirical pricing Kernels', *Journal of Financial Economics*, 64, 3, 341–372.

S. A. Ross (1976) 'The Arbitrage theory of capital asset pricing', *Journal of Economic Theory*, 13, 3, 341–360.

L. Ross (1977) 'The intuitive psychologist and his shortcomings: distortions in the attribution process', in L. Borkowitz (ed.) *Advances in Experimental Social Psychology* (New York: Academic Press).

L. Ross, D. Green and P. House (1977) 'The "false consensus effect": an egocentric bias in social perception and attribution process', *Journal of Experimental Social Psychology*, 13, 3, 279–301.

M. J. Roszkowski, G. Davey and J. E. Grable (2005) 'Insights from psychology and psychometrics on measuring risk tolerance', *The Journal of Financial Planning*, 18, 4, 66–75.

M. J. Roszkowski and J. Grable (2005) 'Estimating risk tolerance: the degree of accuracy and the paramorphic representations of the estimate', *Financial Counseling and Planning*, 16, 2, 29–47.

J. B. Rotter (1971) 'External control and internal control', *Psychology Today*, 5, 1, 37–42, 58–59.

K. Rowlingson and E. Kempson (1993) *Gas Debt and Disconnections* (London: Policy Studies Institute).

A. D. Roy (1952) 'Safety first and the holding of assets', *Econometrica*, 3, 431–449.

M. Rubinstein (2002) 'Markowitz's "portfolio selection": a fifty-year retrospective', *The Journal of Finance*, 62, 3, 1041–1045.

A. Rustichini (2005) 'Neuroscience. emotion and reason in making decisions', *Science*, 310, 1624–1625.

W. Samuelson and R. Zeckhauser (1988) 'Status quo bias in decision making', *Journal of Risk and Uncertainty*, 1, 1, 7–59.

A. Saunders (1999) *Credit Risk Measurement: New approaches to Value-at-Risk and Other Paradigms* (New York: Wiley and Sons).

L. J. Savage (1954) *The Foundations of Statistics* (New York: Wiley and Sons).

N. Schwartz and G. L. Clore (1983) 'Mood, misattribution, and judgments of well-being: Informative and directive functions of affective states', *Journal of Personality and Social Psychology*, 45, 513–523.

R. C. Scott and P. Horvath (1980) 'On the direction of preference for moments of higher order than the variance', *The Journal of Finance*, 35, 4, 915–919.

S. Sears and K. C. John Wei (1985) 'Asset pricing, higher moments and the market risk premium: a note', *Journal of Finance*, 40, 1251–1253.

U. Segal (1989) 'Anticipated utility: a measure representation approach', *Annals of Operations Research*, 19, 1–4, 359–373.

J. R. Seguin, L. Arseneault and R. E. Tremblay (2007) 'The contribution of "cool" and "hot" components of decision-making in adolescence: Implications for developmental psychopathology', *Cognitive Development*, 22, 530–543.

E. Shafir, P. Diamond and A. Tversky (1997) 'Money illusion', *Quarterly Journal of Economics*, 112 (2), 341–374.

W. F. Sharpe (1963) 'A simplified model for portfolio analysis', *Management Science*, 9, 277–93.

W. F. Sharpe (1964) 'Capital asset prices: A theory of market equilibrium under conditions of risk', *The Journal of Finance*, 19, 3, 425–442.

G. A. Shaw and L. Giambra (1993) 'Task-unrelated thoughts of college-students diagnosed as hyperactive in childhood', *Developmental. Neuropsychology*, 9, 1, 17–30.

H. Shefrin (2005) *A Behavioral Approach to Asset Pricing* (Boston, MA: Elsevier Academic Press).

H. Shefrin (2008) 'Risk and return in behavioral sdf-based asset pricing model', *Journal of Investment Management*, 6, 3, 1–18.

H. Shefrin and M. Statman (1985) 'The disposition to sell winners too early and ride losers too long: theory and evidence', *Journal of Finance*, 40, 3, 777–790.

H. Shefrin and M. Statman (1994) 'Behavioral capital asset pricing theory', *Journal of Financial and Quantitative Analysis*, 29, 3, 323–349.

H. Shefrin and M. Statman (2000) 'Behavioral portfolio theory', *Journal of Financial and Quantitative Analysis*, 35, 2, 127–151.

R. J. Shiller and J. Pound (1989) 'Survey evidence on the diffusion of interest and information among investors', *Journal of Economic Behavior and Organizations*, 12, 46–66.

B. Shiv, G. Loewenstein and A. Bechara (2005) 'The dark side of emotion in decision-making: when individuals decreased emotional reactions make more advantageous', *Cognitive Brain Research*, 23, 85–92.

B. Shiv, G. Loewenstein, A. Bechara, H. Damasio and A. Damasio (2005) 'Investment behavior and the negative side of emotion', *Psychological Science*, 16, 435–439.

H. Shui and L. M. Ausubel (2004) 'Time inconsistency in the credit card market', *University of Maryland, Working Paper.*

H. A. Simon (1955) 'Behavioral model of rational choice', *Quarterly Journal of Economics*, 69, 1, 99–118.

H. A. Simon (1957) *Models of Man: Social and Rational* (New York: John Wiley and Sons).

S. B. Sitkin and L. R. Weingart (1995) 'Determinants of risky decision-making behavior: a test of the mediating role of risk perceptions and propensity', *Academy of Management Journal*, 38, 6, 1573–1592.

P. Slovic, M. L. Finucane, E. Peters and D. G. MacGregor (2004) 'Risk as analysis and risk as feelings: some thoughts about affect reason, risk, and rationality', *Risk Analysis*, 24, 2, 311–322.

P. Slovich, B. Fischhoff and S. Lichtenstein (1982) 'Facts and fears: understanding perceived risk' in D. Kahneman, P. Slovich and A. Tversky (eds) *Judgment Under Uncertainty: Heuristics and Biases* (New York: Cambridge University Press).

J.M Smallwood, S. F. Baracaia, M. Lowe and M. Obonsawin (2003) 'Task unrelated thought whilst encoding information', *Consciousness and Cognition*, 12, 3, 452–484.

J. Smallwood, E. Beach, J. W. Schooler and T. C. Handy (2008) 'Going AWOL in the brain: mind wandering reduces cortical analysis of external events', *Journal of Cognitive Neuroscience*, 20, 458–469.

J. Smallwood, R. C. O'Connor and D. Heim (2005) 'Rumination, dysphoria and subjective experience', *Imagination, Cognition and Personality*, 24, 355–367.

J. Smallwood and J. W. Schooler (2006) 'The restless mind', *Psychological Bulletin*, 132, 6, 946–958.

F. A. Sortino and R. Van Der Meer (1991) 'Downside risk', *Journal of Portfolio Management*, 17, 4, 27–32.

F. A. Sortino and L. N. Price (1994) 'Performance measurement in a downside risk framework', *Journal of Investing*, 3, 3, 59–64.

F. A. Sortino and H. J. Forsey (1996) 'On the use and misuse of downside risk', *Journal of Portfolio Management*, 22, 2, 35–42.

F. A. Sortino (2001) 'From alpha to omega', in F. A. Sortino, and S. Satchell (eds) *Managing Downside Risk in Financial Markets: Theory, Practice and Implementation* (Oxford: Buttworth Heinemann).

M. Statman (2003) 'Behavioral portfolios: hope for riches and protection from poverty', *Pension Research Council Working Paper*, 1–24.

B. Steenbarger (2002) The *Psychology of Trading: Tools and Techniques for Minding the Markets* (New Jersey: John Wiley and Sons).

H. Stern (1962) 'The significance of impulse buying today', *Journal of Marketing*, 26, 59–63.

R. J. Sternberg and J. Gastel (1989) 'If dancers ate their shoes: inductive reasoning with factual and counterfactual premises', *Memory and Cognition*, 17, 1–10.

J. Stiglitz and A. Weiss (1981) 'Credit rationing in markets with imperfect information', *American Economic Review*, 71, 3, 393–410.

F. Strack, L. Werth and R. Deutsch (2006) 'Reflective and impulsive determinants of consumer behavior'. *Journal of Consumer Psychology*, 16, 205–216.

T. Suddendorf and J. Busby (2005) 'Making decisions with the future in mind: developmental and comparative identification of mental time travel', *Learning & Motivation*, 36, 110–125.

M. M. Sweitzer, P. A. Allen and K. P. Kaut (2008) 'Relation of individual differences in impulsivity to nonclinical emotional decision making', *Journal of the International Neuropsychological Society*, 14, 878–882.

T. Takahashi (2007) 'Hyperbolic discounting may be reduced to electrical coupling in dopaminergic neural circuits', *Medical Hypotheses*, 69, 195–198.

J. Tatom and D. Godsted (2006) 'Targeting the unbanked-financial literacy's magin bullet?', University Library of Munich, *MPRA Working Paper* n. 4266 (Germany).

L. Telser (1955) 'Safety first and hedging', *Review of Economic Studies*, 23, 1, 1–16.

R. H. Thaler, A. Tversky, D. Kahneman and A. Schwartz (1997) 'The effect of myopia and loss aversion on risk taking: an experimental test', *Quarterly Journal of Economics*, 112, 2, 647–661.

R. H. Thaler (1985) 'Mental accounting and consumer choice', *Marketing Science*, 4, 3, 199–214.

R. H. Thaler and E. J. Johnson (1990) 'Gambling with the house money and trying to break even: the effects of prior outcomes on risky choice', *Management Science*, 36, 6, 643–660.

N. J. T. Thomas (1999) 'Are theories of imagery theories of imagination? an active perception approach to conscious mental content', *Cognitive Sciences*, 23, 207–245.

L. C. Thomas, D. B. Edelman and J. N. Crook (2002) Credit scoring and its applications, Society for Industrial and Applied Mathematics SIAM, Philadelphia.

V. A. Thompson and R. M. Byrne (2002) 'Reasoning counterfactually: making inferences about things that didn't happen', *Journal of Experimental Psychology, Learning, Memory and Cognition*, 28, 6, 1154–1170.

J. Treynor (1961) 'Market value, time and risk'. Unpublished manuscript.

J. Treynor (1962) 'Towards a theory of market value of risky assets'. Unpublished manuscript. A final version in R. A. Korajczyk (1999) (ed.) *Asset Pricing and Portfolio Performance* (London: Risk Books), pp. 15–22.

A. Tversky and D. Kahneman (1973) 'Availability: a heuristic for judging frequency and probability', *Cognitive Psychology*, 5, 2, 207–232.

A. Tversky and D. Kahneman (1974) 'Judgment under uncertainty: heuristics and biases', *Science*, 185, 1124–1131.

A. Tversky and D. Kahneman (1981) 'The framing of decisions and the psychology of choice', *Science*, 211, 453–458.

A. Tversky and D. Kahneman (1986) 'Rational choice and the framing of decisions', *Journal of Business*, 59, 4, 251–278.

A. Tversky and D. Kahneman (1992) 'Advances in prospect theory: cumulative representation of uncertainty', *Journal of Risk and Uncertainty*, 5, 4, 297–323.

M. Unser (2000) 'Lower partial moments as measures of perceived risk: an experimental study', *Journal of Economic Psychology*, 21, 3, 253–280.

D. Vandone (2009) *Consumer Credit in Europe: Risks and Opportunities of a Dynamic Industry* (Berlin: Springer-Verlag).

B. Viswanath, Y. C. Janardhan Reddy, K. J. Kumar, T. Kandavel and C. R. Chandrashekar (2009) 'Cognitive endophenotypes in OCD: a study of unaffected siblings of probands with familial OCD', *Progress in Neuropsychopharmacology & Biological Psychiatry*, 33, 610–615.

J. Von Neumann and O. Morgenstern (1944) *Theory of Games and Economic Behavior* (Princeton, NJ: Princeton University Press).

E. J. Vughan and T. M. Vaughan (2000) *Essentials of Risk Management and Insurance*, 2nd edn (New York: John Wiley and Sons, Inc).

M. Waldron and G. Young (2006) 'The state of British household finances: results from the 2006 NMG research survey', *Bank of England Quarterly Bulletin*, 4, 396–403.

H. Walter, B. Abler, A. Ciaramidaro and S. Erk (2005) 'Motivating forces of human actions. neuroimaging reward and social interaction', *Brain Research Bulletin*, 67, 368–381.

R. Warwick (2003) *The Handbook of Risk* (Hoboken: John Wiley and Sons).

J. Watson (2003) 'The relationship of materialism to spending tendencies, saving and debt', *Journal of Economic Psychology*, 24, 723–739.

B. Weber, A. Aholt, C. Neuhaus, P. Trautner, C. E. Elger and T. Teichert (2007) 'Neural evidence for reference-dependence in real-market-transactions', *Neuroimage*, 35, 441–447.

E. U. Weber, A. Blais and N. E. Betz (2002) 'A domain-specific risk-attitude scale: measuring risk perceptions and risk behaviors', *Journal of Behavioral Decision Making*, 15, 4, 263–290.

N. S. Werner, S. Duschek and R. Schandry (2009) 'Relationships between affective states and decision-making', *International Journal of Psychophysiology*, 74, 259–265.

C. A. Williams, M. L. Smith and P. C. Young (1997) *Risk Management and Insurance*, 8th edn (New York: Irwin McGraw-Hill).

L. Willis (2008a) 'Evidence and Ideology in assessing the effectiveness of financial literacy education, University of Pennsylvania Law School', Research Paper n. 8.

L. Willis (2008b) 'Against financial literacy education, University of Pennsylvania Law School', Research Paper n. 10.

M. Wittmann and M. P. Paulus (2008) 'Decision making, impulsivity and time perception', *Trends in Cognitive Sciences*, 12, 7–12.

World Bank (2005) 'Indicators of financial access (Households Level Surveys)' *World Bank Report.*

W. F. Wright and G. H. Bower (1992) 'Mood effects on subjective probability assessment', *Organizational Behavior and Human Decision Processes*, 52, 276–291.

M. Yaari (1987) 'The dual theory of choice under risk', *Econometrica*, 55, 1, 95–115.

K. C. Yook and R. Everett (2003) 'Assessing risk tolerance: questioning the questionnaire method', *Journal of Financial Planning*, 16, 8, 48–55.

R. B. Zajonc (1984) 'On the primacy of affect', *American Psychologist*, 39, 124–129.

M. Zeelenberg and R. Pieters (2006) 'Feeling is for doing: a pragmatic approach to the study of emotions in economic behavior' in D. De Cremer, M. Zeelenberg and K. Murnighan (eds) *Social Psychology and Economics* (Mahwah, NJ: Erlbaum), pp. 117–137.

M. Zeelenberg, R. M. A. Nelissen and R. Pieters (2007) 'Emotion, motivation and decision making: a feeling is for doing approach' in H. Plessner, C. Betsch and T. Betsch (eds) *Intuition in Judgment and Decision Making* (New York: Erlbaum), pp. 173–189.

A. Zermatten, M. Van der Linden, M. D'Acremont, F. Jermann and A. Bechara (2005) 'Impulsivity and decision making', *The Journal of Nervous and Mental Disorders*, 193, 647–650.

Index

Note: Page numbers in *italics* denote illustrations.